Black Nihilism and Antiblack Racism

Living Existentialism

Series Editors: T. Storm Heter, East Stroudsburg University, LaRose T. Parris, Lehman College, the City University New York, and Devin Zane Shaw, Douglas College

Existentialism is a living, practical philosophy, engaged in contemporary events and responsive to other currents of philosophy across the globe. It can be instrumental to an individual's understanding of themselves as well as to examinations of political, societal, and ecological phenomena.

This series focuses on creative, generative scholarship that expands discussions of existentialism in order to foster an intellectual space for articulating the diverse lineages of existentialism—from Beauvoir's feminist philosophy, to the anticolonial, black existentialism of thinkers like Frantz Fanon and Angela Davis who composed their views of freedom, self, and other from the lived experience of racism and colonialism.

Existentialism has often been miscategorized as a European tradition, limited by the gravitational pull of a few thinkers. Part of the work of this series is to dismantle this incorrect impression of where Existentialism comes from and what its potential is. Existential thought offers a valuable vocabulary for expressing the lived perspectives of colonized, indigenous, and othered peoples. As such, it is increasingly relevant to the ongoing struggle for human freedom the world over.

Philosophy of Antifascism: Punching Nazis and Fighting White Supremacy
Devin Zane Shaw

Sartre on Contingency: Antiblack Racism and Embodiment
Mabogo Percy More

Black Nihilism and Antiblack Racism
Devon Johnson

Black Nihilism and Antiblack Racism

Devon R. Johnson

ROWMAN & LITTLEFIELD
Lanham • Boulder • New York • London

Published by Rowman & Littlefield
An imprint of The Rowman & Littlefield Publishing Group, Inc.
4501 Forbes Boulevard, Suite 200, Lanham, Maryland 20706
www.rowman.com

Copyright © 2021 by The Rowman & Littlefield Publishing Group, Inc.

All rights reserved. No part of this book may be reproduced in any form or by any electronic or mechanical means, including information storage and retrieval systems, without written permission from the publisher, except by a reviewer who may quote passages in a review.

British Library Cataloguing in Publication Information Available

Library of Congress Cataloging-in-Publication Data

Names: Johnson, Devon, author.
Title: Black nihilism and antiblack racism / Devon Johnson.
Description: Lanham, Maryland : Rowman & Littlefield, [2021] | Includes bibliographical references and index. | Summary: "A philosophical analysis of the pessimistic and nihilistic conditions of the existential possibilities for blackness and antiblack racism in 21st century America"—Provided by publisher.
Identifiers: LCCN 2021035484 (print) | LCCN 2021035485 (ebook) | ISBN 9781538153499 (hardcover) | ISBN 9781538153512 (paperback) | ISBN 9781538153505 (epub)
Subjects: LCSH: Racism—United States—History—21st Century. | Blacks—United States—Social conditions—History—21st Century. | Nihilism—History—21st Century. | United States—Race relations—History—21st century.
Classification: LCC HT1521 .J64 2021 (print) | LCC HT1521 (ebook) | DDC 305.800973/0905—dc23
LC record available at https://lccn.loc.gov/2021035484
LC ebook record available at https://lccn.loc.gov/2021035485

Contents

Foreword		vii
Acknowledgments		xi
1	How to Philosophize Black Nihilism	1
2	(European) "Man" and Weak Nihilism	23
3	White Nihilism and Antiblack Racism	67
4	Traditional Black Nihilism: Bell's Pessimism and West's Optimism	83
5	Strong Black Nihilism	119
6	The Future: Black Nihilism, Hip-Hop, and Maturity On God: Black Nihilism and Traditional Black Christianity Black Nihilistic Hip-Hop Music	151
Bibliography		195
Index		201
About the Author		207

Foreword

Nihilism, Friedrich Nietzsche argued, is symptomatic of societies suffering from decay. A decaying society flees from affirmations of life, from the reverie of dance and the ecstasy of the chorus. It retreats into the perceived submerging safety of shared wills to power instead of taking responsibility for values, for the abilities by which thought could be matched by deed without fears of outcomes that offer no guarantees. That philologist now known as a philosopher offered ideas greatly misunderstood by too many over a century. Believing he was the life coach for a set of values that proved to be antipathetic to life, his name was used in proverbial vein by the people he was in fact criticizing. Such is the folly of words carried forth by those imbued with narcissistic fervor. They see and hear what they prefer, and, facing otherwise, what is left but halls of cracked mirrors?

Racism is among the bloated values of Euromodern decay. Yet, as we know, the corpse moves, zombified, with claims of life through persistent practices of disempowerment, destruction, and death. What is racism, after all, but an effort to disempower whole groups of people from the humanity with which they are born but through which they are, under ongoing, structural violence, haunted? As the historical unfolding of Nietzsche's thoughts revealed, his words could be carried on wings of deception, as they were, after all, embraced by Nazis, people with an inflated sense of historical worth. But ironically, given Nietzsche's own racist beliefs, even the messenger can deceive himself from his own message. If the egalitarianism he detested in Christianity was a mark of the nihilism he diagnosed, what could be made of the presupposition of a form of default egalitarianism among whites in the narcissistic fantasies of whiteness? Could not Nietzsche's nightmare, as was the case of so many before and after him, be the realization of truth in a mirror that looked back at him through black embodiment?

As antiblack racism is a form of racism, these queries come to the fore in the text you now hold, Dear Reader: Devon R. Johnson's *Black Nihilism and Antiblack Racism*. It is offered from a Black philosopher who has taken upon himself to face the challenges of nihilism in the rotted age into which he is born, one marked by pandemics of colonialism, dehumanization, environmental degradation, genocide, and mass extinctions many of which, as denials persist, are consequences of irresponsible and often malevolent human misuse of power. As the opposite of decay is life or living activity, then empowerment, humanization, connectedness, sociality, and other forms of creative exemplification of agency should be nurtured. But antiblack racism stands to the contrary. It is a project that pushes life from reaching outward. It squeezes in, forces upon the subjugated a form of closing into the body to a point of implosion. What is that but a death project? What, in addition, happens to purveyors of such maladies if their energy is not directed to what life-affirming projects of empowerment can produce? Wouldn't the irony of life premised upon the production of death not be an underlying death as well, the contradiction of a life of anti-life? Such misdirection is, after all, a foreclosure of possibilities. Too many fail to see that it is possible to die comfortably or practice an easy living death.

So, the discomforting and discomfiting task arises. If nihilism is a value of a decaying society, and antiblack societies are saturated with decadence, then what, in the words of so many who have fought for better worlds over the ages, is to be done?

The *doing* is rich with irony, since all meaningful action is an expression of value. Those who take the nihilistic road out of fear of facing decadence inevitably lie to themselves about the meaning of their actions. They offer a bevy of well-integrated lies from those of history to portraits of the self. They convince themselves of what is, however brutal, must be, and, in doing so, they abdicate agency and responsibility. This abdication is sometimes ironic and paradoxical, since they may even claim a lack of agency as a form of agency: "I at least admit I cannot do otherwise...."

Johnson's concerns, however, are not with those who impose antiblack racism onto black people, which, in their efforts, they attempt to make ontological—that is, a complete reality or permanent state of being. He is concerned with what is to be done by those who are under the heels of that imposition. Their relationship to nihilism is of a different kind, since they face a series of "Catch 22" decisions. If they rely on the agency of their dominators and oppressors—their system—they in effect deny their own agency and responsibility for the values by which they live. If they embark on bringing to fruition the greatest nightmare of all racists—namely, the eventual irrelevance of racists—they face the question of whether they do so as a *reaction* to those values or as a commitment to values beyond them. If the latter, there is the paradox of a lack of faith in the values of their society as an expression of nihilism (those values no longer being meaningful) while affirming the project of building values. On what basis, it would be asked, could such values be built?

As Johnson understands the existential dimension of human beings as, through the production of values, the realization also of our humanity, it means for him that those subjugated to antiblack racism face also constituting at least two possibilities. On one hand, there is the nihilistic value of death projects through which black people are constituted as lowly—in a word, black. As I read him, that is a weak response marked by what W.E.B Du Bois called "double consciousness." Johnson calls it "weak nihilism." It is the acceptance of the abjection that antiblack society imposes on people designated "black." Must black people be what antiblack societies demand? Then there is another possibility, one in which the fallacies of the first are understood as produced by a society that is itself an expression of weak nihilism. That realization demands transcending attachment to the first as a value system. It requires addressing the nihilism through non-evasive transcendence. It is going beyond it through facing its contradictions. This movement is what he calls "strong nihilism." It requires a form of willing connected to a positive consciousness, which, drawing upon the work of Jane Anna Gordon and Paget Henry, is also called "potentiated double consciousness." That movement could be formulated as one from (abject) black to (active) Black. It is a position Fanon espoused in *Black Skin, White Masks* when he declared his project is to offer a path through which black people can become "actional"—that is, becoming Blacks. This latter, existential commitment, although not expressed as such, is an underlying theme of Johnson's provocative critical text.

If one lives meaningfulness in the face of nihilism, would that be optimism? Johnson is aware that optimism is but another side of the coin of pessimism. He examines this problem through exploring ideas from black and Black thinkers who devote their intellectual resources to the quaternity: optimism, pessimism, weak nihilism, and strong nihilism.

The famed Derrick Bell's pessimistic voice returns in an ironic way since his approach to critical legal studies is, as we know today, among the misrepresented models of critical race theory that have occasioned narcissistic rage from white neoconservatives in the USA and those in like-minded countries. That their response—and rage—are more efforts to break the mirror than to look into it is a case in point. We should recall that the title of Bell's most famous work, *Faces from the Bottom of the Well*, already exemplifies the key metaphor: the dark waters below are also mirrors. What may be surprising to readers is the critical discussion of perhaps the most famous diagnostician of nihilism in U.S. black communities: Cornel West. That West's response to at least political nihilism is to assert *Christian* values already brings to the fore the performative contradiction of offering weak nihilism as a response to decadence. Now, of course West, as would many Afro-Christians, would claim there is nothing weak about Christian love, but a response to consider is whether a form of radical love would work without Christian elements. There were those who loved the unloved before Christianity and there are many outside of the Christian tradition who love the unloved from the damned of the earth to what, for many, may be the most insignificant forms of life. What is their non-Christian love but a demonstration of the contingency of Christianity in this endeavor? Wouldn't this be so for those who love beyond any religious or theological identification? Put differently, what must be done even in the absence of the divine?

Johnson asks us to join him on the difficult journey of going further. He raises questions of youth and maturity, of speaking to those in crisis now and not shying away from the challenges they embody. The truth of an imperfect past and present offers a future without guarantees. Why, then, act? Like so many existentialists, from Nietzsche to Fanon, he asks us to get over ourselves. The paradox of commitment through, as Johnson points out, vulgar defiance is a key to opening the door of dignity in the ongoing journey of liberation.

Lewis R. Gordon

Acknowledgments

This book is the summation of my youth, my education, and my experiences; above all, it is a testament to my having survived, and matured, through the gauntlet of blackness in America. I could not have made it through this crucible, thus far, with sound mind and understanding, let alone write this book, without the unwavering protection, support, guidance, and simple kindness of dear people, whom I have come to regard as loved ones, or, simply, "family." I am forever indebted to Lewis Gordon and Jane Anna Gordon. Lewis and Jane have been amazing sources of encouragement and support, for me, throughout the years. Their genuine kindness and generosity cannot be measured in words. Lewis was my doctoral adviser; I do not recall my frameworks for thinking about race before meeting him. The breadth and scope of his scholarship has singularly had the greatest impact on my own. I aim to make him proud. I thank him for his many gifts. In particular, in the absence of my own father, Lewis has, by word, thought, and deed, been somewhat of a fatherly figure for me. He was my philosophy adviser, but also revealed countless, valuable, and unforgettable jewels, insights, into what it means to be a "Man," in the most humanist sense of the term: to be a man for my family, for my people, my community; to be a "Man" for humanity. I am grateful for his dedicated approach to nurturing and demonstrating for his students what it means to, truly, be a *humanist* philosopher. I was an unconventional student. Upon one of our first meetings, I confessed that I wasn't sure how I had made it into a doctoral program. I asked him what he saw in me, and forewarned that I may not be as well-read as some of his other students. He simply replied, with a gentleness of demeanor that anyone who has ever met him falls in love with, "Oh; no worries. I've taught students with far-less background." On another occasion, when I was struggling to pass a preliminary exam, I considered quitting the doctoral degree program after being condescended and verbally abused by a senior professor handling my exam. I called Lewis, and told him, "I might be done." He told me, "Relax." Then, he simply said, "You will not have to work with [that professor], anymore." A few days later, I was assigned a new reviewer. Under their guidance, I passed the exam. There is an immense responsibility that comes along with having the love, support, and belief of your elders: that amazing battery of motivation that comes from simple knowledge that there are those who have prepared a place for you, love you, believe in you, and who gift you with resources to succeed and do well. I write this book in gratitude and solemn respect for all that I have been gifted, and taught, by so many extraordinary teachers, and elders, whom each have prepared me, in various ways, to succeed, and do well.

I am thankful to all of my early education teachers, Ms. Dorothy Dennis; Mr. Robert Starks; the late, Mr. Antonio Henry; Ms. Barbara Henderson; Ms. Barbara Duncan. I am thankful for Dr. Maria Morales, of Florida State University, who took me on, as the only black philosophy major in my graduating undergraduate class, and became my adviser throughout my master's degree. I could not have earned a spot studying with Lewis had it not been for her awesome tutelage. Dr. Peter Dalton, also, was instrumental during my development at Florida State University. Thank-you, both, for the many hours of discussion and encouragement. In particular, thank-you, Kermit Harrison, an advanced graduate student of philosophy I was fortunate enough to meet. He was the first black person I had ever seen speak "academically." He introduced me to critical race theory. He also introduced me to Leonard Harris, who ultimately directed me to Lewis Gordon. In many ways, he was my first Africana philosophy adviser. Thank-you, Kermit. I would like to thank Dr. Paul Taylor; Dr. Jitendra Mohanty; and the late, Dr. Tom Meyer, whom I met while pursuing my doctorate degree at Temple University, for their kindness and generosity in always being willing to meet and discuss ideas with me. Also, thank-you, Sonja Lawson, for always having my back. I was fortunate enough, during this time, to also meet many dedicated graduate students, who I studied alongside and have offered me invaluable critical feedback at various stages of this project's development. Firstly, I must thank my dear friend, Vince Beaver, who has read over numerous versions of this project and has been a rock solid source of support, motivation, and constructive criticism. I am also thankful to Greg Graham for countless hours spent discussing these ideas, and for his genuine friendship. There are many others to thank, including teachers, colleagues, and professional acquaintances, whose comments, thoughts, encouragements, and critical conversations have helped me develop this project. This work benefited from the direct and indirect contributions of many first-class scholars and thinkers I have been lucky enough to meet on my journey. I am thankful for every encounter had.

Acknowledgments

Thank-you, Myron Beasley, Aili Bresnahan, danielle davis, Mireille Fanon-Mendès-France, Leonard Harris, Paget Henry, Rozena Maart, P. Mabogo More, Nelson Maldonado-Torres, Michael Monahan, Marilyn Nissim-Sabat, Lucious T. Outlaw, Jean-Paul Rocchi, and Cornel West, to name a few. I am thankful for the community of people, whom I affectionately refer to as my philosophical brothers and sisters. Thank-you, Tal Correm, Douglas Ficek, Chike Jeffers, Derefe Chevannes, Lior Levy, Qrescent Mason, Tom Meagher, Neil Roberts, Rosemere Da Silva, Colena Sanker, and Ariella Werden-Greenfield. I am grateful to be a part of this wonderful community of scholars, who are each located around the Caribbean Philosophical Association, an organization that I am forever thankful for, a safe and nurturing space for open and critical philosophical engagements with the "underside" of our political realities.

I would also like to thank my colleagues at the University of Tampa, Marcus Arvan, Steve Geisz, Carter Hardy, and Peter Westmoreland. Thank-you all for being genuinely supportive and encouraging of me. Cheers.

I am especially thankful for the editors of this book series, LaRose T. Parris and T. Storm Heter, for all of your work. Thank-you, especially, for creating this platform for critical thought to be shared.

I extend my final thanks to my family, the original site gifting me a strong sense of self-worth and value. This book is dedicated to them, my aunties, uncles, and cousins, and in particular, my maternal grandparents, Jamaican immigrants, who instilled in their progeny the values of family, hard work, and keeping one's head held high. I was taught that "I am not better than anyone," and "no one is better than me." I thank my late grandfather, Reginald "Mr. Martin" Kissoonlal, with whom I spent countless hours driving the coastlines of Jamaica, in his red pickup truck, talking, listening, being listened to; he was the first person to gift me with a book on (Jamaican) colonial history. I miss him; I hope my book is something of which he would have been proud. I thank my grandmother, Thermutis "Ms. Lilly" Kissoonlal, who, through religious contexts, first taught me to philosophize. I remember watching her climb a breadfruit tree when she was well past the ripe old age of seventy. She remains the strongest woman I know. I thank my mother, Anand Kissoonlal, who worked hard, loved, and supports me, unconditionally. To work, and provide, as a single mother, so greatly, so that I could go to college and study, and to instill such an ethic of excellence, so that your son could be a professor (in a field where less that 1% of black people are represented), forever makes you a Heroine, in my eyes. I love you, Mom. To my sisters, Jamelle and Janelle, and my nephew and nieces, Aliyah, Jace, and Ava, I hope this book makes you smile with pride. I strive to be someone you each can look up to, and depend on. I love you all.

To my wife, Gina Antoinette Auxilly Johnson, I write this book for us, our children, and for all black children. Thank-you for loving me, darling. Thank-you for putting up with me, especially as I worked to complete this project. Thank-you for being the most gracious, wonderful, caring, person I have ever met. I love you, Woman. You brought me back from the dead. I hope this book gives us more life.

—Devon R. Johnson, Phd.,
Tampa, Florida, May 27, 2021

Chapter 1

How to Philosophize Black Nihilism

> Of what is great one must either be silent or speak with greatness. With greatness—that means cynically and with innocence.[1]

What attitudes should "Man" have when producing values? Are there values and attitudes that ought to be produced? Modern European philosophy addressed these questions; it also infamously produced antiblack racism. Understanding traditional and nontraditional modern European philosophers' thought concerning human values, in my estimation, helps explain the historical emergence of certain black attitudes that have emerged in response. There is a particular black attitude in response to antiblack racism that I think is valuable, or, at the very least, ought to be carefully considered. I will demonstrate it: fuck antiblack racism; fuck antiblack racists. Fuck that. Black nihilism.

"'Nihilism,' an ideal of the highest degree of powerfulness of the spirit, the over-richest life—partly destructive, partly ironic."[2] What a wondrously spirited, dynamic, rich, potential-filled, and dangerous attitude to have in response to antiblack racism. If you find the above sort of language offensive, I assure you, the absurdities engaged in this book are much more vulgar than any turn of phrase I could muster in response to them. I understand why such attitudes and languages are viewed as offensive; they are "vulgar." However, I want to show that these attitudes can also be constructive for moving through, and beyond, the absurdities of antiblack racism.

The term "vulgar" comes from the Latin term *vulgaris*, meaning of the "mob," the root being vulgus, meaning mob, or common people. In other words, its meaning is associated with the masses, or what are seen as lower classes of unreflective peoples. Through its sixteenth-century, Middle-English origins, the term developed to mean one who produces ignorant, uncultivated, inarticulate, and/or undesirable perspectives. And yet, referring to the undesirability of statements as a basis for rejection amounts to callous refusals to engage alternative perspectives; it is a form of elitism; it is a criticism of language that functions as a denial of perspectives. For instance, in 2008, a player in the National Basketball Association, Josh Howard, a black man, was recorded at an amateur football game, loudly proclaiming during the playing of the American National Anthem what amounts to saying, "Fuck that." He said, "They're playing the National Anthem, right now. I don't celebrate that shit; I'm black, God damn it!" Statements like these are obviously offensive to certain sensibilities. But what was wrong with what Howard said? I heard him as strongly, defiantly, and vulgarly rejecting a symbolic ritual saturated in antiblack racism. How should black people respond in such situations? This book attempts to provide an answer, and is premised around a central question: What attitude should black people have in response to impositions of antiblack racist desires, symbols, and values?

Responses such as Howard's are typically deemed unworthy of addressing on grounds of vulgarity. Among these allegations are charges of ignorance, personal failures of erudition, moral deviance, and simply put, a lack of the right sorts of values. But there is something of momentous importance that can emerge from strong, defiant, attitudes toward traditional forms of valuing. For example, traditionally, the idea of an original consciousness existing within a black body is attacked and demanded to justify its existence in antiblack racist societies. Certain forms of what may be viewed as vulgar responses, although I have another term in mind, maybe conducive for strongly insisting on black humanity. That is, attempts at devaluing traditional values of Western life may necessarily involve being viewed, by those traditions, at least, as vulgar.

In light of historically well-documented white-normative ideals on nearly every level of life in Western reality, especially in the United States, the fact is, if one wants to understand antiblack racism and certain responses to it, it becomes necessary to understand the presumed legitimacy of traditional Western Humanism. Africana philosophy is multifaceted, but on this front, it generally commits itself to two paths: a critique of the claims of traditional Western philosophy and analyses of the question of black liberation from antiblack racist oppression.

Most people consider "racism," in terms of what critical race theorists call, "racial essentialism," which is an assertion of there being essential traits, essences, or ways of being, necessarily inhering in people, due to their race.[3] Racial essentialism is the imagining of what races of people *really* are. They employ Aristotle's conception of essence, where certain properties are deemed inherent to the meaning of an object, in this case, the "raced" person.[4] From this perspective, "antiblack racism" merely suggests a qualifying of the object of reference. However, according to black existentialist approaches, the prefix, "antiblack," adds more than a specification for a type of racism. "Antiblack racism" is an existentially descriptive term that designates the phenomenon of racism itself.[5] In particular, "antiblack" connotes denials of one's subjective capacities. "Black," here, assumes an ontologically descriptive meaning, denoting situations of existential invisibility, where one is seen as a nonexistence in relation to normative conceptions of humanity, that is, "white." Thus, terms such as "black existential life" resists charges of essentialism, because whether or not one exists as "black" is not, in an existential sense, a matter of personal identity formation. There are subjective dimensions of personal identity formation, or what one might call, phenomenal activity, involved in living blackness; there are also objective existential dimensions of blackness in spite of which one lives. Frantz Fanon illuminated the philosophical uniqueness of phenomenal perspectives developed from spaces of black existential invisibility, where critical dimensions of subjective capacities develop in relation to objective, lived, experiences of blackness.[6]

There is textual evidence of antiblack racism in European philosophy, dating back as far as the medieval period, through the "discovery" of the "new world," and modern European colonization of Africa. There, one finds obsessions with the category of "Man," understood as Humanity, but grossly reduced to the perspectives of (European) "Man," understood as (white) Humanity. This reduction entails axiomatic conceptions of white-normative and antiblack racist ideals and is a consequence of (European) "Man's" innermost existential struggles. I use a capital "H," in Human being, and a capital "M," in "Man," to designate philosophies, descriptions, and thoughts developed and understood to be true of all Humankind. However, I use the parenthetical and quotations, in (European) "Man," and (white) Humanity, to designate philosophies, descriptions, and thoughts developed and understood to only be true of European descended, racially white people. The results of those attempts are reflective of failures, and weaknesses, evident in the struggles and desires of (European) "Man," which further resulted in European Enlightenment philosophies producing antiblack racist practices and institutions, all under the banner "civilized (white) Humanity."

Disregarding the first paragraph of this book as "vulgar," and perhaps being tempted not to read further, may indicate an appeal to traditions championed by people who, along with claiming to "know" philosophical ideals stratifying human beings along racial and sexual lines, also claimed to occupy a transcendent position from which to discern the vulgar. This amounts to the claim that certain forms of expression fail to beget any real meaning. The antiblack racist, for example, simply announces that expressions such as the ones above have no valuable meaning, and if they have any meaning at all, it is vulgar, violent, and unnecessary. This is another way of saying, "We should not care about what that person says; that person has nothing to say." That someone who has just made an expressive utterance has nothing to "say," depends upon the idea that what that person says is of no relevance; even worse, it implies that person thinks "nothing."

Vulgar black rejections of antiblack racism suggest both a failure and an achievement. At the symbolic level, "vulgar" expressions of blackness might signal an achievement in resisting one's presumed invisibility. If black people are signifiers of nonexistence in antiblack racist societies, then black "vulgar" rejections potentially become reasonable responses to an unreasonable situation. It is unreasonable to respond to unreason with reason. An attempt to reason with the unreasonable can lead to a debilitating neurosis. This is a crushing realization for one whose sole means of defending oneself against invisibility is the deployment of reason. Reason, it seems, must become creative.

Black people in antiblack racist societies are not simply a part of society. We are a part of society's underside: the underbelly bolstering its frontal dimensions. We embody the cultural limits of antiblack racist societies, displaying everything they *are*, by virtue of what they *are not*. Black perspectives in the United States, for example, are typically seen as "vulgar." "Vulgarity," however, need not necessarily be associated with inarticulateness, ignorance, lack of thought, erudition, and/or perception. Black vulgarity in an antiblack racist society can also take the form of highly articulate, theoretical questions about the relation of black invisibility to the ontological and epistemological dimensions of Western society and humanist thought, in general.

Some, who are genuinely interested in the question of black liberation, are misguided as to the role of vulgarity and violence contained therein. They only conceive vulgarity and violence in terms of impropriety and physical assault. They fail to recognize ways in which the position stating that there is a need for black liberation is itself "vulgar and violent," against traditional conceptualizations of (white) Humanity. "Vulgarity," in the case of black liberation, also means *any* undue alteration. Furthermore, "violence" does not have to be restricted to physical assault, and may refer to forms of existential erasure, anguish, and angst, that attenuate, and often precipitate, physical assaults. In such contexts, expressing a need for black liberation functions as a demand for an undue alteration of reality, or an affront to traditional senses of decency and justice. Hence, there is a general undesirability for articulations of the need for black liberation. I want to suggest that vulgarity and physical violence are among the first reactive moments of strong, healthy, and mature responses to antiblack racism and quests for black liberation. Thus, black vulgarity, here, can be understood as crude, but rich, gestures toward critiques of values underpinning antiblack racism. Consider the context in which, for example, Howard's comments were made. He was faced with a decision of whether or not to solemnly pledge allegiance to an antiblack racist society through a ritualistic ceremony of expressive solidarity for a symbol, a flag. He chose, in that moment, to insist upon the value of black vulgarity in such contexts. His actions, as well as his words, were inherently "vulgar."

What does it mean when the way for black people to not be considered vulgar involves saluting values in allegiance with antiblack racist symbols? It means that one is in an antiblack racist society, and it means one is in the midst of a value system that denies that one is a human being capable of producing values, to which, perhaps, a great initial response is "Fuck that." There is a peculiar irony at play in raising the question of the humanity of black people in antiblack racist societies. The question of black humanity raises the paradox of dehumanized humans. How can a human be dehumanized? Does this mean that the subject in question is no longer human after dehumanization? The short answer to the latter question is "no." Black people are, have always been, and remain human beings. Dehumanization does not erase the humanity of the dehumanized; rather, it provides an absurd, perverse, and contradictory existential context through which the subject's humanity must be articulated. The answer to the former question is more complicated but sheds a great deal of light on the latter question. Blacks are dehumanized by the white-normative organization of traditional Western theories of Humanity, including the construction of moral, ethical, political, economic, and social contracts ordering antiblack racism.[7] As a result of histories of commitments made on behalf of traditional Western Human discourses, whereby the miseries of black life becomes symptomatic, a necessary output, there exists an overarching white-normative theoretical structure for producing value that continues to undergird lived black realities today.

Modern European philosophy produced colonial ideals of a rationalistic duty to colonize the "primitives" of the world. Such rationalizations ultimately established symbolic orderings of life dialectically placing the thesis of "whiteness," culture, understanding, rationality, morality, and normativity against the antithesis of "blackness," primitivism, lack of understanding, irrationality, immorality, and deviance. Such frameworks conditioned epistemological systems which served as rationalizations for the enslavement and forced labor of African people, thus turning them into "black" people. I use the term "black," in "black people," to designate the views and subjugated perspectives of African diasporic peoples born after and within the modern European colonial moment. The project of Western imperialism established vast colonial regimes, of which the United States now stands as an exemplar, whereby the introduction of chattel slavery and the forced labor of Africans into capitalistic modes of production seriously invests in a cultural world of meaning, from which blackness functions as a symbolic negation of all that is desirable in human life. Stating that Africans became "black" moves the discussion from the level of geography, morphology, and biology to questions of symbolic meaning, value construction, and existential life. Since the pigmentation of one's skin can function as a marker of primitivism, signaling the absence of culture and capacities for transcendent thought, in such societies, the meaning of blackness becomes a matter of lived fact for those locked in a dialectical semiotic framework of white-normative conceptions of humanity and black deviancy. If one's deviance from society's normative conception of humanity is betrayed by something as unavoidable as the appearance of one's skin, then, it seems, one's existence potentially faces constant bombardment from oppositional reactions to one's humanity by virtue of social values constructed around skin color. That is, one experiences one's body as existentially locked at the level of a negative semiotic marker. To put it another way, in antiblack racist societies, the very appearance of black skin marks one's inhumanity.

I am black. I discovered I was black. Then, I discovered what "black" was taken to mean in my society. Most black people born in antiblack racist societies can recount when those constellations of negative predetermined meanings, fixed around the hues of our skin, first began to crystalize. My consciousness emerged into this world "imbued with a will to find meaning in things."[8] However, I was arrested, literally and figuratively, in my process of discovery, only to learn that, like Frantz Fanon, I was taken to be an "object in the midst of other objects."[9] I needed something to save me from that crashing feeling of dispossession; but tradition, the obvious place to go, seemed but a waning vestige of ideals that, too, were shattered in the wreckage of my assault. I was indignant; like Fanon, I "burst apart."

A demand for answers will soon follow, but first, I must pick up my pieces. In the sharded fragments of the first item considered for reconstitution, I caught a glimpse of a reflection that was supposedly my own. And the drama began: What should I value when facing the project of human valuing? As if the question of what I should value when facing the project of constructing myself isn't hard enough, my first painful realization was that through an initial bursting of the positive certainties of my consciousness, my earliest recollections of experiences and expectations for myself and others, my society does not typically offer black people a genuine encounter with the project of human valuing. The question became, for me, what should be valued when facing (European) "Man" attempting to intercept the processes of human valuing? More succinctly, what does it make sense for black people to value in the face of whiteness? Should black people persist in valuing blackness? Does that make sense? Is there a way to value blackness that isn't saturated in weakness and reactivity? I feel myself getting dizzy. Vertigo? No. I am forced to start from an absurd beginning. Why bother? Because. Fuck it; black nihilism.

Why "black" nihilism? This book attempts to answer that question. As a black person, I must consider an absurd version of the question, "Do I exist?" If René Descartes were right, then I would have answered the question simply by formulating it. To think entails to exist; "I think; therefore, I am."[10] My beliefs, projections of values, out of which reflections are produced, judgments are made, and knowledge is formed, entail my existence. To think, as a human being, is to be pre-reflectively aware of my existence. And, every time I think to myself, "I exist; right?", I am presented with what feels like an incessant train of subsequent "moments" to potentially consider the question. But, what about when I am taken hold of, possessed, dispossessed, seized by antiblack authorities of my society; when I am commanded, under penalty of torture, chains, and death, to cease and desist all expressions of my freedom; what about when I am successfully made to "burst apart," and doubt my own existence as a subjectivity? Is Descartes's *cogito* correct in those moments? Does my body become less known to me than my consciousness and my thoughts? No; in those moments, it is my body that is forcibly moved by something other than me, and through which I become painfully aware of myself as a negative truth. There is a positive truth; another "man," enforcing and militarizing against me, reminding me that my consciousness *must* be a negativity. My coming to awareness of the positive certainties constituting myself as a consciousness runs counter to the schema described by Descartes. For one thing, modern European philosophy, in general, relied upon idealist frameworks where rationalism and empiricism were dominant. But, regardless of whether Cartesian rationalism or Lockean empiricism, or neither, for example, strikes one as correct, the idea that black people can be understood as lacking existential subjectivity, or phenomenal existence, remains incredible.[11]

I only need to look into reality, toward some other thing or being, to realize, immediately, that my existence, and that of every other person, is a point of departure for determining the potential meaning of something which we are not. The ability to distinguish what one is not signals that one exists. And yet, my society points me toward my powers of negation, my abilities to determine myself in terms of what I am not, solely in relation to European "man," who continuously insists that I am *not*. Implicit to the activities of consciousness is the ability to discern an object as distinct from itself, as what it is not; but under some circumstances, this interaction positions an existential erasure. I am simultaneously drawn to the realization of myself as an object of reflection through realizations of what I am not, and yet, a part of what I am not is "Man," in my society.[12] Can I doubt that I exist? Perhaps I can think *what* I am not, but I cannot think *that* I am not, and still, black people in an antiblack racist society are demanded to live, and will, as though we are *not*.

Are there realities that militate against black existence? Yes. Do they challenge fundamental ways of relying on consciousness and thought as indubitable indications of one's human right to existence? Without a doubt. So, then, what does it mean to value one's life in a society that fundamentally denies one's humanity? What does it mean to doubt one's own existence, or to be commanded to? Is this tantamount to doubting that one thinks? Is it possible not to think? Not to doubt? Not to affirm? Deny? Love? Hate? These questions require reflection on the existential condition of blackness and problems faced in constructing "free" and "responsible" meanings for human existence in antiblack racist societies. The "self," or "consciousness," conceived in existential terms, is a paradoxical nonentity, nothingness, that finds being through continued series of choices regarding itself, constituent reconstitution of itself, and reality perceived. As Lewis Gordon wrote the following:

> I think about who I am. I consider my name and my biography (what I have been up to this point), and I ask myself, Am I identical with all these phenomena? As I reflect upon them, I am aware of them as, to some extent, out of my reach except as bits of knowledge. They appear frozen. They appear complete. Yet I wonder about what I can become, and I realize a multitude of possibilities . . . I am an unfinished story, a story in progress, of which I am the author. I can choose an end. But I can never know the end in advance, for I could choose at the last moment to change it . . . I can try to find myself, but I can never declare myself as having been found without making the decision continuously to preserve the version discovered. Myself will always be my responsibility. . . . This is because there is no fixed self. . . . There are only semblances, chimera, social constructions, manifested wishes of definite self-hood. In short, outside of these constructions, there is no self; there is, so to speak, a perspective that is, in itself, "nothing." Facing myself as nothing, I am free to present myself under a variety of interpretations . . . I am freedom. As a freedom, I seem to have nowhere to settle down. Wherever I land is always an object to me and is therefore not identical with what I am.[13]

Antiblack racism attempts to deny developmental processes of black consciousness by collapsing the meaning and dynamism of black selfhood into a base objectivity. Consciousness experiences itself through continuous series of subjective "moments," the way a video game character might hop from surface to surface before each disappears. Each fleeting moment of positive footing is the hallmark of human conscious experience. Thus, human consciousness is capable of profound types of doubt in terms of the value, meaning, and constitution of its phenomenal activities.

No matter what ideals my environment, my society, my world proclaims, I should always look around, take stock of the entire affair of reality, as it presents itself to me. I should bear in mind that "the appearance refers to the total series of appearances and not to a hidden reality, which would drain itself of all the *being* (Emphasis in original) of the existent."[14] As Jean-Paul Sartre wrote, "[If we can manage to get beyond] what Nietzsche called the 'illusion of worlds-behind-the-scene,' and if we no longer believe in the being-behind-the-appearance, then the appearance becomes full positivity; its essence is an 'appearing' which is no longer opposed to being but on the contrary is the measure of it."[15] Within antiblack racist societies, there seems to be a form of doubt stitched into the ephemeral fabrics of its being; nothing seems secure; everything seems capable of being spontaneously devalued and destroyed. My experience of being demanded to doubt the validity of black existence, expression, and "appearance" requires elucidation. At first, there was a struggle to reconstruct the forms of positivity that were burst apart; but in the process, I realized, as Fanon put it, "The fragments have been put together again by another self."[16] The existential credo of existence preceding essence becomes nauseatingly apparent. The question, "What should man value in the face of the project of valuing?", confronts black people, who must "exist," in part, by deciding the meaning of a previously shattered self, while constructing one's "self," anew. In this sense, as Sartre put it, "Consciousness is not a mode of particular knowledge which may be called an inner meaning or self-knowledge; it is the dimension of transphenomenal being in the subject."[17] We are faced with the task of having to construct a value for blackness without the luxury of our society's ideals. In effect, I am forced to face my consciousness, to become conscious of my consciousness constructing itself, to face my own nothingness in becoming; but, under what conditions?[18] As Lewis Gordon suggested, such approaches: to determine, what kind of a self a human being chooses as his project is to determine not only what kind of human being the chooser is, but also *who* (Emphasis in original) the human being may be in his particularity in virtue of the choices which make his life meaningful.[19] For my contribution, an account of black nihilism and antiblack racism is here demanded, and hopefully, supplied.

The philosophical anthropology undergirding Western society is founded on "Man" seeking "man in his definition," and this search has traditionally sought a metaphysical foundation for human knowledge, hypothesized to exist solely by virtue of our rationalistic capacities, or experiences of the certainties surrounding mathematics and sciences in relation to the physical and metaphysical world.[20] For instance, what is the nature of the presumed identity relationship between two different types of being, "mind" and "body," experienced as "sameness?" What connects our experiences of the body and our experiences of the mind as substance, that is, consciousness? Descartes's delicate partitioning of himself in addressing these questions was an interrogative inquiry voluntarily and freely undertaken. He was not demanded to "burst apart" before putting himself back together; he was not demanded to defend his existence at the behest of some other being. Nonetheless, Descartes's ushering in of modern rationalistic discourses for European human philosophy, on the heels of the scientific discoveries of Galileo and Copernicus, introduced centuries long, globally expanded, European quests to secure a basis for knowing and establishing "truth," according to a positive certainty emanating from "Man." Cartesian rationalism, in other words, marked the dawn of the "spirit of modern Europe."

Friedrich Nietzsche's philosophy of Nihilism directly questioned Enlightenment attitudes producing traditional ideas of (European) "Man." He questioned the fortitude and ability of European men to face themselves outside constructions of their traditional values. Nietzsche's philosophy can be read as, in part, asking, "What attitude should (European) 'Man' adopt when producing values?" On the other hand, I ask, "What attitude should black people have toward those who have traditionally chosen not to face themselves outside of their traditional values, and who have done so in the form of attempting to block anyone else from facing themselves outside of the traditional values of (European) 'Man'?" What should I do with one who not only seeks to obliterate my black sense of self, but also seeks to impede my path from genuine questions and encounters concerning what is outside of the values of "European Man"? I ask myself, "What attitude should I have toward the traditional ideals of (European) 'Man,' whiteness, which blocks the path to questioning what is outside of, perhaps beyond, the antiblack racist world?" In other words, "What attitude should be taken toward the nihilism of white-normative Human ideals undergirding antiblack racism, or what I call, 'white nihilism'?"

The modern European search for a method of discovering a universal basis for human reality can be read hermeneutically as describing the experiences of consciousnesses trying to ground philosophical projections in terms of science, and yet the reliability of "science" depends upon a philosophical grounding of the basis on which one should accept the conclusions of math and logic. In other words, the "Cartesian Circle" needs a metaphysical basis for assurance *beyond* what is afforded in the presumably closed sets of logical derivation. For instance, if I imagine two brackets, and a series of items with an observable pattern in between, with the last instantiation being left blank, that is, [X, Y, 4, 7, X, Y, 4, 7, X, Y, 4, _], it is possible for me to be reasonably reliant on the logic of sameness in difference, identity in patterns, that strikes my consciousness immediately, as the next item in the series being "7." But, if I remove either, or both brackets, my context disappears. At this point, any patterning projected onto the series becomes possible; even further, I am faced with the possibility of infinity, where patterns disappear. But aren't all meanings forms of patterns cast against a potential infinity of nothingness through which they must substantiate themselves? Aren't all realities, and philosophies, attempts at bracketing or patterning, making *something* knowable against the possibility of the infinite, or the unknowable? What is that unknown infinite that might threaten, or determine human patterns of reality? According to the dramas of my society, at this point, the Christian "God" enters. For, only God, or perhaps a Devil, might possess the power to determine or deceive regarding our most fundamental experiences of ourselves.[21]

My society, my world, seems to be ordained by the God of Europe. Is the God of Europe the guarantor of the rational against the irrational? Is the God of Europe rational? Has he been? The tradition of modern European philosophical anthropology proceeded from a metaphysical presumption of the Christian God as a symbolic referent for infinite being, which was conceived as a perfection, completion, or positivity, a consummate "beyond," that ensures and reinforces the powers and potentials of "rational" human consciousness. If modern Europe's conception of a Christian God is the metaphysical basis upon which human knowledge is affirmed through our rational and logical capacities for reflection, then God functions as the guarantor of a dualistic human world, wherein the realm of the philosophical and scientifical offers certainty. The postulation of a metaphysics beyond the limits of human philosophy in terms of that which we cannot represent as an object of consciousness, but which simultaneously situates our ability for knowing and projecting in general, is a hallmark of the spirit of modern Europe. That is, modern European understandings of humanity were greatly influenced by choices to keep "in order," maintaining in the proper place, a realm of human reality against the metaphysical domain of God.[22]

What more of that unknown, infinite, force lurking in the background of European modernity? This is not to ask about the reality of God, or to question the sincerity of modern European religious beliefs, but rather to ask about existential desires indicated by their dominant philosophies. If each reality is a form of choice, and if Nietzsche is right that Europe's traditional forms of reality have been constrained and bracketed by rationalistic conceptions of reason and scientific reductions of "truth," then the question can be asked: What is *beyond* those particular rationalistic and scientific schemas of traditional values developed by (European) "Man," which continue to deny and burst apart black humanity in the process of affirming its own? What are the conditions of that form of denial? What about its disgusting, noxious, stinky elements, where I, not Descartes, or any of *them*, was *made* to remind myself that I *need* to exist; I *must* exist. What about antiblack racism? Is black suffering some part of God's ultimate enlightenment program for Humanity? Does this mean that I ought to acquiesce to my own suffering in the name of goodness, objectivity, and truth? Everywhere I turn, the mundane functioning of my society insists on me, "Yes; you are a sufferer." Perhaps God has willed it so. Something must have gone wrong. Something always goes wrong. Maybe I wasn't paying attention. I feel myself getting dizzy, again; but I am determined to hold on to something, to brace against something, anything, even if just for a moment. I need footing; but I am beginning to suspect that all footing is temporary, chimerical, or only good enough to get me to the next chimera. One thing seems clear, if I want to avoid dizziness, I have got to keep it moving.

All philosophies respond to the limits of human consciousness; but where does the realm of the phenomenal end? Where should one conceive the line to be drawn? If all truths may be equally chimerical, then the activities of choosing and desiring remain elements of projection that can be described. Nietzsche's critique of the spirit of Europe, for example, evaluates modern philosophical-anthropological traditions in terms of choices made through confrontations with existential being. His analysis did not restrict consciousness to terms of truth and falsity, or good and evil, but rather in terms of categories of activity and passivity. For example, he considered it a passive activity of consciousness to reduce the dynamism of human life to a correlate of metaphysical being exclusively in terms of rationalism and moralism; he considered active consciousness by inverting the dialectic of Cartesian dualism and making freedom the thesis of human life against an infinitely unknowable beyond. This question of making life meaningful and free in spite of a potentially limiting meaninglessness is the foundation for a philosophy of nihilism.

How should one choose to exist in the face of nihilism? How should I *be* in relation to the fact that whatever way I choose, there is never meaning in itself, but always a nothingness that simultaneously seems *beyond* my choices, *and* lying at the center of my choices? I seem to be a nothingness that experiences reality, a consciousness. I project my nothingness as negations against an inherent nothingness of existence that precedes me, which I experience as apart from me, existing in itself: all of which, brings about the paradoxical occasion for experiencing myself as a simultaneous being and nothingness. Or, as Sartre wrote, "Consciousness is an abstraction since it conceals within itself an ontological source in the region of the in-itself, and conversely the phenomenon is likewise an abstraction since it must 'appear' to consciousness."[23] I am a nothingness that comes into being by negating myself against a further nothingness, discovering what I am in virtue of what I am not, in which and through which I am constantly having to perform a nihilating activity. "The concrete is man within the world in that specific union of man with the world. . . . Is there any conduct which can reveal to me the relation of man with the world?" asked Sartre. His answer strikes me as correct: "[It] is a human attitude filled with meaning." But, the question remains, "What does this attitude reveal to us?"[24] If all meaning is chosen, then what about thoughts of my black meaning? What about thoughts of my blackness in the face of antiblack racist denials and threats of the cessation of my being? It seems that I am anything, everything, and *nothing* I choose to be, which comes with a nauseating realization that I am simultaneously a choice to be, whose choices of being constantly elude my grasp.

I feel another piece of reality slipping away. I am like a psychiatric patient wondering if I should have myself recommitted. How do I live; how does anyone, knowing deep down that we are all nothing? Am I made to fight against being made into nothingness in the antiblack racist world only to realize that I am a nothingness in any schema beyond it? This is the final straw; I can't go on anymore. I am in a death spin. I need to rest. There is nowhere to rest. Where can I rest? Anywhere, I don't care. Idealism. Rationalism. Empiricism. Colonialism. Whiteness. Where is my suit and tie? They are all starting to look appealing; Christianity, God? I'll take it all! "But just as I reached the other side, I stumbled, and the movement, the attitudes, the glances of the other fixed me there."[25] Should I have accepted that "civilizing deluge" of modern European rationality, morality, respectability, and above all, Christ? Even if I so desired, may I? Or would those particular ideals stand in need of justification for their original exclusions of blackness from the purview of who exactly counted as earth's human population?

We are inundated with antiblack racist desires cloaked in objectivist, idealist languages. I read John Locke's universalistic pronouncements claiming insight into Humanity and natural rights and wondered how he still managed to value being a shareholder in England's largest African slave-ship building enterprises, "The Royal African Company." I read Kant's insights into the rationalist nature of human morality, and his analytic-synthetic articulations of human epistemology, and wondered how he still managed to value producing an antiblack racist anthropological taxonomy alongside essays instructing on how to properly flog Africans.[26] I read Hegel's depictions of rationalism in relation to metaphysical movements, conflicts, and potential reconciliations between human consciousness and universal will, and wondered how he still managed to value depicting black bodies (Africa) as being a site where consciousness, literally, does not exist.[27] The philosophical impact of these luminaries of whiteness, among others, are well-known to any student of Western Humanism. The ways in which each of the above thinkers, and others, committed to certain forms of antiblack racist ideals in nihilistic ways, thereby situating traditional ideals of whiteness continuing to operate today, will be explored.

"Nihilism" can be used to describe engagements attempting to face or retreat from, that is, be active or passive in response to, absurdities within the situation of human valuing. Nietzsche's critique of European philosophy, for example, raised questions relevant for considerations of strength and freedom in human life against potentially debilitating conceptions of that which is "beyond" traditional values. Value projections, from this viewpoint, are cast against what might inevitably be a despairing, if not horrible, yet surmountable, nothingness of meaning at the center of the predicament of human existence. Nietzsche raised the question of what is beyond the rationality and science, reasonability and goodness, God, and ultimate value of modern Europe? What is that which is beyond the horizon of the phenomenal world conditioning the incompleteness of meaning at the center of human understanding? What is that nothingness against which I experience myself as consciousness by virtue of a negative activity, negation, identifying myself as that which I am not? What is this process of nothingness finding its being through acts of nihilation? What should we call this entire affair of describing experiences of consciousness induced to profound forms of pessimism concerning the existence of all human meaning; yet, against which one must, to avoid dizziness, suicide, or potentially murder, continue to produce meaning? Nihilism.

I am interested in nihilism as a phenomenon describing engagements questioning reality, and as an attempt to live freely and strongly in relation to its absurdities. I struggle to understand, as I simultaneously struggle to live through, my antiblack racist society. However, my struggle is not against what Arthur Schopenhauer conceived as "universal will," or the cosmos itself, or any of that. As I have said, the antiblack racist world does not typically offer black people a genuine encounter with such dilemmas. What I mean is that black people struggle against an irrational force of human willing, which appeared to me the moment I became aware of myself as a social being beyond the contexts of my family and the marginal spaces of my community. A great shadow cast an eclipse of nothing less than the sun holding my systems of belief in goodness and fairness together in orbit; something forcibly, violently, and repeatedly penetrated my world, thrusting meaninglessness, uncertainty, and doubt, into the annals of my existence. Something impedes my theorizing of a world of meaning beyond this one. A shadowy figure, God? No, antiblack racism. There is only "Man"; yet the shadow of (European) "Man" is expansive. He blocks my way. Maybe he doesn't know it; maybe he does. What I *know* is that he patrols for me, hunts me, and develops elaborate systems designed to make me doubt that I am a human.

In an antiblack racist society, it is easy to imagine, anticipate, and even develop well-rehearsed schemas of response, to any of the myriad of potential ways the structural, institutional, and, in particular, police and military wings of society can swoop down and instantly make what is left of one's life a living hell. "Hell," here, can take on Fanon's meaning in his consideration of Dante's *Inferno* as compared to the experiences of nonbeing in black life." In most cases, the black man lacks the advantage of being able to accomplish this descent into a real hell.[28] It is hell for consciousness to exist within reality as situated beyond the borders of reason and rationality, or beyond morality and ethics, by Kantian deontological extension, and right and law, by Lockean liberal extension. That black peoples, families, and communities, entire localized and globalized organizations and systems of human values, can be assaulted, pillaged, damaged, destroyed, incarcerated, if not outright taken away, and killed for a rationality that defies reason, a morality that defies goodness, and for a justice that defies fairness, all carried out with the coolness and calmness of avowedly free beings, makes it difficult to conclude otherwise than that antiblack racism, its proponents and apologists, depend upon an initial supplanting of the role of the metaphysical in relation to black life, underneath which certain forms of black knowledge, ethics, and "survival" may be possible. However, survival can be a form of passivity in the form of subsistence.

I am not interested in survival; I am interested in activity. My question is, "How does one actively affirm black selfhood in an antiblack racist world, especially when rationalistic and moralistic means have proven historically futile, if not silly?"[29] How can my belief and desires not draw down on me with the crushing weight of the universe, especially, if I do not have a legitimate possibility for philosophically making sense of them, or publicly demonstrating and having reciprocally recognized as a constitutive participant in political society, my projections, values, and expressions, through which to share, engage others, and become engaged by others. How do I affirm myself when something about my antiblack racist society outlaws me as an "impurity?"[30] What is it about this world that requires blackness to be viewed as an impurity? White nihilism. The next two chapters seek to explain white nihilism mainly through an exposition of Arthur Schopenhauer's philosophy of pessimism and Friedrich Nietzsche's philosophy of nihilism. The existential phenomenon of "Pessimism" is explained as a process of devaluing decadent, no longer sustainable, values. "Nihilism" is explained as the process of attempting to forge newer values in light of pessimism. Schopenhauer's and Nietzsche's thoughts on the existential phenomena of pessimism and nihilism are illuminating for thinking about the existential struggles of European "Man," however, I will only focus on these struggles in terms of their historical roles in constructing the ideal of "whiteness," and as a result, antiblack racism and black nihilism.

Part I of this book does not undertake an exhaustive genealogy of (European) "Man." I do, however, elucidate the production of values necessitating antiblack racism, what Cornel West considered, the white "gaze," from which the perspectives of (European) "Man" emanate.[31] Then, I will show how antiblack racism is undergirded by modern European philosophical frameworks with ontological presumptions, axiological determinations, and existential commitments to values abysmally delimiting consciousness while restricting the boundaries of Humanity to peoples recognized as racially white.

In chapter 2, I offer a sketch of traditional modern (European) "Man" as a nihilist. Delineations between passive and active, and weak and strong, forms of nihilism are explained and discussed in relation to (European) "Man." These connections between modern European philosophies of "Man," and nihilism, are explained as "weak nihilism."

In chapter 3, I offer an analysis of weak nihilism and antiblack racism, or what I call, "white nihilism," which is identified as inherent in the axiological structures of antiblack racist values. Chapter 3 explains that antiblack racism is borne of a basic form of weak nihilism, or "white nihilism." It concludes by demonstrating historical Western commitments and gestures supporting white nihilism and antiblack racism, and that this phenomenon continues to drive antiblack racist commitments in the twenty-first century. I end part I by raising the question of the potential for the category of "black nihilism" to be a healthy response to white nihilism and antiblack racism.

Part II of this book seeks to develop a fundamental framework for theorizing about black nihilism. Chapter 4 offers an analysis of two traditional pillars of black American cultural responses to antiblack racism. The question of strong versus weak black nihilism in response to antiblack racism is raised in light of a discussion of what I call Derrick Bell's pessimism and Cornel West's optimism. To achieve this goal, their philosophies are explored in terms of their convergence on the existential and socioeconomic plights of black people in America. Divergences in their thought are explored in terms of Bell's advocation for a pessimistic attitude, whereas West advocated for optimism in favor of traditional black Christian ideals, as a counter-posit to antiblack racist realities. The divergence between Bell's and West's thoughts is used to support a theoretical framework establishing at least two dominant poles of black responses to antiblack racism. Bell's pessimism is distinguished from West's optimism as more conducive for considering the strengths of black nihilism; however, I interrogate both positions in light of previously established categories of nihilistic strength and weakness. I argue, for instance, that nihilistic attitudes in response to antiblack racism are only viewed negatively when collapsing the inherent dynamism of the phenomenon into a singular modality. In this way, I argue, black Christian optimism, for example, has traditionally played a militating role against certain forms of black nihilism and pessimism. I believe West's classical critique of the political and philosophical dimensions of black Christianity are validated; however, I also question the limitations of what can be argued as the Kierkegaardian elements of his response to antiblack racism. By demonstrating the shortcomings of Kierkegaard's philosophy for responding to pessimism and nihilism, I hope to provide a useful context for reconsidering the values of traditional black optimistic attitudes in response to today's antiblack racist world. The Kierkegaardian elements of black Christian optimism are interrogated in Jean-Paul Sartre's languages of "anguish," "bad faith," and "freedom."

Derrick Bell's pessimism is contrasted with Schopenhauer's philosophies of resignation. Important distinctions between Schopenhauer and Bell's black pessimism are identified and discussed.[32] It is determined that weak nihilistic frameworks motivate black optimistic responses to antiblack racism, and that black pessimism, while running the risk of producing weak black nihilistic responses, can lead to strong black nihilism. I begin chapter 4 explaining two traditional forms of black responses to antiblack racism in the United States, theorizing Bell's pessimism as a paradigmatic correlate of West's optimism. I conclude the chapter by citing several critics of West's philosophy on black nihilism.

Chapter 5 explores the potential for strong black nihilistic attitudes to be a valuable response to antiblack racism through a discussion of Frantz Fanon's existential philosophy. A direct answer to the question "What kinds of values should black people produce in the face of whiteness?" is attempted. Can strong black nihilism be a healthy response to antiblack racism? Frantz Fanon's thought on the subject is the center of this chapter. Although Fanon never mentioned "nihilism," in his work, there are various points where his thought can be used to support my theoretical framework identifying nihilism as attenuating antiblack racism and how to strongly respond to it. Fanon's thought can be used to illustrate the complete processes of black nihilism responding to white nihilism and antiblack racism. Journeying through Fanon's optimistic ascents, and pessimistic crash and burns, as depicted in his chapter on "the lived experience of the black," for instance, can be used to situate reflections on the ultimate fates and limitations of strengths and weaknesses awaiting such protagonists.[33] Fanon's thought addresses the freedoms and limitations of black existential subjectivities in antiblack racist societies. For instance, his critique of Sartre's "Black Orpheus," and its dialectical evaluation of *negritude*, suggested that Sartre missed crucial points about the lived experiences of blackness. There are absurdities abounding in the black existential situation that make its theorization imperceptive to purely dialectical methodologies. The lived experiences of antiblack racist rationalities inverting and perverting the terms necessary for dialogical consideration of the black experience, the fact that certain forms of political irony, violence, and contradictory existential movement, vulgarity, may become necessary from the space of blackness in an antiblack society, are considered in Fanon's terms. These forms of reasoning are at the center of my critique of Western philosophy and European "Man," which I find support for in Fanon's writings, and articulate through the aforementioned categories of pessimism and nihilism. Fanon's responses to antiblack racism are offered as an illustration of strong black nihilism. His depiction of the concept of "existential freedom" can be used to illuminate a link between strong black nihilism and mature responses to antiblack racism.

I consider the conclusions of my analysis within a vibrant debate in black American scholarship on the issues of black pessimism and black optimism. I explain what is sometimes called the Afropessimism debate in terms of the philosophies of Stephen Best, Saidiya Hartman, Achille Mbembe, Frank Wilderson, III, Jared Sexton, Steven Martinot, Fred Moten, and others, each of whom are explained in terms of their positioning within the Afropessimism debate and my theorization of black nihilism. After demonstrating how black nihilism can fundamentally accommodate the terms of the Afropessimism debate, I end chapter 5 by introducing the notion of aesthetic responses to pessimistic realities (initially raised through my discussion of Schopenhauer and Nietzsche). Here, I set up the final chapter's theorizing of certain black aesthetic productions, reflective of struggles for human freedom faced while living through nihilistic processes of transitioning from dying to living values.

The final chapter of this book attempts to track the black nihilistic twists, turns, and series of developments previously raised, through the categories of "youth," "maturity," and "hip-hop music and culture," understood as a dominant mode of aesthetic expression, reflections and projections, which may be indicative of potentially strong nihilistic ways of future being for generations of black adults. I offer a critique suggesting that the circumstances of antiblack racism eviscerate the existential category of black youth in such a way that traditional elements of optimism otherwise to be found therein succumb to a profound pessimism. I argue that the lived realities of pessimism situate the nihilism of black American youth, which involves a hidden suspicion of weak nihilism both on the parts of antiblack racism and black Christianity, alike. Furthermore, since creativity in hope is the domain of youth, black youth are particularly in need of the most protection and cultivation as a space where strong nihilistic possibilities, not weakness, is nurtured. Engaging the aesthetic productions of black youth is a fundamental and necessary means for achieving this goal.

Finally, I conclude this monograph by arguing that black nihilism is a force for the future of black youth, one that uses freedom in expression, vulgarity, creativity, art, literature, music, dance, and so on, all as vehicles through which new, strong, healthy, and mature values for blackness can emerge. The role of music, in particular, as a form of value production is discussed by Nietzsche in *The Birth of Tragedy from the Spirit of Music*, where it is suggested that certain forms of tragic poetry set to melodies over Attic stage productions may be our best means for aesthetically representing the pessimism of the human existential situation while simultaneously depicting our nihilistic struggles to forge newer values for its meanings.[34] I illustrate connections between Nietzsche's conceptions of nihilistic art and certain forms of hip-hop music productions through a discussion that focuses on works by the artist, Kendrick Lamar. For example, similarities and differences are drawn and discussed between Kendrick's albums, *Section 80* and *Damn*, and the nihilistic travails of optimism and pessimism found in Fanon's work. After articulating the need for philosophical engagements with certain hip-hop productions as a means for bolstering and facilitating the development of strong black nihilistic attitudes among black youth, I offer some concluding remarks concerning my hope-filled prayers for contemporary generations of youth who are striving through the situation of nihilism and antiblack racism in the twenty-first century, envisioning and constructing future anti-racist, humane, political, and social human worlds: the youth who deserve every ounce of support and scholarly wisdom we can offer as they are at the frontlines of today's struggles to potentially make politically and socially reified those long-held ideals of Humanity and freedom for which so many people have fought, for centuries, and continue to fight for, today.

So, why "nihilism"? Why choose the term first popularly used by Jacobi, in 1799, which is derived from the Latin, *nihil*, meaning nothing, colloquially understood as a rejection of all religious and moral principles, or a belief that life is meaningless? Why should that term involve a productive response to antiblack racism? Well, if "nihilism" simply means an attitude of wanton individualism, or destruction, then there is no good reason for supporting it. However, there are forms of nihilism that can be strong, productive, and worthy of our support. If one persists, "But, isn't there some other way, besides nihilism?" I respond, if I am asked to choose between nihilism and not, in the sense that attitudes and beliefs can be chosen, then I think it is a mistake to consider the question, or even the questioner, as having any other alternative. There is no decision to be made between nihilism and not; there are only choices to be faced concerning which forms of nihilism, and why. Nihilism, considered as a responsive attitude, amounts to more than the paradoxical formulation of a philosophy that profoundly rejects all philosophies.[35] What about that which occasions those kinds of attitudes in people? Does the question, "Why choose nihilism?", entail a presumption that there is some positivity that nihilistic choices negatively tear themselves away from? I ask the questioner, is there some inherent positive meaning in things that nihilists simply fail to grasp? Or might the nihilist grasp an inherent meaninglessness at the center of the appearance of meaning in things? This formulation of the question establishes inquiries into nihilism as a subject of philosophical study. So, how should I answer the questioner, "Why nihilism?" Any answer one could supply will depend on the multitudinous elements of consciousness and lived experiences, and judgments of those experiences, constituting and concerning each individual. I can only attempt to make you see reality as it appears for many of us: perhaps to inform you, but primarily to render undeniable, or at least intelligible, the value of some of our choices. You may or may not recognize yourself in the analyses provided throughout the rest of this book. In the meanwhile, I ask you, the reader, the questioner, to lend yourself to the thoughts, experiences, feelings, travails, frustrations, joys, accomplishments, defeats, contoured twisting and turnings, growths and pains of optimisms, pessimisms, doubts, fissures, disruptions, reconciliations, resiliencies, and nihilisms of consciousnesses that may or may not be other than their own.

NOTES

1. Friedrich Nietzsche, *The Will to Power*, trans. Walter Kaufmann (New York: Vintage Books, 1967), 1: 3. Originally published (posthumously) in 1901.
2. Ibid. 14: 14.
3. For an example of this kind of critical race theory, see, K. Anthony Appiah and Amy Gutmann, *Color Conscious: The Political Morality of Race* (New Jersey: Princeton University Press, 1996), 74–105.
4. "It should be borne in mind that 'essence' does not here mean the traditional, Aristotelian, notion of an identity-relation between a thing and the property without which a thing cannot be what it 'is'—that is, a substance." Lewis Gordon, *Fanon and the Crisis of European Man* (New York: Routledge, 1995), 15. See, also, Aristotle, *The Basic Works of Aristotle: Metaphysics*, trans. W.D. Ross, ed. Richard McKeon (New York: Random House, 1941), Z, 1029b12–1032a10.
5. Lewis Gordon, *Bad Faith and Antiblack Racism* (New York: Humanity Books), 1–6.
6. Frantz Fanon, *Black Skin; White Masks*, trans. Charles Lam Markmann (New York: Grove Press, 1967), 109–140.
7. Charles Mills, *The Racial Contract* (New York: Cornell University Press, 1997).
8. Fanon, *Black Skin; White Masks*, 109.
9. Ibid.
10. René Descartes, *Meditations on First Philosophy*, trans. Michael Moriarty (England: Oxford University Press, 2008). Originally published in 1641.
11. Inherent to both theories is an essentialized notion of "self," or "subject," that reflects and determines "objective" meaning. This ontological dualism is a hallmark of modern European philosophy and is traditionally understood through the respective epistemologies of rationalism and empiricism, wherein conscious activity is understood to result in projections that are representatively reflected by consciousness

as epistemically true, or false, in relation to material reality. For Locke's empiricism, see John Locke, *An Essay Concerning Human Understanding* (Oxford: Clarendon Press, 1979), originally published in 1695.

12. See, Tommy Curry, *The Man-Not* (Philadelphia: Temple University Press, 2017).

13. Gordon, *Bad Faith and Antiblack Racism*, 9.

14. "[To] the extent that men had believed in noumenal realities, they have presented appearance as a pure negative. It was that which is 'not being'; it had no other being than that of illusion and error. But even this being was borrowed, it was itself a pretense, and philosophers met with the greatest difficulty in maintaining cohesion and existence in the appearance so that it should not itself be reabsorbed in the depth of non-phenomenal being."

See, Jean-Paul Sartre, *Being and Nothingness*, trans. Hazel e. Barnes (New York: Washington Square Press, 1956), 4.

15. Ibid.

16. Fanon, *Black Skin; White Masks*, 109.

17. Ibid. 10.

18. Sartre, *Being and Nothingness*, 9–17.

19. Gordon, *Bad Faith and Antiblack Racism*, 5.

20. Descartes sought a universal foundation for human knowledge in logical and mathematical terms: his identification of "consciousness (mind)," "identity (a priori)," and "substance (body)," as the fundamental ontological categories within which human existence comes to apprehend and know itself. Our a priori capacities provide an understanding of "identity" that enables human knowledge concerning material reality, including our own concerning bodies, occasioning the famous "mind-body" problem.

21. See, for example, Descartes's Third Meditation, in his *First Philosophy*, where he argued that God is the source of the human ideal of perfection, understood through the a priori, and therefore not a source of deception (Devil). See Descartes's discussion of "perfection" and "God."

22. It should be noted, despite Descartes's insistence that the rational realm is guaranteed by God, his scientific rationalism still raised the ire of the church. Seeing what happened to Galileo, and considering Descartes's own admirations of Galileo's work, it can be questioned to what extent Descartes saw himself as advancing grounds for the removal of divine understanding in scientific inquiry, or perhaps erecting a rationalistic Christian God to compliment the influence that Francis Bacon's scientism, for example, clearly had on him.

23. Sartre, *Being and Nothingness*, 34.

24. Ibid. 35.

25. Fanon, *Black Skin; White Masks*, 109.

26. Emmanuel Chukwudi Eze, "The Color of Reason: The Idea of Race in Kant's Anthropology," in *Postcolonial African Philosophy: A Critical Reader*, ed. Emmanuel Eze (Oxford: Blackwell Press, 1997), 103–140.

27. Georg Wilhelm Friedrich Hegel, *The Philosophy of History*, trans. John Sibree (New York: Dover Publications, 1956), 174–175.

28. Fanon, *Black Skin; White Masks*, 8.

29. Lewis Gordon, *Existentia Africana* (New York: Routledge, 2000), 41–61. In particular, see his discussion of violence while analyzing Frederick Douglass's famous fight with the "slave breaker," Covey. There, Gordon explains ways in which the fight was "a moment of scratching through [a] veil of nonseeing and raising the question of pushing the stakes up to otherness."

30. "In the *weltanschauung* [worldview] of a colonized people there is an impurity, a flaw that outlaws ontological explanation." Fanon, *Black Skin; White Masks*, 110.

31. Cornel West, *Prophesy Deliverance!* (Louisville: London Westminster Knox Press, 2002), originally published in 1982. See, especially, chapter two, entitled, "A Genealogy of Modern Racism."

32. Derrick Bell, *Faces at the Bottom of the Well: The Permanence of Racism* (New York: Basic Books, 1992).

33. Fanon, *Black Skin; White Masks*, 109–140.

34. Friedrich Nietzsche, *The Birth of Tragedy*, trans. Francis Golffing (New York: Anchor Books, 1956).

35. Webster's Dictionary, for example, traditionally defines nihilism as a "rejection of all religious and moral principles, in the belief that life is meaningless" or "an extreme skepticism maintaining that nothing in the world has real existence." "Nihilism," *Merriam-Webster.com Dictionary*, Merriam-Webster, https://www.merriam-webster.com/dictionary/nihilism.

Chapter 2

(European) "Man" and Weak Nihilism

> There is a physical difference between the white and black races which I believe will forever forbid the two races living together on terms of social and political equality . . . there must be superior and inferior . . . I, as much as any other man, am in favor of having the superior position assigned to the white race.[1]

The fact of antiblack racism, today, is less in need of demonstration than it is in need of enumeration and illumination. Antiblack racism remains the hue of mundane reality, at least in the United States, and its tentacles are well-documented as having gripped the globe. How do ideals generated by peoples centuries ago continue to color our reality? Black people have always been able to see the contradictions of antiblack racist logics, but, today, are able to socially respond and make known in a variety of publicly discursive ways the contradictory nature of the illusions supporting the phenomenon. I do not find it difficult to ascertain the philosophical and moral illegitimacy of antiblack racism; however, there is difficulty in explaining a preponderance of fallacies from the seventeenth through nineteenth centuries and their legitimacy in the twenty-first. How does antiblack racism, which has been laid bare, dramatized, and satirized in plain view of the public, continue to dominate contemporary cultural realities? Veils have fallen, it seems, and yet antiblack racism persists; how can that be? Another way of asking this question is, "Why do antiblack racists insist upon the veil of white supremacist values so desperately?"

I have come to exist within a world enshrouded by veils of modern European thoughts, philosophies, and perspectives, which smother my humanity in ideals of whiteness. These veils are so cold, so thin; yet I cannot breathe through them. I cannot believe these veils are sought, by some, in their quest for life, and warmth. I imagine that whatever the constructors of these veils were facing, they found it to be absolutely frigid, horrifying, and for them, ought to be avoided at all cost. What is that which antiblack racist ideals of whiteness seeks to cloak itself from? Pessimism and nihilism. Underneath antiblack racist veils of whiteness stands a nihilistic human being, responding to the fundamental existential conditions of Humanity, with weakness. Life beyond antiblack racism involves facing nihilism. "Nihilism" references the process of attempting to construct newer values in the place of fallen ones. I aim to show it is also a constitutive feature of antiblack racism. As a subject of European philosophical reflection, "nihilism" is genealogically akin to the historical emergence of antiblack racism in Western life; both proceed from the cultivation of existential categories pertaining to Enlightenment forms of imperial reasoning and colonization, or the construction of (European) "Man."[2] (European) "Man" has historically imposed himself upon the world by colonially establishing systems of white supremacist social, political, and cultural values, alongside antiblack racist institutions, structuring those realities. The result has been an attempt to make the ideals of (European) "Man" function like the primordial will of the universe, out of which black life might, perhaps, construct alternative realities in order to make this tragic fact of black existence bearable.[3]

The apparent permanence of antiblack racism challenging each of my attempts at constructions of selfhood is experienced, by me, to be as far-reaching, vast, and inextricable from reality, as time and space. My positioning within the space of blackness in a white universe, on this level, is an existential and geographical affair. I write this book from a location physically centered in the middle of my city's black space, or ghetto; I also read Charles Mills explain that the blackness of my positioning results, in part, from an ontological chasm dividing race in this society, one that is prescribed by moral, political, and epistemic norms, or a "racial contract."[4] In particular, Mills described an epistemological contract undergirding Western society, a tacit agreement among antiblack racists, wherein the sphere of human knowledge production is limited to white bodies and spaces.[5] What would (European) "Man" say for himself regarding my encounter with this absurd dimension of his existence, out of which it seems, his chosen way of making life bearable demands that my life be made unbearable, if not completely erased? What are the fundamental features of the valuations of (European) "Man" that requires eradicating me as a source of value production?

Where should I look for an honest account of (European) "Man?" I want to hear him speak for himself, honestly, and in his own words; but that man rarely ever chooses to speak to me plainly, least of all regarding his own trials and tribulations. So, I read what they wrote among themselves, when they were most certain someone like me wasn't literate or erudite enough to attend their conversation, let alone grasp and challenge its meanings.

There I was, reading European philosophers. I was a fly on the wall; I was pitched too high and nestled too perfectly in the forgotten backdrop to be noticed or swatted at. Here is what I have learned.

The weaknesses and self-doubts of (European) "Man" are plainly admitted among some of its nontraditional philosophers. They met in an undisclosed backroom of European philosophy. There, I learned of their consideration that nihilism, in the case of Nietzsche, and pessimism, predominantly, in the case of Schopenhauer, was believed to be an indispensable, if not natural, feature of the Human developmental process, which required developing responses for facing absurdities in existence. As to be expected, mentions of antiblack racist values appear only incidentally. The center of their thought is not on justifying white supremacy, which is already presumed, but on how (European) "Man" ought to produce value in the face of absurdities. Phenomenal consciousness in black bodies, here, are not considered as part of human reality. What one finds is (European) "Man" asking the question of how to make life valuable in spite of a tacitly acknowledged realization that life has no meaning. As I will explain, I observed conditions under which modern traditions of whiteness were developed, resisting apprehensions of the meaninglessness of its own existence, and negatively deflecting that meaninglessness onto blackness; I observed whiteness rendering itself as a positivity in Human existence by virtue of that which it must negate itself against, which in this case, is blackness. On this view, black consciousness becomes a surrogate nothingness to be dominated, and overcome, in place of the immutability of the primordial universe of cosmic will, which can be denied, avoided, or perhaps hidden from, so long as there are black *bodies*, as overly determined objects, against which white consciousness can affirm the value of its projections. I call this entire affair "white nihilism."

It would be beyond the scope of the present study to give an exhaustive account of (European) "Man's" proclamations of positivity regarding the knowable orders of reality, against which, (European) "Nihilistic Man" ultimately emerged in the backroom of modernity and began disclosing serious doubts. Nonetheless, this chapter offers a theorization that fundamental traditions of (European) "Man" can be designated as "weak nihilistic."

In the final analysis, Nietzsche's and Schopenhauer's words struck me as among the most honest and in-depth philosophical attempts at wrestling with the doubts of (European) "Man," but there were precedents. As a clandestine observer, I had witnessed each of Europe's major philosophers pass through the room, at some point. Some stayed and entertained the conversations longer than others. I couldn't make out all of the voices or discover every merit of each conversation. Some voices I had heard before, and some conversations I could easily recognize; others I knew only by name, and book titles. I can trace, for you, a sketch of some of the varied conversations concerning doubt, pessimism, nihilism, and existential attitudes of (European) "Man," observed through my serendipitously fly positioning. Here are a few noteworthy discussions, and admissions of doubt, within (European) "Man," that I found most useful.

Traditional modern European philosophy depends upon the idea that human existence involves the capacity to rationally order the world.[6] Ancient Mediterranean philosophies grew through medieval Christian theologies and Islamic thought that eventuated into modern European philosophical and scientific ideals.[7] In other words, modern European thought emerged through a struggle between religious belief and rational knowledge.[8] René Descartes famously positioned philosophy in the middle of the modern fight between science and theology by introducing a philosophical framework for the thinking "ego," as the site of preeminent cognitive representations where representative human knowledge of the external world is possible.[9] His was the first voice I heard. He argued that scientific knowledge required legitimization through a priori understanding, because human knowledge needed to meet conditions of epistemic certainty premised on one as a thinking and willing being.[10] In other words, scientific truth, on this view, needs philosophical legitimization; human knowledge requires certainty *beyond* rational doubt. Rationality is ultimately defended by Descartes, but only after being considered against a contextualizing *beyond*, which, for him, was "God."[11]

Descartes introduced modern questions concerning epistemic conditions for human knowledge. He championed the certainty of reason as the foundation of human knowledge's triumph over metaphysical skepticism. He introduced the modern philosophical moment in traditional European thought. This view challenged, for example, the religious traditionalism of St. Augustine, who argued, in *Against the Academics*, Christian faith is primary for human knowledge. In other words, St. Augustine argued that metaphysical skepticism required faith in divine revelation to be overcome.[12] For Descartes, however, skepticism is not overcome by faith but rather by rational proofs. He rationalized medieval conceptions of religious faith.[13] His dualist rationalist epistemology was able to maintain a conception of God's ontological existence, and moral goodness, alongside certainties of mathematics and logic, by attributing a rational nature to the metaphysical universe that works in accordance with traditional Christian theologies.[14]

> When we consider the immensity of God, it is manifest that there can be nothing at all that does not depend on him: not only any subsistent being, but no order, no law, no reason of truth and goodness.[15]

Descartes's thought was not merely a theological proof of God's existence. Although he affirmed Christianity, he envisioned a metaphysical cosmos of limitless perfection alongside a realm of perfectly human knowledge impervious to divine intervention. He effectively removed God from human affairs.[16] The modern European philosophical conversation began with Cartesian affirmations of the potency of reason to definitively determine the "truths" of metaphysical and physical reality. Descartes's carved out a basic framework of Christian faith and pure reason.

The next voice I heard was Immanuel Kant's. He offered a *Critique of Pure Reason* (1781), where he exposited transcendental conditions for rational understanding, alongside antinomies between imperatives of reason and freedoms of will. He investigated reason's potency to ethically effect human willing. In *Critique of Practical Reason* (1788), he framed the question of human knowledge in terms of tension between human experiences of phenomena and things beyond phenomena, or "noumena." He argued, in response to Descartes, that there is an impassible barrier between phenomenal experience and noumenal reality.[17] Kant resolved the tension between noumena and phenomena by presuming a positive logical order within metaphysical reality but dividing the universe into practical and pure parts. On this view, Humanity uses practical reason to understand the universalistic principles of pure reason, or synthetic a priori judgments, which amounts to non-tautological, nonempirical knowledge, as "truth."[18] For example, in his *Groundwork for the Metaphysics of Morals* (1785), Kant said, "Where do we get the concept of God as the highest good from? Solely from the idea of moral perfection that reason lays out for us a priori and which it ties, unbreakably, to the concept of a free will."[19] Human understanding, he argued, uses practical reason to ascertain universal principles, that is, "the highest good."[20] He described a dualism entailed by human experience. He admitted, though, that human perspectives on metaphysical reality are necessarily limited.[21]

Kantian and Cartesian thought fundamentally shaped the modern European philosophical conversation and its traditional proclamations. It is traditionally based on a rationalistic form of optimistic hypostasizing regarding "truth." Traditional European philosophy proclaimed knowledge of universal truths, although Kant acknowledged important epistemological limitations, and Descartes died before he could develop a succinct resolution for the mind/body problem.[22] The spirit of modern (European) "Man" is traditionally articulated in light of such declarations claiming to know universal truth, and natural order, by which, as it goes, Humanity ought to be socially and politically ordered.

Johann Fichte's criticism of Kant's idealism was the next voice that I discerned. He made a gesture that there may be an unavoidable pessimism attenuating both Descartes and Kant's proclamations concerning (European) "Man" and his knowledge. When it was Fichte's turn to speak, he openly wondered whether universal truth and order were nothing more than products of imagination, ultimately produced for purposes of keeping purposelessness at bay. He, at first, agreed with Kant that humans could not, properly speaking, *know* noumena; but Fichte rejected Kant's claim that phenomenal projections needed to know noumena to be meaningful. Fichte argued that freedom in *imagination*, not noumena, was the justificatory grounds for knowledge. Fichte proposed abolishing the role of noumena in human knowledge formation. Kant suspected an internally rational, ordered metaphysical universe. Fichte imagined noumena as indefinable. Thus, he resolved problems of dualism by developing an ontological monism that is only *experienced* as a dualism. He distinguished between the world of human experiences and the world of cosmological universality. He labeled phenomenal perspectives of human experience an "I," which orders all that is beyond it, or the noumenal "not-I," of the empirical and metaphysical worlds. According to Fichte, the phenomenal "I" finds its limits beyond the noumenal world of the "not-I," by attempting to logically order the metaphysical world of the "absolute-I."[23] In this way, he imagined, the limitations of human life are necessarily limited by the absolute-I's *annihilation* of the meaning of the not-I.[24]

Fichte's words struck me immediately. He was describing the activities of (European) "Man's" value projections, which included pure reason, as being primarily manifested through imagination. Point duly noted. According to the private testimonies of Fichte, Kant, and Descartes, thus far, (European) "Man" has admitted his projections and desires for universal "truth," but as Fichte is about to reveal, he finds himself overwhelmed, exhausted, and rejected in the process. Existential exhaustion, according to Fichte, results from tension between I and not-I, where (European) "Man" experiences himself through his investigations of mystifying dimensions of human experiences as weak in his capacities for transcending the conflict.[25]

Fichte challenged optimistic idealism within Enlightenment thought when proclaiming that Humanity confronts the exhaustion of its own mechanisms in attempting to represent the absolute-I to itself. On his view, Humanity reaches its limitations when engaging metaphysical reality, and in revulsion projects repulsiveness onto the not-I. I listened, carefully, "The returning motion of the I from its repulse by the infinite . . . and the feeling that it engenders is attributed to the object, to the not-I."[26] In other words, exhaustion results from pursuit of universal meaning; one experiences exhaustion through a longing for universality that one can never attain.[27] I wonder, what valuation Fichte is going to attach to that which is beyond the imagination of (European) "Man," which enables his processes through an energy and activity of imagination that guarantees support for modern European orderings of antiblack racist world? "God," is invoked by (European) "Man," this time through Fichte, as a symbolic referent for the *beyond*.[28] Fichte said that to avoid existential exhaustion, the tension between noumena and phenomena "must be cut rather than loosened, by an absolute decree of reason, which the philosopher does not pronounce, but merely proclaims: since there is no way of reconciling the not-I and the I, let there be no not-I at all."[29] He suggested dispensing with reliance on universal grounds for constructing the meaning of Humanity, allowing metaphysical reality to be whatever it is *not*, or not-I.

I listened closely to Fichte; the words coming from him were stirring. He appeared stirred, but unshaken. Did I detect a sense of positive assuredness in him still? He appeared conflicted, but comforted, naively perhaps, by the "truth" of a darker horizon he was gesturing toward. What is clear, to me, is that Fichte admitted profound doubt concerning the optimistic grounds upon which (European) "Man's" traditional assertions rest. By extension, such doubt serves as a basis for doubt concerning assertions of the antiblack racist and white supremacist structures and ideals by which such societies are founded. Through Fichte, I heard (European) "Man" admit a metaphysically affirmed basis for his traditional philosophies that he knows is impossible; perhaps, as Fichte suggested, he should have focused on how human life *experiences* the not-I, and not on bridging a presumed gap in meaning.[30]

(European) "Man," then, is very well aware that human beings make sense of reality by viewing it through a phenomenally limited lens, which entails exhausting realizations of finitude, despair, and pessimism.[31] The ironic situation of realizing human finitude through an engagement with universality induces exhaustion. Fichte showed how, in exhaustion, (European) "Man" encounters ultimate meaninglessness as a paradox that is emotionally rejected. Exhaustion is human existence being driven beyond itself and beyond the veils of its meanings. This exhaustion, Fichte argued, was experienced as inevitable; what in all truth is a finite being, enabled with transcendent capacities but unable to complete innate universal drives, (European) "Man" necessarily exhausts himself through a longing for forms of meaning that he can never achieve, and for which it seems, antiblack racism has become his chosen consolation.

The only recourse for existential exhaustion, according to Fichte, is imagination in forming alternative ways to justify human value of human finitude. Imagination is a uniquely human capacity to conjure radical forms of meaning beyond limitations. According to Fichte, since value projections are not produced by the not-I, (European) "Man" need not refer beyond himself in order to ground the legitimacy of his meanings. In response to exasperating feelings of incompleteness, (European) "Man" can construct uniquely creative alternatives whose legitimacy is grounded exclusively in the realm of imagination.[32] Is Fichte, here, admitting that the values of (European) "Man," no matter how positivistic and rationally pronounced, are at base known to be nothing more than conjuring orienting human life into one of any number of its potential configurations? Fichte seemed confident; one can experience freedom and not liberation, and not limitation, through producing values rooted in imagination. However, given the necessary incompleteness of human willing and desire, imagination provides only transient moments of existential contentment, and needs to be constantly reimagined.

Have I been listening correctly? I have heard European men implicitly admitting among themselves that their traditional ideals, the metaphysical bases upon which antiblack racist institutions have been built, are a sham: desired imaginings. As if that isn't absurd enough, it is the other part that I found more disturbing. I also heard an implicit acceptance of the need to continually reinforce projections of their desired imaginings alongside acknowledgments of their inherent meaninglessness, and the valuelessness of any life considered *beyond* that. Madness. I am listening to unapologetic neurotics, who *know* it is not humanly possible to accomplish their desires, and yet who depend upon incessantly trying, reinforcing images of their imagination onto me, in order to sustain the value of their being.

My stomach was beginning to turn, but I continued to listen and observe. According to Fichte, (European) "Man" faced a world of unreality and imagination premised upon emotional longings stemming from exhaustion. Constructing imaginative possibilities for meaning in human life is all one can do in response. Here, an indefinable flux of being necessarily exhausts the nature of the human condition once the veils of human meaning fall. This creates theoretical space for denying the potential of (European) "Man's" certainty regarding the rationality involved in his claims to epistemically ground universal truths: an important admission, or perhaps, omission. (European) "Man" confronts existence and defines freedom in terms of endlessly pursuing ideals that can never be attained, though one remains motivated, by staggered recurrences of contentment, to continue the effort of justifying one's life.

Resisting existential exhaustion requires producing values strong enough to resist the weaknesses, that is, limitations and incompleteness, of human life. From this perspective, consciousness displays weakness when attempting to deny the transient and incomplete nature of human willing by fixing the meaning of reality according to an absolute-I. Fichte's contribution challenged optimistic idealism by arguing that dependence on noumena to produce value is a recipe for existential exhaustion; perhaps beyond the veils of optimism, there is only an emotional longing for universality that ends in frustration when not effectively buffered by imagination.[33] Indeed, much of what (European) "Man" says in justification of antiblack racist societies, at least when he knows I am present, and wishes to be polite, I hear as *rationalistic* "nonsense," perhaps desires and imaginations, utterly meaningless, devoid of any real considerations for the problems of my lived reality, or how to address them.

While Descartes's and Kant's conceptions of human being allowed for a theological metaphysics where cognition of the logical unity of the universe is presumed compatible with God's being, Fichte completely usurped Christian metaphysics, replacing it with incomprehensible universal flux. Thus, Fichte's philosophy did not depend on the role of noumena to legitimize human values; he ultimately considered religious theologies superfluous. Here, we can see (European) "Man" facing the *beyond* as something that resists definitive interpretation, not from a sense of certainty attenuating the rationality of his values, but rather, from a sense of knowledge concerning a profound sense of uncertainty attenuating the creativity of his imagination.

These dimensions of the existential life of (European) "Man," elucidated by Fichte, are developed further through Arthur Schopenhauer's and Friedrich Nietzsche's contributions to the conversation. In fact, it was Fichte's description of the meaninglessness of the universe that inspired Friedrich Heinrich Jacobi to label him as a "nihilist." The term "Nihilism" appears in Jacobi's 1799 criticism of rational idealism.[34] His critique was far-reaching, extending to Spinoza and Kant, but it was his specific mention of Fichte that produced a colloquial understanding of the term "nihilism."[35] Jacobi argued that philosophical idealism, in general, was "nihilism" because it annihilated or, at least, reduced the meaning of the Christian world to nothingness. Since rationalism entails questioning universal truth apart from the divine will of God, following St. Augustine, according to Jacobi, idealism is heretical. God's will simply *is* universal Truth:

> Man has this choice and this alone: nothing or God. Choosing nothing he makes himself God; that means he makes God an apparition, for it is impossible, if there is no God, for man and all that is around him to be more than an apparition. . . . God is and is outside of me, a living essence that subsists for itself, or I am God. There is no third possibility.[36]

The main concern for Jacobi was that if human values were not grounded in the divine will of God, or if reduced to astronomy and physics, humanity will be left bereft of religious, that is, moral standards by which to measure itself. Jacobi's Christianity interpreted Fichte's thought as promoting a dangerous subjectivity that threatens God's omnipotence. Fichte, on the other hand, claimed to be liberating human freedom from exhaustion, pushing the boundaries of "Man's" existential life, which in modern Europe also meant thinking beyond traditional Christian values. This is why, as Jacobi observed, Fichte's nihilism could easily embrace crime, immorality, and atheism. Jean Paul, a student of Jacobi's, wrote, "In an age where God has set like the sun, soon afterwards the world too passes into darkness. He who scorns the universe respects nothing more than himself and at night fears only his own creations."[37] For Jean Paul, and Jacobi, any epistemology not explicitly reliant on Christian metaphysical ontology, whether Descartes's rationalistic dualism or Fichte's creative pluralism, was blasphemy against God.[38] As we will see, there is perhaps another form of blasphemy involved in replacing God's will with white supremacy.

I focused on the fact of Fichte's potential admission of weakness, perhaps for so long, that I may have missed some other interlocutor before I heard Schopenhauer's voice, whom Nietzsche wasted no time in following.[39] Schopenhauer and Nietzsche expanded the doubt expressed in Fichte's discussion, especially the parts concerning values and creativity in imagination. For them, aesthetic productions of art, that is, music and poetry, were among the greatest and highest human expressions of value. On their view, art is among the only potential remedies for enduring an otherwise cruelly meaningless existence. For them, nihilism and pessimism toward life could be tolerated, if not overcome, through aesthetic production and absorption.

The thoughts of Nietzsche and Schopenhauer on the existential developments of (European) "Man" are instructive for illuminating the creative desires standing behind antiblack racism. From this perspective, it makes sense that antiblack racist productions tend to promote themselves in terms of illusions and representations of the objectivity of values, which *seriously* insist upon themselves. Perhaps it is through further representations, that is, illusions of equality and progressiveness, perhaps, or aesthetic representations of art, music, and poetry, especially tragic poetry, that antiblack racist values seek to simultaneously instantiate and hide the basic nature of themselves.

I shift my attention to Schopenhauer's and Nietzsche's respective conversations on pessimism and nihilism. Schopenhauer's discussion of an existential pessimism attenuating (European) "Man" prepared the floor for Nietzsche's concerning nihilism. The convergence of their thought on the constellation of the cosmos as *beyond*, indefinable, immutable, constant, and meaningless, enabled a profound divergence of their thought on the value associated with the worth of existence. Schopenhauer's articulation of the fleeting nature of human life and the ultimate meaninglessness of its values within the grand scheme of things, for Nietzsche, signaled conditions for a grander human achievement, the inversion of all values. This move by Nietzsche led to his philosophy of "the eternal recurrence," out of which would emerge his suggestion that (European) "Man" adopt the existential attitude of a "will to power."[40] Nietzsche's philosophy of an eternal recurrence theorized that the universe has been occurring and recurring out of and into infinity. As a result, universal reality has no beginning or ending state, and no definitive meaning, only a finite amount of being such that there may be an infinite number of arrangements, and potentially, recurrences of particular arrangements.[41] He described "the eternal recurrence," and the pessimism of universal meaning therein implied, as a horrifying and burdensome weight attended by a realization of the inverted value of all human values, and yet, he shifted the burden of that weight by avowing its embrace. From this point of view, the ultimate affirmation of life could only lie in willing its continuity, including all of its pessimistic particularity.

To embrace pessimism may signal the highest form of greatness in the human species; Nietzsche called it "amor fati," or the love of fate. Affirming life, on this view, however, involves more than simply accepting pessimism; it calls for a willing of life in spite of pessimism. For instance, in *Ecce Homo* (1908), Nietzsche said the following:

> My formula for human greatness is amor fati: that one wants to have nothing different, not forward, not backward, not in all eternity. Not merely to bear the necessary, still less to conceal it—all idealism is mendaciousness before the necessary—but to love it.[42]

However, Schopenhauer's discussion of (European) "Man's" pessimism must be more fully explained in order to understand Nietzsche conversation on nihilism.

Schopenhauer began by confessing that (European) "Man" was situated within a cosmological universe, in which reality beyond the human world of projected values consists purely of blind, contradictory, immutable, self-justified, universal will. He rejected Kant's claim that we cannot know *noumena*, or "things-in-themselves." For Schopenhauer, the "thing-in-itself" is universal will, and we have access to it through our faculties of human intuition and reason. On this view, reason is one of the many instruments shaped by will to accomplish its end, which is, again, mainly to keep hidden from us that our existence is pointless. The primordial will of the universe exists and wills for no reason; thus, for Schopenhauer, reason did not function as an epistemological ground for moral law, as it did in the philosophy of Kant, or the idiom through which the pursuit of happiness and the notion of goodness can be understood, as it did in Socratic and Platonic thought. Reason, here, is an illusion of universal will, a representation filling human life with ambitions, desires, and illusions of knowledge. Schopenhauer informed that modern European desires were products of ultimately meaningless wills.

At this point, I am not sure whether it was a blessing or a curse to have become a fly on the wall of the backroom of modern European doubt, to become privy to the inner turmoil of European "Man," to see the weaknesses leaking from the value sources dominating my society. What I know for sure is that I have confirmed a profound suspicion of the entire category of that "Man's" objectivity. Schopenhauer admitted that in (European) "Man's" quest to achieve means for his objectively given values, he rarely questions whether the things he wants are actually "good." The result of such an authentic inquiry, according to Schopenhauer, is that the objective goodness of human desires and endeavors consists entirely in an *illusion*, a representation of universal will, which conditions the emergence and emptiness of human desires. In other words, (European) "Man" is an author of the concept of objective value, not the translator of it. If universal reality is a blind, irrational force willing existence for absolutely no reason at all, then nothing (European) "Man" wills can have objective value; thus, according to Schopenhauer, he is aware that there are no values that can be said to be valued for their own sake. Yet, one can challenge the truth of this conditional by objecting to the consequent in light of the antecedent. That is, it might be the case that despite an immutable, groundless, universe, Schopenhauer's claim that one ought not to invest any level of value into what ultimately makes no difference, nevertheless, relies on an implicit advocacy for at least the values of intelligence and freedom in valuing. In other words, in the face of pessimism, or perhaps antiblack racism, it may be unintelligent and further oppressive for human beings, especially black people, to follow Schopenhauer's advice of essentially valuing not valuing. Furthermore, there is a fundamental paradox in Schopenhauer's thought regarding the possibility of willing a non-willing, and this would have been the first problem of Schopenhauer's philosophy inherited by Nietzsche.[43]

While Nietzsche agreed with the premises of Schopenhauer's pessimism, he pronouncedly disagreed with its conclusion. For Nietzsche, value structures that will a non-willing are to be condemned as "nihilistic."[44] His philosophy of nihilism was a way to redeem the value of (European) "Man" against the pessimism implicit in confronting universal will. Nietzsche inherited the question of individuation versus individuality. If individuation is regarded as an illusion, it is not clear how one ought to understand the individuality involved in willing the cessation of one's individuation. In Schopenhauer, there is a distinct resentment toward the impossibility of universal reconciliation alongside an admonishment for (European) "Man" to surrender to that resentment. Nietzsche's conversation broke with Schopenhauer's, here, by reinvigorating the question of individuality in terms of necessity. Nietzsche took as his starting point the search for the value of human life; he attempted to value the necessity of phenomenal life in spite of pessimism, which ultimately led to him raising the question of the positive value of phenomenal valuing.

Nietzsche described the first reaction of (European) "Man's" exposure to the universe beyond his traditional values as pessimism. However, for Nietzsche, pessimism conditions a unique possibility: the process of the devaluation of values. This process removes the Apollonian veil of Socratic philosophy, which Nietzsche famously argued is taken over by Judaic and

Christian value systems; it reveals Schopenhauer's pessimistic fact of existence: there is only the suffering will. Yet, Nietzsche radically transformed Schopenhauer's pessimism. On Nietzsche's view, the human world, albeit representation, claims its space as an equal if not elevated site for unique manifestations of the universal will, that is, human phenomenal will. The individuality of the phenomenal will may be illusory against the backdrop of the oneness of the universe; however, it is again endowed with a near endless agility against the backdrop of the human world. From that point onward, Nietzsche suggested (European) "Man" simply refuse to ascend from the unreality of a human world he creates. According to Nietzsche, that, indeed, is the only *real* world.

If Fichte appeared, to be stirred, by what was now being revealed as beyond the positive valuations of European "Man," then after Nietzsche spoke, Schopenhauer looked straight up shook. He shook his head toward the floor and raised his hands as if to say, "No, no, no . . . nothing further can be done." He seemed defeated by what was beyond the traditional values of (European) "Man." Nietzsche, on the other hand, was grinning, he sat comfortably in that stark backroom of modern European doubt. I was beginning to see why. Nietzsche's response to Schopenhauer involved a radically new kind of valuing where one effectively raises the meta-axiological question of the value of values: a devaluation of traditional values that leads to a revaluation of valuing, or the process of transvaluation. Schopenhauer raised the question of the devaluation of values, pessimism, but, it seems, was too shook to proceed to value beyond the failure of the traditional values. I suppose, for him, either (European) "Man" was valuable in himself, or we should all go and apprehend art, or perhaps become monks?

In *Thus Spoke Zarathustra* (1883), Nietzsche developed a more interesting response to the pessimistic devaluation of values by transvaluing the concept of value production according to a new conceptualizing of human possibility and excellence. However, much like Schopenhauer on human suffering, Nietzsche conceded that one can never be truly satisfied with any achieved level of excellence; to become a *source* of value, the creator of standards, one has to always be on the way to overcoming and creating further values and standards for excellence. Any claim to excellence that fails to recognize its own inevitable transience is not excellence, but decadence.

Nietzsche considered phenomenal projections as mirrors for the nature of primordial will; they are the illusion through which universal will realizes itself. Nietzsche infused the unreality of the phenomenal world with the reality of the metaphysical universe. He searched for the strength of will in (European) "Man." Nietzsche understood the human condition to contain the possibility of human achievement. Instead of being a project of failure through suffering, human life became an original project of phenomenal will, power, and mastery. What remains is a healthy dose of uncertainty and fatalism enjoyed by possibilities for achievement. The insufficiency of considering European philosophy by itself notwithstanding Nietzsche's thought, informed by that of Schopenhauer, is an excellent starting point for examining constitutive elements of antiblack racist values and, ultimately, the black nihilism they engender.

I have seen and heard enough to establish the fact of modern (European) "Man's" doubts, his pessimistically and nihilistically facing that which is beyond his valuations of himself. I focus on Schopenhauer's and Nietzsche's voices exclusively. I listen to their discussion of ways to face what is beyond their values. Nihilism is a philosophy that fundamentally rejects the epistemic claims of identity relations between representative meanings and ontological reality found in both rationalist and theological philosophies; that is, nihilism is a philosophy that fundamentally rejects value structures relying upon what I call "metaphysical affirmations" for establishing the value of human values. Fichte could be considered among the first modern European nihilists because he rejected metaphysical affirmations of the value of (European) "Man." However, it was Nietzsche, but first through Schopenhauer, who offered the most explicit and honest descriptions of the nihilism of (European) "Man," as dependence on metaphysical affirmations.

Schopenhauer's pessimism expressed doubts about metaphysical affirmations. He insisted that all products of human experience were representations borne of consciousness presenting illusions, in some cases, as knowledge.[45] To be clear, he still considered scientific, or empirical, knowledge to be an illusion worth believing in. He claimed that although reality is ultimately a representation within European "Man's" consciousness, a particular class of representations remain grounded according to the "principle of sufficient reason."[46] Thus, for Schopenhauer, Kant's transcendental idealism, for example, described certain forms of shared human value projections worth believing in; but, he continued, transcendental idealism, nevertheless, remains an imaginative illusion.[47] On this view, (European) "Man" projects rational form onto noumena while brutes, but not animals, may share in something resembling phenomenal consciousness. As Joshua Foa Dienstag explains, in *Pessimism: Philosophy, Ethic, Spirit*, the temporality involved in (European) "Man" enjoying his illusions, according to Schopenhauer, is also a source of his suffering. Of (European) "Man," Schopenhauer's position is that "our self-consciousness has not space as its form, but only time; therefore, our thinking does not, like our perceiving, take place in three dimensions, but merely in one."[48] Consciousness is able to organize representations and project them forward or backward thereby recalling a past or planning a future; but, powers of consciousness to reflect, recall, and conjure representations entail desires and will, which, according to Schopenhauer, necessarily brings about suffering and boredom in time. Apprehension of the phenomenon of time is axiomatic to consciousness and its experiences of itself; it forms the basis of life as suffering. So, if I am hearing correctly, Schopenhauer is saying that existential suffering is a unique reality for humans, read as (European) "Man," over animals and "brutes," because they, alone, have "time" to reflect on suffering.[49]

The suffering of (European) "Man" is due, apparently, to his struggles to metaphysically affirm meaning within a universe that inherently rejects such meaning. Schopenhauer insisted that if the values of European "Man" were to have meaning at all, they would have to "point to something . . . that is not a representation but the thing-in-itself."[50] But, the "thing-in-itself" is a nothingness, in constant flux, transcending the time-ordered logic of human consciousness. Thus, on Schopenhauer's view, humans suffer a disposition toward ordering something that cannot be ordered. The crucial question, according to Schopenhauer, was, "How can one best reconcile with the void of meaning in human life? Or, in other words, how can (European) 'Man' justify valuing?" His response was that "Man" cannot. "Time is that by which everything becomes nothingness in our hands and loses all real value."[51]

I have heard (European) "Man" admit (in presumed privacy) that he knows his phenomenal projections are inherently devoid of value. He knows that, from the perspectives of human consciousness, a disconnection exists between experience and reality. (European) "Man," through Schopenhauer, is revealed to be Pessimistic (European) "Man." Here, rationality in cognition, while being a criterion for human existence, is also the source of its inescapable suffering.[52] Because (European) "Man" can never reconcile phenomena and noumena, in other words, he can never fulfill the existential desires causing his suffering. Suffering cannot be eradicated from his condition because universal will never reaches an end, despite the time-ordered activity consciousness vainly strives to assign to its movements.[53] Suffering unfulfilled desire is the baseline of (European) "Man's" existence, on this view. "All enjoyment is really only negative, only has the effect of removing a pain, while pain or evil, on the other hand, is the actual positive element and is felt directly."[54]

Temporary reprieves from (European) "Man's" suffering are possible. To make life bearable, according to Schopenhauer, he must learn the art of living a life that wills in a simpatico relationship with the meaningless will of the universe. That is, on this view, he ought to will against willing altogether; he must become Pessimistic (European) "Man." He suggested aesthetic absorption and asceticism for making suffering bearable for Pessimistic (European) "Man."

In the aesthetic moment of art absorption, I observed Pessimistic European "Man" claiming momentarily release from time-ordered logic and drawn away from the self-awareness and suffering of conscious experiences. Contemplating great works of art may transform phenomenal being into a will-less subject, and since willing is the source of suffering, will-less-ness may be the best means for quasi-avoidance, on this picture. Only when phenomenal will and its desire to create meaning are abandoned, claimed Schopenhauer, can one have peace.[55] The only intelligent response to human existence is phenomenal resignation, he urged. Whereas Fichte urged giving up on metaphysical affirmations of reality, Schopenhauer argued for giving up on the value of phenomenal willing altogether. Apprehending art, he claims, is a moment of scratching through the veil of human reality. In moments of pure aesthetic contemplation, "The artist," Schopenhauer said, "lets us peer into the world through his eyes," and "that he has these eyes . . . is the gift of genius."[56] Here, aesthetic experiences are forms of being "absorbed entirely in the object . . . through pure contemplation," which elevates one, momentarily, beyond our original condition.

Great art is an achievement because it reflects the capacity for consciousness to represent itself abstracted from the category of time; yet, in metaphysical terms, aesthetic absorption remains a fleeting, meaningless phenomenon.

> There always lies so near to us a realm in which we have escaped entirely from all our affliction; but who has the strength to remain in it for long? As soon as any relation to our will, to our person, even of those objects of pure contemplation, again enters consciousness, the magic is at an end.[57]

Great artists are gifted with insight into complex relationships between phenomenal reality and metaphysical reality. They often possess abilities to suppress individuation in offering artistic reflections of ultimate universal will. Thus, in the moment of aesthetic appreciation, the contemplator is drawn outside the human condition.[58] Despite temporary reprieve, however, human life is "a pendulum [swinging] between pain and boredom, and these two are in fact [life's] ultimate constituents."[59] Pain and suffering is the basis of the existence of Pessimistic (European) "Man," and where the suffering manages to be imperfectly avoided, boredom takes its place.[60] Boredom entails suffering inabilities to conquer desiring: settling for the dullness of previous accomplishments. Boredom is a form of decadence resting on comforts of previously achieved desires. The appropriate response to the inevitable suffering of Pessimistic (European) "Man," according to Schopenhauer, is phenomenal resignation.

Speaking of boredom, the inner workings of (European) "Man" don't thrill me to expound. However, as mentioned in the previous chapter, I am forced to start from absurd beginnings. Boredom, here, continues in the form of the ascetic life of saints in the monastery, Schopenhauer's preferred analogy for phenomenal resignation. The phenomenal will of the saint is theoretically opposed to desire since it aims to abide only by God's universal will. However, the irony is that phenomenal will-less-ness, even for a saint, requires constant willing because pessimistic doubt requires constant activity.[61] Schopenhauer also added that pessimistic asceticism entails an implicit moral code. Although he rejected religious interpretations of moral law, that is, Christianity, and metaphysical affirmations of moral law, that is, Kantian idealism, he nevertheless considered morality a consequence of the subdued self-interest implicit to phenomenal resignation.[62]

Pessimistic morality accomplishes indirect virtuous ends through its selfless-ness. Schopenhauer's pessimism, and his overall denial of positive meaning in human life, culminate in a contradictory desire for death as a means for living. He viewed death as an ultimate release from human suffering. It is a complete cessation of phenomenal willing. In this sense, Schopenhauer argued, Pessimistic (European) "Man" ought to welcome death. Dread and fear of death is part of the time-ordered suffering of human existence; death is a cessation of phenomenal will, a return to the primacy of universal oneness, bringing about the nothingness that phenomenal will exhaustively seeks. Yet, fear and dread of death while living, like valuing, seem two fallacies of existence.[63] Death is not the end of existence; it is the end of phenomenal individuation, which is the cause of suffering. Conceiving death as a disconnection, and not a reconnection, as Schopenhauer does, prioritizes the unreality of phenomenal will over the reality of metaphysical will, making fear of death a fallacy, or weakness, based on traditions of imagined metaphysical affirmations.[64]

After listening to Schopenhauer, it is clear to me, (European) "Man" has not historically followed his advice. Perhaps my society would not be the oppressive cauldron of antiblackness that it is, had only Pessimistic (European) "Man" admitted his doubts to himself and decided to resign or, at least, humble himself before an existence he knows he cannot master, instead of doubling down. Schopenhauer's suggestion was an attempt to expand on Fichte's critique of rationality, but where Fichte turned against reason as a way of finding phenomenal liberation, Schopenhauer turned against it by rejecting phenomenal life altogether. Where Fichte reveled in the possibilities of imagination, Schopenhauer abhorred valuing and sought ultimate resignation. The stage has now been entirely set for the emergence of "Nihilistic (European) Man," whom (European) "Man" can now only imaginatively feign that he has not become.

(European) "Man" has admitted that he suffers the task of creating value in a world that pessimistically destroys meaning and value, and if resignation of will through the practices of asceticism and aestheticism is the only way that consciousness can find reprieve, then, ultimately, life is not worth living, but can be made bearable. Friedrich Nietzsche listened intently to all of this. He adopted Schopenhauer's rejection of metaphysical affirmations, while challenging the claim that the value of life is not ultimately worth living. The perspective that there are no universal truths inspired Nietzsche's nihilism. Pessimism regards the logical form of human projections and their accompanying powers of rational judgment as indispensable tools for human life and its affairs, but not as apparatuses for uncovering universal truth. For this reason, Nietzsche considered the whole enterprise of modern European philosophy to be wholly fallacious. Despite his initial agreement with Schopenhauer's pessimism, however, he went on to consider him as displaying a weakness of will, which he called "passive nihilism." His final evaluation of Schopenhauer's pessimism is what led Nietzsche to pejoratively consider all traditional modern Western philosophy, even Schopenhauer's pessimism, as "European nihilism."[65]

"Nihilism," for Nietzsche, is a term describing human life as it lives the death of traditional values and attempts to transvalue modes of valuing to replace them. It entails the situation of realizing the meaning and significance of one's projections cannot be metaphysically affirmed. Thus, "traditional" values can no longer sustain belief. There were historical epistemes, for instance, medieval Europe, where it perhaps made sense to believe in God for lack of better explanations for phenomena. Nihilism denotes the situation of realizing the decadence of dying values and a host of possible responses therein.[66] A nihilistic situation can be either complete or incomplete, and "active" or "passive," which I consider either "strong" or "weak."[67] "Incomplete nihilism" describes what we have previously stated as pessimism. In other words, pessimism admits a devaluation of traditional values while struggling to adequately replace them.[68] "Complete nihilism" faces the project of valuing in the absence of metaphysically affirmed values and can be divided into two categories: passive and active.[69] I reference this distinction in terms of "strength" and "weakness." Activity signals strength, on my view, and an ability to remain insistent on the value of one's values, active against impositions of denial, takes strength. Passivity signals weakness, an inability, or unwillingness, to insist upon the value of one's values in the face of denials. In other words, what I call "weak" nihilism responds to the fall of traditional values by denying the value of human valuing altogether. Schopenhauer's pessimism is an example of weak nihilism, on my view. "Strong" nihilism, on the other hand, not only rejects decadent values, but seeks creation of ways of valuing beyond weak nihilism.

If complete nihilism is the situation of facing and attempting to value within pessimistic devaluations of values, then weak nihilism responds to pessimism by either seeking to resurrect a monistic form of valuing, as in the case of Kant, or by entirely denying the value of valuing, as in the case of

Schopenhauer. Weak nihilism can be both optimistically and pessimistically conceived as willing against human willing, according to Nietzsche's view. Then, there remains the possibility of producing strong nihilistic responses to the absurdities of human life.

What a novel, and dangerous, standard Nietzsche has proposed for evaluating the values of (European) "Man." He suggests we evaluate values according to standards that promote willing, not for the sake of universal truth, or as an attempt at liberation from suffering, but purely as a means of testing our strength, of testing which of our values will withstand; which values will prove valuable for no other reason than their being valued by us. Here, Kant's positive rationalism *and* Schopenhauer's negative pessimism each represent pillars of the weak nihilism of modern (European) "Man." Rational idealism, for instance, is a form of weak nihilism because it limits consciousness by negating the value in the dynamism of human willing, and by making the value of human will subordinate to categories of pure reason, rationalism also destroys the dynamic value of freedom in human life. Schopenhauer's phenomenal resignation potentially avoids Kant's weaknesses but remains a denial of the freedoms of consciousness in other ways and is weak by virtue of his inability to value beyond pessimism. Kant and Schopenhauer represent weak and incomplete nihilistic statuses of (European) "Man," because both philosophies amount to moralistic rejections of the vitality of life:

> The logic of pessimism down to ultimate nihilism: what is at work in it? The idea of valuelessness, meaninglessness: to what extent moral valuations hide behind all other high values.
>
> Conclusion: *Moral value judgments are ways of passing sentence, negations; morality is a way of turning one's back on the will to existence.*[70]

Metaphysical affirmations of moral philosophies inherently presuppose negative judgments concerning the value and dynamism of human freedom. By confining the value of human freedom to rationalism and morality, as in the case of Kant, or pessimism and suffering, as in the case of Schopenhauer, (European) "Man" rejected fundamental freedoms entailed by the human existential condition. Behind either the idealism of optimism or the "intelligence" of pessimism, (European) "Man" sought to hide.

Nietzsche's thought supports my theorization that the idea of Humanity governing traditional (European) "Man" is based on a weak nihilistic subterfuge. He described European "Man's" pessimism, a burdening realization of his meaninglessness in the cosmos, through stages of nihilism:

> Nihilism as a psychological state will have to be reached, *first*, when we have sought a "meaning" in all events that is not there: so the seeker eventually

becomes discouraged. Nihilism, then, is the recognition of the long *waste* of strength, the agony of the "in vain," insecurity, the lack of any opportunity to recover and to regain composure—being ashamed in front of oneself as if one had deceived oneself all too long. This meaning could have been, the "fulfillment" of some highest ethical canon in all events, the moral world order; Or the growth of love and harmony in the intercourse of beings; or the gradual approximation of a state of universal happiness; Or even the development toward a state of universal annihilation—any goal at least constitutes some meaning. What all these notions have in common is that something is to be achieved through the process—and now one realizes that becoming aims at *nothing* and achieves *nothing*—thus, disappointment regarding an alleged aim of becoming as a cause of nihilism: whether regarding a specific aim or, universalized, the realization that all previous hypotheses about aims that concern the whole "evolution" are inadequate (man no longer the collaborator, let alone the center, of beginning).[71]

Next, he described "European" (Man's) weak nihilistic response to pessimism:

Nihilism as a psychological state is reached, *secondly*, (Emphasis in original) when one has posited a totality, a systemization, indeed any organization in all events, and underneath all events, and a soul that longs to admire and revere has wallowed in the idea of some supreme form of domination and administration. . . . Some sort of unity, some sort of monism: this faith suffices to give man a deep feeling of standing in the context of, and being dependent on, some whole that is infinitely superior to him, and he sees himself as a mode of the deity.—"The well-being of the universal demands the devotion of the individual"—but behold, there is no such universal! At bottom, man has lost the faith in his own value when no infinitely valuable whole works through him; he conceived such a whole in order to be able to believe in his own value.[72]

Nietzsche's testimony is the proverbial "headshot." He admitted that modern (European) "Man" responded to pessimism, which was inadvertently introduced by René Descartes's development of transcendentalist conceptions of "truth," in full light of religious traditions, locating the value of human values outside the sphere of human willing. He said, (European) "Man" "lost faith in his own value when no infinitely valuable whole works through him," which he needs, "in order to be able to believe in his own value." This spirit of (European) "Man" entails moralistic judgments concerning universal reality and is what links both Kantian optimism and Schopenhauerian pessimism each as weak nihilistic philosophies. Weak nihilistic values directly, as in the case of Kant, or indirectly, as in the case of Schopenhauer, depend on metaphysically affirmed conceptions of truth; they are the opposite of human values rooted in the freedoms of consciousness and powers of the phenomenal will. From this perspective, Kant's idealism optimistically posits a rationalistic, metaphysical, "real world," which Schopenhauer's pessimism only manages to incompletely reject. Schopenhauer's pessimism is weak, on this view, because it indirectly makes a metaphysical affirmation in terms of its judgments against the value of phenomenal willing through its ethics of resignation. In other words, according to Nietzsche, pessimism represented the final stage, the death gasp, of modern (European) "Man," or, in response to the threat of becoming normal man, if you will, they have chosen to embarrassingly limp onward, shrouded in decrepit, decadent, weak nihilistic banners representative of old yearnings for fallen traditions, which continue to find voice, today, through the languages of antiblack racism and white supremacy.

Nietzsche has fully assumed the floor. Through his tattling, and my own black fly positioning, it has been revealed that (European) "Man" depends upon optimistic and pessimistic denials of his existential situation for valuing himself, which have resulted in the weaknesses I have suspected lying at the center of his antiblack racist impositions. The philosophy of modern (European) "Man" began with Descartes's rationalistic Christianity, which extended through Kant's idealism, positively evaluating the phenomenal world, but ultimately ended in Schopenhauer's pessimism, negatively evaluating the phenomenal world. Nietzsche asked the following question:

> To what extent Schopenhauer's nihilism still follows from the same ideal that created Christian theism.—One felt so certain about the highest desiderata, the highest values, the highest perfection that the philosophers assumed this as an absolute certainty, as if it were a priori: "God" at the apex as a *given truth* (Emphasis in original). "To become as God," "to be absorbed into God"—for thousands of years these were the most naive and convincing desiderata.[73]

There was a hidden crisis concerning the value of rationality in modern European philosophy. The historical sagas over the traditions of (European) "Man," which have yielded multiple forms of pessimism, reveal the rise and potential fall of Weak Nihilistic (European) "Man." Nihilism emerged in modern European thought, in part, through the rationalism of Descartes's philosophy, which continued through the transcendental idealism of Kant. These modern forms of rationalism, and their insistence on valuing absolute truth held over from medieval Christian theology, have run their course and were exposed by Fichte and Schopenhauer, for example, as illusions and desires. The role of rationality in modern Enlightenment philosophy nevertheless continued to serve as metaphysically affirming for the values of European ideals. Modern (European) "Man" attempted to construct a bulwark against the pessimism revealed through the crises of rationalism.

Schopenhauer, for instance, responded to the crises by denying the metaphysical value of rationality, meaning, and therefore purpose, in human valuing. Nietzsche, on the other hand, rejected Schopenhauer's pessimism alongside the rational idealism it opposed because both failed to conceive of a redeemable quality for the value of human freedom outside of metaphysical affirmations:

> Extreme positions are not succeeded by moderate ones but by extreme positions of the opposite kind. Thus the belief in the absolute immorality of nature, in aim and meaninglessness is the psychologically necessary affect once the belief in God and an essentially moral order becomes untenable. Nihilism appears at that point, not that the displeasure at existence has become greater than before but because one has come to mistrust any "meaning" in suffering, indeed in existence. One interpretation has collapsed; but because it was considered *the* (Emphasis in original) interpretation it now seems as if there were no meaning at all in existence, as if everything were in vain.[74]

Pessimism need not necessarily result in an opposing idealism, weakness, or resignation. But, more importantly, pessimism can invigorate human life and support valuations affirming the dynamism of phenomenal will—that is, pessimism can lead to strong nihilism. For example, In *The Birth of Tragedy* (1872), Nietzsche argued that ancient Greek societies accomplished healthy relationships in valuing through a symbolic juxtaposition of the Dionysian spirit of music and the plasticity of Apollonian art, imagery, and lyrics.[75] The Dionysian represents the eternally fluid nature of universal will, on this view. Dionysus, the God of wine, is symbolized through the sound of music, which is reflective of the disembodied transcendence of universal will.[76] The Apollonian, contrastingly, represents the formal world of order. Apollo, the God of light and illumination, symbolizes rationality and order through the plasticity of art forms.[77] Nietzsche praised pre–Socratic Greek society for their Dionysian strength of will in facing pessimism through aesthetic constructions of music, imagery, lyricism, and plasticity in Attic tragedies.[78] For Nietzsche, combining the Apollonian and the Dionysian in aesthetic representations of tragedy were the highest cultural responses to the human condition.

Greek tragedies, in their earliest form, had for its sole theme the sufferings of Dionysius, according to Nietzsche, which remained "the sole dramatic protagonist," despite variations, in its later forms.[79] Pre-Socratic Greeks, Nietzsche claimed, healthily faced pessimistic truth and universal flux by dramatizing the affair. Contrasting the pessimism of ancient Greek interpretations of tragedy with the optimism of Socratic interpretations, Nietzsche wrote as follows:

Once the optimistic element had entered tragedy, it overgrew its Dionysiac regions and brought about their annihilation and, finally, the leap into genteel domestic drama. Consider the consequences of the Socratic maxims: "Virtue is knowledge; All sins arise from ignorance; Only the virtuous are happy"—these three basic formulations of optimism spell the death of tragedy.[80]

He further wrote, "[Socrates was] the prototype of an entirely new mode of existence. He is the great exemplar of that theoretical man," that theoretical optimist, who, with his faith that the nature of things can be fathomed, ascribes to knowledge and insight the power of panacea.[81] On this view, moral interpretations of aesthetic productions are to be rejected for the same reason that rationalistic interpretations of universal reality are to be rejected, both depend upon metaphysical affirmations. Attic tragedy, alternatively, laid bare the human condition of facing indeterminate projects of meaning. The heroes of Attic tragedy symbolize the imminent failures of human life attempting to order reality. The tragic hero demonstrates the limits of human will against the usurping and immutable powers of the universe.

> Tragedy . . . is in its essence pessimistic. Existence is in itself something very terrible, man something very foolish . . . the hero of tragedy does not prove himself . . . in a struggle against fate, just as little does he suffer what he deserves. Rather, blind and with covered head, he falls to his ruin.[82]

According to Nietzsche, pre-Socratic Greeks gave birth to formalized conceptions of tragedy in order to respond healthily to pessimism, but Socratic rationalism brought about the decline of the vitality of Greek life by devaluing tragedy. He claimed that healthy Greek relationships with the existential dissipated after the influence of Socratic rationalism:

> Is pessimism necessarily a sign of decline . . . as it once was in India and now is, to all appearances, among us, "modern" men and Europeans? Is there a pessimism of strength? . . . And again: that of which tragedy died, the Socratism of morality, the dialectics, frugality, and cheerfulness of the theoretical man—how now? Might not this very Socratism be a sign of decline . . . is the resolve to be so scientific about everything perhaps a kind of fear of, an escape from, pessimism?[83]

Metaphysical meaninglessness did not diminish the value of human life for pre–Socratic Greeks; it made life more precious. Nietzsche continued his critique of modern (European) "Man." I listened as he described a fear-driven continuation of Socratic thought and faith into the primacy of modern science and rationalism. Where modern (European) "Man" resolved to be "scientific about everything," according to Nietzsche, he demonstrated a fearful fleeing from pessimistic truth. In this way, European philosophy from Socrates through Kant, extending to Schopenhauer, can be read as a revelation of fear, weakness, and flight from the pessimistic truths of human existence.

Nietzsche agreed with Schopenhauer that human life could be buffered against its absurdities through aesthetics. However, Nietzsche augmented his position, by insisting on the value of valuing. In *The Twilight of the Idols: Or How One Philosophizes with a Hammer* (1859), Nietzsche argued for the value of human valuing in spite of pessimistic knowledge, and *not* simply as a way of coping with it. In the preface to the second publishing of *The Birth of Tragedy*, he likened this form of valuing to laughing in the face of the absurd; he advised, "One ought to learn how to laugh, if one is bent on being a pessimist."[84] Where Nietzsche's earlier thoughts followed Schopenhauer by trying to make life bearable through aesthetic absorption, he later argued for the value of "laughing," or valuing, in spite of the meaninglessness.

Nietzsche's mature analysis considered Schopenhauer's phenomenal resignation as a form of moral resentment against human existence. Moral *ressentiment*, for Nietzsche, means to value impotence and weakness as "good," when it is actually one's recourse in the face of superior power:[85]

> What does the etymology of the terms for good in various languages tell us? ... The basic concept is always *noble* in the hierarchical, class sense, and from this has developed, by historical necessity, the concept *good* embracing nobility of mind, spiritual distinction. This development is strictly parallel to that other which eventually converted the notions common, plebian, base into the notion *bad* (Emphasis in original).[86]

He further wrote as follows:

> It was the Jew who, with frightening consistency, dared to invert the aristocratic value equations good/noble/powerful/beautiful/happy/favored-of-the-gods and maintain, with the furious hatred of the underprivileged and impotent, that only the poor, the powerless, are good; only the suffering, sick, and ugly, truly blessed.[87]

From this perspective, Schopenhauer's pessimism is seen as a form of weak nihilism harboring *ressentiment* against the power of the universe. Schopenhauer displayed the quintessence of Nihilistic (European) "Man," a philosopher promoting an inherent weakness: a noxious pessimism mixed with a disfigured moralism, that is, weak nihilism.[88] He displayed moral *ressentiment* against the immutable will of the universe by valuing phenomenal resignation. His devaluation of traditional values was done out of impotence and weakness, not activity and strength, or intelligence. His philosophy concerning the intelligence of resignation attempted to make his weak pessimistic nihilism "good" in relation to the "bad" immutability of universal will. His phenomenal resignation depended on moralistic appraisal of existence. Nietzsche claimed as follows:

> Schopenhauer wanted it otherwise and therefore had to conceive of this metaphysical ground as the opposite of the ideal—as 'an evil, blind will,': that way it could be that 'which appears,' that which reveals itself in the world of appearances. But even so he did not renounce the absoluteness of the ideal—he sneaked by.[89]

Although Schopenhauer rejected metaphysically affirmed conceptions of morality, his move to value resignation nevertheless involved moralistic condemnation of universal will as deceptive, false, or "evil." In Nietzsche's words, Schopenhauer was "a pessimist, a world-denier and God-denier, who *comes to a halt* before morality—who affirms morality and plays the flute [a pastime of Schopenhauer's] affirms *laede neminem* [hurt no one] morality: what? Is that actually a pessimist? (Emphasis in original)"[90]

Schopenhauer's resignation was a moral indictment against the universe camouflaged within pessimistic truth. Without the moralistic overtures, Nietzsche advanced pessimism as a primordial confrontation with the universe that does not evaluate but either affirms or rejects. Pessimism accepts that universal will "aims at nothing and achieves nothing."[91] Pessimistic knowledge, however, does not entail a judgment against universal will.[92] Rather, pessimism refers to the "innocence of becoming":[93]

> Suppose we realize how the world may no longer be interpreted in terms of these three categories, and that the world begins to become valueless for us after this insight: then we have to ask about the sources of our faith in these three categories. Let us try if it is not possible to give up our faith in them. Once we have devalued these three categories, the demonstration that they cannot be applied to the universe is no longer any reason for devaluing the universe.
>
> Conclusion: The faith in the categories of reason is the cause of nihilism. We have measured the value of the world according to categories *that refer to a purely fictitious world.* (Emphasis in original)[94]

To believe in morality is to pass sentence on existence, according to this view. Schopenhauer, for example, endorsed the wisdom of Silenus: "Not to be born is best . . . the next best thing by far is to go back . . . where [man] came from, as quickly as he can."[95] However, his endorsement was representative of weak desires to keep the absurdities of human existence at bay, judging them. Since the pessimistic truth is that human life admits of no universal truth, it follows that there is no perspective from which to judge universal existence. Schopenhauer contradicted the logical trajectory of pessimism by making moralistic judgments against universal will. His pessimism relied on such judgments in order to render the wisdom of resignation as valuable. However, reliance on vast generalizations of metaphysical values, or what I call, "metaphysical affirmations," in order to establish the value of human life, is a form of weak nihilism that reflects "pathology," at the very least:

> Nihilism represents a pathological transitional stage (what is pathological is the tremendous generalization, the inference that there is no meaning at all): whether the productive forces are not yet strong enough, or whether decadence still hesitates and has not yet invented its remedies. . . . That there is no absolute nature of things nor a "thing-in-itself." This, too, is merely—even the most extreme nihilism. It places the value of things precisely in the lack of any reality corresponding to these values and in their being merely a symptom of strength on the part of the value-positers, a simplification for the sake of life.[96]

Nihilism involves several stages of the situation of facing an absence of universal truths. How one responds to that absence may indicate presence or absence of one's existential strength. "Values and their changes are related to increases in the power of those positing the values."[97] The human condition is a situation where one must necessarily create meaning out of meaninglessness, and those who cannot do so, in relation to others, without metaphysical affirmations demonstrate weakness. Or, in Simone De Beauvoir's words:

> Conscious of being unable to be anything, man then decides to be nothing. We shall call this attitude nihilistic. The nihilist is close to the spirit of seriousness, for instead of realizing his negativity as a living moment, he conceives his annihilation in a substantial way. . . . Nihilism is disappointed seriousness which has turned back upon itself.[98]

Similarly, according to Nietzsche, a strong will is needed to pessimistically value traditional ideals, while still valuing human life without metaphysically affirmed bases for doing so. "Nihilism," Nietzsche said, is "an ideal of the highest degree of powerfulness of the spirit, the over-richest life—partly destructive, partly ironic":[99]

> [Given insights], that becoming has no goal and that underneath all becoming there is no grand unity in which the individual could immerse himself completely as in an element of supreme value, an escape remains: to pass sentence on this whole world of becoming as a deception and to invent a world beyond

it, a *true* world. But as soon as man finds out how that world is fabricated solely from psychological needs, and how he has absolutely no right to it, the last form of nihilism comes into being: it includes disbelief in any metaphysical world and forbids itself any belief in a true world. Having reached this standpoint, one grants the reality of becoming as the only reality, forbids oneself every kind of clandestine access to afterworlds and false divinities—*but cannot endure this world though one does not want to deny it* (Emphasis in original).[100]

He described the stages of nihilism as exhaustive and often in need of reprieve. The exhaustive situation of having pessimistic knowledge and not wanting to know it, but being unable to deny it, is the potentially debilitating circumstance of pessimistic nihilism; the weak "perish" of it:

What is a *belief*? How does it originate? Every belief is a considering-something-true.

The most extreme form of nihilism would be the view that *every* belief, every considering-something-true, is necessarily false because there simply is no *true* world. Thus: a *perspectival appearance* whose origin lies in us (insofar as we continually *need* a narrower, abbreviated, simplified world).

—That is the measure of strength to what extent we can admit to ourselves, without perishing, the merely *apparent* character, the necessity of lies.

To this extent, nihilism, as the denial of a truthful world, of being, might be *a divine way of thinking*.[101]

This is why I choose the term "strong nihilism."

It is a measure of the degree of strength of will to what extent one can do without meaning in things, to what extent one can endure to live in a meaningless world because one organizes a small portion of it oneself.[102]

Thus, on my view, weak pessimistic nihilism amounts to a form of phenomenal resignation, but what I call, "strong pessimistic nihilism," is a stage in development toward strong nihilism.

Traditional (European) "Man" demonstrates classic weak nihilism refusing to strong nihilistically value in response to pessimism. Since rational idealism is a weak nihilism that seeks to replace one set of monistic, metaphysically affirmed beliefs, Christianity, with another, that is, the categorical imperative, traditional Western philosophy can be viewed as a prolonged response of weakness and incompleteness to the pessimistic truths of the human existential condition, that is, optimism.[103] Western philosophers, from Socrates through St. Augustine, Descartes, Jacobi, Kant, are "weak optimistic nihilists." The pessimist, Schopenhauer, betrays a pathological dependence on metaphysical affirmations for valuing, or denying, human life while devaluing optimism. Schopenhauer represents Europe's "weak pessimistic nihilism." He forbade himself access to false divinities, as it were, but was unable to provide value for human life in their absence and responded with implicit moral condemnation.

Where (European) "Man" traditionally produced a weak optimistic nihilism cavaliering with positive certainties of universal truth over Humanity, Schopenhauer proposed a weak pessimistic nihilism through his asceticism. Schopenhauer was perhaps noble to face the truth of pessimism by at least identifying it. Yet, valuing against willing out of a sense impotence is *ressentiment*, pessimism, and weak nihilism. Motivated by Schopenhauer's discussion, Nietzsche argued that having acquired pessimistic knowledge, one must not only learn to laugh but also how to philosophize. He considered pessimism a "hammer" that dismantles traditional beliefs and values, but which must ultimately learn to construct newer values. In *Beyond Good and Evil* (1886), Nietzsche wrote, "We, who have different beliefs. . . . Where have we to fix our hopes? In new philosophers—there is no other alternative: in minds strong and original enough to initiate opposite estimates of value, to transvalue and invert "eternal valuations."[104] Pessimism hammers and destroys metaphysically affirmed "eternal valuations." It is a form of nihilism that destroys traditional values by rejecting human valuing altogether. Strong nihilism, however, is pessimism that destroys weak values through an active construction of stronger ones. Strong nihilism is the healthy end of pessimism; weak nihilism is pessimism borne out of resentment. According to Nietzsche, pessimism "in the hand of the strongest becomes . . . [an] instrument with which one can make oneself a new pair of wings."[105] Pessimism transformed into strong nihilism enables unique creations and new forms of meaning. Nietzsche referenced pessimistic knowledge as a sensibility through which truly new values and meanings are sought; it is pessimism *and* strong nihilism that is "precisely how we find the pathos that impels us to seek new values."[106]

In *Thus Spoke Zarathustra* (1885), Nietzsche wrote extensively on what can be called the weak pessimistic nihilism of the "last man," of modern Europe, and the struggles of what can be called the strong nihilism of the "higher man," that brings into existence the *Ubermensch*, or *Dionysian* man, or what I consider as (European) "Man" being revealed as a nihilist. Through the demon, Zarathustra, Nietzsche disparaged the weakness of (European) "Man," the jesters masquerading as "masters of the present," as decadents pursuing the question: "How is man to maintain himself best, longest, most pleasantly?"[107] The "last man" is (European) "Man," who *seriously* wishes to remain the *last*, that is, *final* man. That is, weak nihilistic (European) "Man," masquerading, sought to write the final chapter on human becoming, an absurd feat, and he knew it. He wishes to appear as (European) "Man," the strong optimist, but that is impossible. Before the dusk of the day, he was revealed as pessimistic (European) "Man," whose antiblack racist attempts at erasing me may lie in him desperately needing to deny that he is, in fact, nothing more than a weak nihilistic (European) "Man."

Nietzsche's observations encompassed all of the optimism and pessimism that passes before (European) "Man." "The most cherished beliefs of the last man are those of 'freedom,' 'progress,' 'justice,' and 'great events.'"[108] However, (European) "Man" deifies the quasi-completeness of his system of ordering and proceeds to treat his values as metaphysically affirmed. In his traditional garb, that is, he is a weak nihilist that deifies human freedoms in value. His nihilism is reactive against pessimistic meaninglessness, but weak; it responds with ideals abhorrent to and in denial of human freedom.

Nietzsche envisioned the strong nihilist, or the (European) "higher man," as displaying a strong pessimistic nihilism. The "higher man" rejects the optimism of the last man's weak pessimistic nihilism. The higher man, however, goes through two stages: Initially, he is a strong pessimistic nihilist who negates and destroys traditional values, perhaps struggling to produce newer values while facing pitfalls of collapses into forms of weak nihilism. Potentially, the strong pessimistic nihilist becomes a strong nihilist, positively struggling to continually affirm and build newer values.

It may be argued that it is a mistake to attribute destruction to this form of what Nietzsche called "Dionysian man" and what I call the strong nihilist. However, this is avoided through my distinction between "strong pessimistic nihilism" and "strong nihilism." Perhaps the activity of Dionysian man is a pure instantiation that is removed from the negating activity of the pessimistic higher man seeking to devalue traditional values. Giles Deleuze, for instance, addressed this concern when he defined reactivity as "that relation of primary forces that is involved in conservation, adaptation, and utility. Activity on the other hand, refers to those forces that subjugate, dominate, appropriate, and possess."[109] For Deleuze, human consciousness is inherently reactive and responds to the activity of external stimuli, including existing values.[110] The fall of the last man, on this view, is his allowing of the active elements of values to become permeated by the reactive constitutions of the mind. For the last man, reactivity gets asserted as a form of activity. For example, in *Thus Spoke Zarathustra*, Nietzsche claimed that after the pessimistic "higher man" wanders into the wilderness beyond traditional values, a demon approaches and affirms his journey; but then, the demon leaves him! The demon later returns to find the higher man praying before an "all-affirming ass."[111] That is, after the advance of rejecting optimism, the higher man tends to grow weary in pessimism, and struggles to simultaneously be a destroyer of existing values while creating newer ones. From this perspective, (European) "Man" can be understood in terms of "the reactivity of his valuations," or, he who allows human values to lose their active elements.[112] "With the higher man the reactive will has become conscious of itself."[113] As a pessimist the higher man understands the last man as in need of spiritual comfort from pessimistic truths. Yet, the higher man cannot share in the last man's traditional comforts because he rejects metaphysical affirmations. At the same time, the higher man, becoming conscious of his own will, feels the existential need to construct values for himself, but "fears regressing back to reactivity."[114] "This is why he despises himself. Each higher man has in his own way fallen from grace with both God and Man."[115] At this moment, the higher man is most prone to risks of collapsing back into the last man. This capacity of the higher man to revert back to reactivity marks the difference between the strong nihilism of higher man and the strong pessimistic nihilistic activity of the character of Dionysian man. The higher man, strong nihilism, is the goal of the last man.[116]

Dionysian man is by definition a strong nihilist but cannot be considered apart from the pessimistic activity; he is, on my view, a strong pessimistic nihilist. He requires an "alliance with the force of reactivity . . . as a means to his own enhancement."[117] In other words, "becoming-active is affirming and affirmative, just as becoming-reactive is negating and nihilistic."[118] Where, for example, Michael Gillespie drew lines of demarcation between the activity of Dionysian man and the reactivity of the last and higher man, Byron Williston argued as follows:

> Nietzsche thinks that the passive nihilist's very knowledge of the perspectival character of all truths must be denied at [the stage of Dionysian man] and this denial is a characteristic element of all becoming-reactive. Without this move to reactivity "life itself would be impossible."[119]

In other words, on Williston's view, nihilism is a feature of the human life process where pessimistic destruction of traditional values and strong nihilistic productions of newer values fit a Dionysian description, which entails reactivity *and* activity. To use Nietzsche's analogy, Dionysian man ought to value with the seriousness of a child at play, but with an adult understanding of childhood play. Another point duly noted.

The seriousness of a child at play represents pure activity, but adult understanding of that activity is molded by the reactivity of its disposition against seriousness. This is what I understood when Nietzsche said, "Innocence is the child, and forgetfulness, a new beginning, a game, a delf-rolling wheel, a first movement, a holy Yea."[120] An adult understanding of the seriousness of child's play means interpreting human meanings as innocent, or without appeal to metaphysical affirmations, while also retaining an element of reactive nihilism to the extent that consciousness is aware of its own potential (perhaps need) for ideals, pretending, or as we say, for "play-play."

It had long since gotten dark. The conversations that began on a bustling dawn, confidently and optimistically declaring the day, have long since descended into the pessimistic twilight of night. And now, here, (European) "Man" leans against the wall awkwardly, half clad in the disheveled robes of his previous certainties, in the dead and still of night, talking about art.

So, the value of values cannot be metaphysically affirmed without appealing to some version of *ressentiment*, and that is weak nihilism. Nietzsche then claimed that life is only justifiable as a type of aesthetic achievement. Unlike Schopenhauer, who thought art could lift humans beyond human existence, Nietzsche suggested that "strong" art does precisely the opposite.[121] Strong art does not avoid human values; it seeks to impose them onto universal reality. Strong art recalls Fichte's sense of creative imagination in accepting pessimism while valuing the aesthetic possibilities of value projections. That is, despite insignificance on a metaphysical level, strong art relies on a uniquely human capacity to forge meaning. Strong art, then, is not a means for militating against human existence; it is an empowered reflection of that existence; it aesthetically symbolizes the fragmentation of universal will experienced as human will. For Schopenhauer, the fragmenting of universal will was the source of human suffering; but for Nietzsche, this suffering simply requires what we can call "phenomenal affirmations" rather than "metaphysical affirmations."

Although human value productions are doomed to decay or lack permanent meaning in a metaphysical sense, the eternally recurrent moment to produce newer values at each instant of reality requires a certain aesthetic, or style, to be gone through strongly. Perhaps (European) "Man" should have approached his existence as an artist approaches art. As artists, we know our productions inherently lack universal significance and metaphysical permanence, yet we find affirmative meaning in our productions, nonetheless. Furthermore, upon completion, each artistic piece reminds the artist of an ever emergent need to create newer art and of the evanescent nature of each constructed piece. The artist cannot, and should not, ever cease to produce art as long as he or she is alive and able. Likewise, phenomenal life requires constant production; it becomes pathological when it attempts to "finish" the processes of making life valuable. The weak nihilism of modern (European) "Man," as "the last man," from this perspective, attempts to "finish" the project of human valuing.

Each moment of human existence creates an opportunity for choosing meaning. The eternal recurrence of the phenomenal moment perpetually places human life in relation to "other" moments.[122] It constitutes the nihilistic condition of human freedom and choice. Because each moment is experienced as a relationship to some other configuration of reality, conscious life involves perpetual representations. Pessimism results, initially, from seeing life through this lens. The pessimist, or weak pessimistic nihilist, can grow weary or unable to continue valuing in light of knowledge of the eternal recurrence; but the strong nihilist embraces the situation as, potentially, the "greatest elevation of the consciousness of strength in man as he creates the overman."[123]

Strong nihilists do not avoid the truth of pessimistic knowledge, or the eternal instability of human freedom and choice, by valuing in submission to absurdities of existence; rather, strong nihilists value the project of valuing in spite of, and perhaps in accordance with, it. The strong nihilist values with meaninglessness already accounted for. In other words, pessimism and some elements of reactivity are requisite for strong nihilism, initially, however, as Nietzsche said, if pessimistic knowledge is not accompanied by strong wills, it can be the most oppressive thought, that is, if transvalued values have not been developed:

1. The idea [of the eternal recurrence]: the presumptions that would have to be true if it were true. Its consequences.
2. As the *hardest* idea: its probable effect if it were not prevented, that is, if all values were not revalued.
3. Means of *enduring* it: the revaluation of all values. No longer joy in certainty but in uncertainty; no longer "cause and effect" but the continually creative; no longer will to preservation but to power; no longer the humble expression, "everything is *merely* subjective, but "it is also our work!—Let us be proud of it! (Emphasis in original.)"[124]

Strong nihilistic wills enable processes of transvaluation necessary to turn the destruction of pessimism and weak nihilism into, at least, strong pessimistic nihilism. Strong nihilism succeeds in transvaluing traditional values by not only devaluing their metaphysically affirmed bases, but also creating values that do not depend on metaphysical affirmations to replace them. The transvaluation of all values requires nihilistic strength to value without metaphysical affirmation.

The phenomenon of the eternal recurrence does not proscribe any predetermined sets of values to be "proud" of. However, it reveals that which must be taken into account if conscious life is to be strongly and freely valued. Nietzsche's ethical philosophy, for example, did not depend on moralistic conceptions of goodness, or badness, as did Schopenhauer and Kant, but invoked existential notions of strength and weakness in their place. For example, where Kant championed the a priori goodness of the metaphysical category of rationality in constructing pure reason as the basis of values, Nietzsche championed strength and freedom:

My new path to a "Yes."—Philosophy, As I have hitherto understood and lived it, is a voluntary quest for even the most detested and notorious sides of existence. From the long experience I gained from such a wandering through ice and wilderness, I learned to view differently all that had hitherto philosophized: the *hidden* history of philosophy, the psychology of its great names, came to light for me. "How much truth can a spirit *endure*, how much truth does a spirit dare?"—This became for me the real standard of value. Error is cowardice—every achievement of knowledge is a consequence of courage, of severity toward oneself, of cleanliness toward oneself—Such An experimental philosophy as I live anticipates experimentally even the possibilities of the most fundamental nihilism; but this does not mean that it must halt at a negation, a No, a will to negation. it wants rather to crossover to the opposite of this—to a Dionysian affirmation of the world as it is, without subtraction, exception, or selection—it wants the internal circulation: The highest state a philosopher can attain: to stand in a Dionysian relationship to existence—my formula for this is *amor fati* (Emphasis in original).[125]

"Amor fati," here, describes strength through a love and embrace of the fated eternal recurrence. This indicates that the strong nihilist rejects false comforts and uses pessimism as a means to live without a need for certainty; this is a feat that only the strongest of will, Dionysian man, perhaps, according to Nietzsche, who love the eternal recurrence, could withstand.

For Nietzsche, the strong advance the horizons of freedom in human life by demonstrating amor fati through a strong nihilistic will to value life in spite of absurdity. Pessimism and nihilism, on this view, are attitudes that can justify existence despite its metaphysical meaninglessness. Nihilistic strength begins with pessimistic rejection of traditional values and moves to construct values grounded in a love of possibility and freedom. Jacobi's fears, it seems, are fully realized in nihilistic philosophies. However, I read the immorality and destructiveness of nihilistic populations as perhaps a dizzying representation of what the process of transvaluation actually looks like. The point of nihilism, however, is not simply to pessimistically endorse destruction and chaos, as Jacobi wrongly suggested; strong nihilism draws on the dynamism and freedom of human will to construct a valuable existence not premised upon decadence. Strong nihilism advocates neither for blind destruction nor for blind disdain for others; but it does caution against idealist values rooted in otherworldly sources.

Nihilistic (European) "Man" emerged with a pessimistic hammer forcing a confrontation with traditional (European) "Man." "The greatest struggles: for this a new weapon is needed. The hammer: to provoke a fearful decision, to confront Europe with the consequences: whether it's will "wills" destruction. Prevention of reduction to mediocrity. Rather Destruction!"[126]

European nihilism, is a consequence of a leveling-down to mediocrity of modern culture, according to Nietzsche, a posturing of rationalism that belies a weak nihilism.[127] But, the existential fragilities of (European) "Man" have presented for us an even more fundamentally damning threat, one that threatens to do more to our humanity besides "leveling down." European nihilism desires a leveling-down of the freedom found in the dynamism of phenomenal will by constructing values for human life which have historically denied the majority of the world's human beings from theoretical inclusion into the "human" category, while concomitantly building a world of antiblack racist values around such exclusions. In other words, weak nihilistic European existential dispositions have historically played a fundamental role in the construction and maintenance of the traditional values of antiblack racism and white supremacy.

Alright; I have heard enough. I have spent countless hours listening to (European) "Man" divulge his desires, and limitations, through a notable rat pack of voices; at least, Descartes, Kant, Fichte, Schopenhauer, and Nietzsche have confessed, on various levels, the traditional values of modern (European) "Man," the current bases of construction for my society, were in fact lived and experienced, by them, within fluid matrices of meaning and desires centered on their own weaknesses and flights from reality. Philosophical systems attempting to arrest the inevitable, eternal processes of structuring meaning within reality are precisely what is admitted as weak nihilism. From the perspectives developed so far, one could ask, "Is antiblack racism a form of weak nihilism?" Yes. Let us call it "White nihilism."

NOTES

1. Albert P. Blaustein and Robert L. Zangrando, eds., *Civil Rights and African Americans* (Evanston: Northwestern University Press, 1991), 171–174. During his fourth debate with then Democratic presidential nominee, Stephen A. Douglass, Abraham Lincoln spoke these words, at Charleston, Illinois, on September 18, 1858, and again at Alton, Illinois, on October 15, 1858.

2. See, Cornel West, *Prophesy Deliverance!* (Louisville: Westminster John Knox Press, 1982), 47–67.

3. Lewis Gordon, *Fanon and Crisis of European Man* (New York: Routledge, 1995).

4. Charles Mills, *The Racial Contract* (New York: Cornell University Press, 1997).

5. Ibid. 41–89.

6. Bertrand Russell, *The History of Western Philosophy* (New York: Simon and Schuster, 1945), 3–24.

7. For geo-philosophical considerations of the historical emergence of "Europe," see Lewis Gordon, *An Introduction to Africana Philosophy* (Cambridge: Cambridge University Press, 2008), 1–18.

8. The first serious irruption of science was the publication of the Copernican theory in 1543; but this theory did not become influential until it was taken up and improved by Kepler and Galileo in the seventeenth century. Then began the long fight between science and dogma.

   Russell, *The History of Western Philosophy*, 492.

9. I am conscious that I possess a certain faculty of judging [or discerning truth from error], which doubtless I received from god. . . . [And] since it is impossible that he should will to deceive me, it is likewise certain that he has not given me a faculty that will ever lead me to error, provided I use it right.

René Descartes, *Meditations on First Philosophy*, trans. Michael Moriarty (England: Oxford University Press, 2008), 38. Originally published in 1641. See, also, Walter Kaufmann, *Philosophic Classics: Bacon to Kant* (Englewood Cliffs: Prentice-Hall, 1961), 26–91.

10. When I lately considered whether aught really existed in the world, and found that because I considered this question, it very manifestly followed that I myself existed, I could not but judge that what I so clearly conceived was true, not that I was forced to this judgment by any external cause, but simply because great clearness of the understanding was succeeded by strong inclination in the will. . . . I not only know that I exist, in so far as I am a thinking being, but there is likewise presented to my mind a certain corporeal nature.

Descartes, *Meditations on First Philosophy*, 38. See, also, Kaufmann, *Philosophic Classics*, 57.

11. [As] often as I so restrain my will within the limits of my knowledge, that it forms no judgment except regarding objects which are clearly and distinctively represented to it by the understanding, I can never be deceived; because every clear and distinct conception is doubtless something, and as such cannot owe its origin to nothing, but must of necessity have God for its author—God, I say, who, as supremely perfect, cannot, without a contradiction, be the cause of any error; and consequently it is necessary to conclude that every such conception [or judgment] is true. . . . I will assuredly reach truth if I only fix my attention sufficiently on all the thing I conceive perfectly, and separate these from others which I conceive more confusedly and obscurely.

   Descartes, *Meditations on First Philosophy*, 44–45.

12. Michael Gillespie, *Nihilism Before Nietzsche* (Chicago: University of Chicago Press, 1996), 26.
13. Ibid. 42.
14. Do not hesitate, I tell you, to avow and to proclaim everywhere, that it is God who has established the laws of nature, as a King establishes laws in

his Kingdom. . . . You will be told that if God has established these truths, he could also change them as a King changes his laws. To which it must be replied: yes, if his will can change. But I understand them as eternal and immutable. And I judge the same of God. But his will is free. Yes, but his power is incomprehensible. And in general we can rest assured that God can do everything that we can comprehend, but not that he cannot do what we cannot comprehend. For it would be overly bold to think that our imagination has as great an extent as his power.

René Descartes, *Philosophical Essays and Correspondence*, ed. Roger Ariew (Indianapolis: Hackett Pub, 2000), 28–29. See also, Gillespie, *Nihilism Before Nietzsche*, 30–32. For the original French translation, see, Charles Adam and Paul Tannery, eds., *Ouvres de Descartes* (Paris: Vrin Press, 1957), 1: 135–136.

15. Descartes, *Philosophical Essays and Correspondence*, 206. See, also, Gillespie, *Nihilism Before Nietzsche*, 31. For the original French translation, see, also, Adam and Tannery, *Ouvres de Descartes*, 7:435.

16. Michael Gillespie summarized Descartes's conception of human knowledge in relation to God's existence. Gillespie wrote as follows:

> The human will, which is in essence the same as the will of God, thus discovers that it is limited, that it is not God. The discovery of such a limitation, however, is simultaneously the recognition of the necessity of the unlimited, that is, man, only is as the negation of the unlimited, that is, as the negation of God. . . . Deception requires self-consciousness, which is the basis for distinguishing oneself from others. God, however, is not self-conscious. God thus is no deceiver. If God is no deceiver, then the truths of mathematics cannot be doubted and the only thing that stands in the way of man's perfection is man himself. Through science, man can expand the sphere of his knowledge and his power until it is identical with that of his will, that is, until he becomes master and possessor of nature. . . . Descartes thus demonstrates that God cannot be the God he was traditionally understood to be, since as infinitely infinite and therefore non-self-conscious he cannot have intentions or will in a traditional sense.
>
> Gillespie, *Nihilism Before Nietzsche*, 60–61.

17. Appearances, so far as they are thought as objects under the unity of categories, are called phenomena. But if I admit things which are objects of the understanding only, and nevertheless can be given as objects of intuition, though not of sensuous intuition (as *coram intuiti intellectuali*), such things would be called noumena (*intellegibilia*). . . . For if the senses only represent to us something as it appears, that something must by itself also be a thing, and an object of a non-sensuous intuition, that is, of the understanding. That is, there must be a kind of knowledge in which there is no sensibility, and which alone possess absolute objective reality, representing objects as they are, while through the empirical use of our understanding we know things only as they appear. . . . In fact, quite a new field would seem to be open, a world, as it were, realized in thought, which would be a more, and not a less, worthy object for the pure understanding.

Immanuel Kant, *Critique of Pure Reason*, trans. Paul Guyer (Cambridge: Cambridge University Press, 1998), 347. Originally published in 1781. See, also, Kaufmann, *Philosophic Classics*, 475.

18. The concept Phenomena . . . suggested by itself the objective reality of the Noumena, and justified a division of objects into phenomena and noumena, and consequently of the world into a sensible and intelligible world (*mundus sensibilis et intelligiblis*); and this in such a way that the distinction between the two should not refer to the logical form only of a more or less clear knowledge of one and the same object, but to a difference in their original presentation to our knowledge, which makes them to differ in themselves from each other in kind.

Kaufmann, *Philosophic Classics*, Ibid.

19. Immanuel Kant, *Groundwork for the Metaphysics of Morals*, trans. Allen W. Wood (New Haven: Yale University Press, 2002), 15. Originally published in 1785.

20. Only a rational being has will—which is the ability to act according to the thought of laws, i.e., to act on principle. To derive action from laws you need reason, so that's what will is—practical reason. When reason is irresistible in its influence on the will, the actions that a rational being recognizes as objectively necessary are also subjectively necessary; i.e., the will is the ability to choose only what reason recognizes, independently of preferences, as practically necessary, i.e., as good.

Kant, *Groundwork for the Metaphysics of Morals*, 18.

21. "[It's] an island, enclosed by nature itself within unalterable limits. It is the land of truth . . . surrounded by a wide and stormy ocean, the native home of illusion, where many a fog bank and many a swiftly melting iceberg give the deceptive appearance of farther shores, deluding the adventurous seafarer ever anew with empty hopes, and engaging him in enterprises which he can never abandon and yet is unable to carry to completion." Kant, *Critique of Pure Reason*, 339. See, also, Kaufmann, *Philosophic Classics: Bacon to Kant*, 469.

22. Descartes suspected that the pineal gland might be a specific region of the brain where epistemic representations of secondary qualities are housed.

23. Gillespie, *Nihilism Before Nietzsche*, 64–100.

24. Michael Gillespie, for example, supports this understanding of Fichte's philosophy of the not-I. Gillespie explained as follows:

> The existence of the not-I poses an unavoidable problem for the I. The not-I is the opposite of the I and annihilates it. Where the not-I is the I is not. Yet, the not-I is posited by the I and thus presupposes it.
>
> Ibid. 81.

25. Ibid.
26. Ibid.
27. Regarding Fichte's idea of longing, for instance, Gillespie explains the following:

> Longing arises out of a dissatisfaction with the limits of the I, that is, out of its feelings of incapacity. This feeling arises however, because in longing the I is already in some sense beyond its limitations and thus feels the contradiction between what it is as an absolute activity and what it is as an empirical being.
>
> Ibid. 91.

28. Gillespie further explains the role of "God" as that which situates the "beyond" in Fichte's philosophy, he wrote as follows:

> From the perspective of the absolute-I, the not-I is only an internal disruption of the I itself. The empirical-I, however, experiences this disruption as a feeling. The primordial-I, as Fichte understands it, is both everything and nothing. As pure, unconditioned activity, it is totally without internal distinctions and encompasses everything whatsoever. . . . This pure activity is disrupted by an alien element that appears within the I. . . . This other undermines the self-identity of the I by establishing a boundary between what it is and what it is not. The I experiences this boundary as a feeling that curbs its activity. As a result of this feeling, the I does not want to extend itself any further in the direction closed off by the boundary. It thereby ceases to be absolute and becomes merely an empirical-I. . . . The limitation of the I is also the source of self-consciousness. The primordial I is a pure activity, a point that wants to become an infinite plane . . . it is pure will. This outreaching however is checked at a particular point by the not-I. The will meets a resistance which it cannot overcome. . . . The I comes to recognize itself as an I in consequence of its encounter with the not-I or object. The inner experience of the empirical I undergoing this experience is a feeling of incapacity that sets a limit for the I. . . . The I strives for the infinite but the infinite cannot be attained. At some point short of the infinite, the I reaches the limits of its strength, and can go no further. At this point it is repulsed from the infinite. . . . [This] is the source of the feeling of incapacity in the I, the feeling that the will is limited, that it is not God.
>
> Ibid. 88–89.

29. Johann Gottlieb Fichte, *Foundations of the Science of Knowledge* (Cambridge: Cambridge University Press, 1970), 137. Originally published in 1795.

30. For instance, Gillespie explains as follows:

> Fichte attempts to resolve this apparent contradiction by properly distinguishing. . . . The not-I is real and restricts the empirical-I. . . . Both the empirical-I and the not-I, that is, both individual human subjects and the objective world, in Fichte's view, are expressions of the free activity of the absolute-I, of the infinite will that is essential to both God and man.
>
> Gillespie, *Nihilism Before Nietzsche*, 79–83.

31. According to Fichte, "The mutual necessity and mutual contradiction of the I and not-I is the essence of the problem that manifests itself in Kant's antinomies." Fichte, *Foundations of the Science of Knowledge*, 217.

32. Gillespie described Fichte's conception of imagination in response to pessimism. He wrote as follows:

> [The] new image engenders a new boundary and a new feeling of limitation. . . . As a result it is driven forward from one image to the next along a dialectical path

by the repeated negation of successive realities. At each moment of liberation, "harmony exists and a feeling of inclination ensues, which in this case is a feeling of contentment, of repletion, of utter completeness," but this harmony "lasts only a moment . . . since the longing necessarily recurs."

Gillespie, *Nihilism Before Nietzsche*, 79–83.

33. Of Fichte's perspective on Kantian idealism, Gillespie wrote as follows:

[Kant] partitions reason in a way that allows space for both science and morality, for both the finite-I and the objective world on one hand and the infinite-I and subjective freedom on the other. Fichte, however, believes that he has discovered that Kant's island of truth is itself only an illusion, that there are no fixed and immutable forms, and that everything is merely the projection of the imagination upon the banks of fog where one image gives way to another. This confusion, of course, is exactly what Kant predicted would engulf those who left the shelter of his island.

Ibid. v85.

34. The first historical appearance of the term "nihilism" was F. L. Goetzieus's *De Nonisismo et nihilismo in theologia* (1733). However, this text is relatively unknown and seems to have had little or no influence on the term's later emergence.

35. In an open letter to Fichte, Jacobi wrote, "Truly, my dear Fichte, it should not grieve me, if you, or whoever it might be, want to call chimerism what I oppose to idealism, which I reproach as nihilism." Gillespie, *Nihilism Before Nietzsche*, 65.

36. Ibid. 66.

37. Ibid. 106.

38. It was under these religious-philosophical conditions that Descartes famously produced a defense of God's existence (by disproving the possibility of an evil deceiver demon) alongside his rationalistic epistemology.

39. I am not offering a genealogy of "Nihilism" in modern Europe, but a sketch of the thought of certain undeniably influential thinkers.

40. Friedrich Nietzsche, *The Will to Power*, trans. Walter Kaufmann (New York: Vintage Books, 1967). Originally published (posthumously) in 1901.

41. Friedrich Nietzsche, *Thus Spoke Zarathustra*, trans. Thomas Common (Hertfordshire: Wordsworth Editions Limited, 1997). Originally published in 1883.

42. Friedrich Nietzsche, *On the Genealogy of Morals* and *Ecce Homo*, trans. Walter Kaufmann and R. J. Hollingdale (New York: Knopf Doubleday Publishing Group, 2010), 258. *Ecce Homo* was originally published (posthumously) in 1908.

43. When it comes to the philosophical consideration of art . . . I cannot follow [Schopenhauer] . . . in so far as the subject is an artist, he is already liberated from his individual will and has become a medium through which the only truly existent subject celebrates his redemption through illusion . . . the whole comedy of art is not at all performed *for* (Emphasis in original) us . . . we are images and artistic productions for the true creator . . . it is only as an aesthetic phenomena that existence and the world are eternally justified.

See. *The Birth of Tragedy Out of the Spirit of Music*, trans. Shaun Whiteside (London: Penguin Books, 2003), 5: 31–32. Originally published in 1872.

44. [Schopenhauer] interpreted in turn art, heroism, genius, beauty, grand sympathy, knowledge, the will to truth, tragedy, as phenomena consequent upon the "denial" of or the thirst to deny the "will"—the greatest piece of false-coinage in history, Christianity alone excepted. Looked at more closely he is in this merely the heir of the Christian interpretation: but with this difference, that he knew how to take what Christianity had rejected, the great cultural facts of mankind, and approve of them from a Christian, that is to say nihilistic, point of view (—namely, as roads to "redemption," as preliminary forms of "redemption," as stimulants of the thirst for "redemption." . . .)

See, Friedrich Nietzsche, *Twilight of the Idols*, trans. R. J. Hollingdale (England: Penguin Books, 1968), 89–90. Originally published in 1889.

45. The world is my representation: this is a truth valid with reference to every living and knowing being, although man alone can bring it into reflective, abstract consciousness. If he really does so, philosophical discernment has dawned on him. It then becomes clear and certain to him that he does not know a sun and earth, but only an eye that sees a sun, a hand that feels the earth. . . . If any truth can be expressed a priori, it is this.

Arthur Schopenhauer, *The World as Will and Representation, vol. I*, trans. E. F. J. Payne (New York: Dover Publications, 1968), 3. Originally published in 1819.

46. [Time], space, and causality. . . . While each of these forms, which we have recognized as so many particular modes of the principle of sufficient reason, is valid only for a particular class of representations, the division of object and subject, on the other hand, is the common form of all those classes; it is that form under which alone any representation, of whatever kind it be, abstract or intuitive, pure or empirical, is generally possible and conceivable . . . everything that exists for knowledge, and hence the whole of this world, is only object in relation to the subject, perception of the perceiver, in a word, representation.

Ibid.

47. For instance, Schopenhauer argued that space, time, and causality do not belong to the thing-in-itself, but only to the phenomenon. See, Schopenhauer, *The World as Will and Representation, vol. I*, 1–13. For further explication of this point, see, Joshua Foa Dienstag, *Pessimism: Philosophy, Ethic, Spirit* (Princeton: Princeton University Press, 2006), 88.

48. Arthur Schopenhauer, *The World as Will and Representation, vol. II* (New York: Dover Publications), 137.

49. Every state of welfare, every feeling of satisfaction, is negative in character; that is to say, it consists in freedom from pain, which is the positive element of existence. It follows, therefore, that the happiness of any given life is to be measured, not by its joys and pleasures, but by the extent to which it has been free from suffering. . . . If this is the true standpoint, the lower animals appear to enjoy a happier destiny than man. . . . The chief source of all this passion is that thought for what is absent and future. . . . In his powers of

reflection, memory and foresight, man possesses, as it were, a machine for condensing and storing up his pleasures and his sorrows. But the brute has nothing of the kind. . . . [Besides] the sources of pleasure which he has in common with the brute, man has the pleasures of the mind as well . . . the most innocent trifling or the merest talk up to the highest intellectual achievements; but there is the accompanying boredom to be set against them on the side of suffering.

Arthur Schopenhauer, *Studies in Pessimism*, trans. By T. Bailey Saunders (New York: Cosimo, 2007), 8–10. Originally published in 1851.

50. Schopenhauer, *The World as Will and Representation*, vol. *I*, 119.

51. Dienstag, *Pessimism: Philosophy, Ethic, Spirit*, 92. See, also, Arthur Schopenhauer, *Essays and Aphorisms*, trans. R. J. Hollingdale (England: Penguin Books, 1970). Originally published in 1890. In particular, see, "On Vanity."

52. The absence of reason restricts the animals to representations of perception immediately present to them in time, in other words to real objects. We, on the other hand, by virtue of knowledge in the abstract, comprehend not only the narrow and actual present, but also the whole past and present together with the wide realm of possibility.

He further wrote, "[Animals] are much more satisfied than we by mere existence . . . primarily due to the fact that [they remain] free from care and anxiety together with their torment." See, Schopenhauer, *The World as Will and Representation*, vol. *I*, 84.

53. Absence of all aim, of all limits, belongs to the essential nature of the will in itself, which is an endless striving . . . the same thing is also seen in human endeavors and desires that buoy us up with the vain hope that their fulfillment is always the final goal of willing. But as soon as they are attained, they no longer look the same, and so are soon forgotten, become antiquated, and are really, although not immediately, always laid aside as vanished illusions . . . the will always knows . . . what it wills her and now, but never what it wills in general. Every individual act has a purpose or end; willing as a whole has no end in view.

Schopenhauer, *The World as Will and Representation*, vol. *I*, 164.

54. Schopenhauer, *Essays and Aphorisms*, 168.

55. Instead of the restless pressure and effort; instead of the constant transition from desire to apprehension and from joy to sorrow; instead of the never-satisfied and never-dying hope that constitutes the life dream of the man who wills, we see that peace that is higher than all reason, that ocean-like calmness of the spirit, that deep tranquility, that unshakable confidence and serenity, whose mere reflection in the countenance . . . is a complete and certain gospel. Only knowledge remains; the [phenomenal] will has vanished.

Schopenhauer, *The World as Will and Representation*, vol. *I*, 411.

56. Only through pure contemplation . . . which becomes absorbed entirely in the object, are the ideas comprehended; and the nature of the genius consists

precisely in the preeminent ability for such contemplation . . . this demands a complete forgetting of our own person.

                Schopenhauer, *The World as Will and Representation*, vol. *I*, 185.

57. Schopenhauer, *The World as Will and Representation*, vol. *I*, 197–198.
58. On the occurrence of an aesthetic appreciation, the will thereby vanishes entirely from consciousness . . . this is the origin of that satisfaction and pleasure that accompany the apprehension of the beautiful . . . to become a pure subject of knowing means to be quit of oneself.

Arthur Schopenhauer, *Parerga and Paralipomena,* trans. E. F. J. Payne (Oxford: Clarendon Press, 2000), 415.

59. Schopenhauer, *The World as Will and Representation*, vol. *I*, 312.
60. Dienstag, *Pessimism: Philosophy, Ethic, Spirit*, 98.
61. We must not imagine that after the denial of the will-to-live has appeared through knowledge . . . such denial no longer wavers or falters, and that we can rest on it as an inherited property. On the contrary, it must always be achieved afresh by constant struggle . . . that whole will-to-live exists potentially so long as the body lives, and is always striving. . . . We therefore find in the lives of saintly persons that peace and bliss we have described, only as the blossom resulting from the constant overcoming of the [phenomenal] will . . . for on earth, no man can have lasting peace.

                Schopenhauer, *The World as Will and Representation*, vol. *I*, 391.

62. Stoic ethics is originally and essentially not a doctrine of virtue, but merely a guide to the rational life, whose end and aim is happiness through peace of mind. Virtuous conduct appears in it, so to speak, only by accident, as means, not as end.

                Schopenhauer, *The World as Will and Representation*, vol. *I*, 86.

63. As far as you are an individual, death will be the end of you. But your individuality is not your true and innermost being: it is only the outward manifestation of it. It is not the thing-in-itself, but only the phenomenon presented in the form of time; and therefore with a beginning and end. But your real being knows neither time, nor beginning, nor end, nor yet the limits of any given individual. . . . So when death comes, on the one hand you are annihilated as an individual; on the other, you are and remain everything.

                Schopenhauer, *Studies in Pessimism*, 50–54.

64. See, Schopenhauer's, "The Vanity of Existence," in *Studies in Pessimism*.
65. Dienstag, *Pessimism: Philosophy, Ethic, Spirit*, 163.
66. Byron Williston, "'Complete Nihilism' in Nietzsche," *Philosophy Today* 45, no. 4 (Winter 2001): 357–369.
67. Nietzsche, *The Will to Power*, 22: 17. Originally published (posthumously) in 1901.
68. Gillespie, *Nihilism Before Nietzsche*, 179.

69. Ibid.
70. Nietzsche, *The Will to* Power, 11: 11.
71. Ibid. 12: 12.
72. Ibid.
73. Ibid. 17: 15.
74. Ibid. 55: 35.
75. Friedrich Nietzsche, *The Birth of Tragedy*, trans. Francis Golffing (New York: Anchor Books: 1956).
76. Gillespie, *Nihilism Before Nietzsche*, 208.
77. Ibid. 209.
78. Ibid.
79. Nietzsche, *The Birth of Tragedy*, 10: 65.
80. Ibid. 14: 88.
81. Ibid. 15: 92.
82. Dienstag, *Pessimism: Philosophy, Ethic, Spirit*, 169.
83. Ibid. 171.
84. Ibid.
85. Friedrich Nietzsche, *The Genealogy of Morals*, trans. Francis Golffing (New York: Anchor Books: 1956), IV: 162–163.
86. Nietzsche, *The Genealogy of Morals*, IV: 162.
87. Ibid. VII: 167.
88. Dienstag, *Pessimism: Philosophy, Ethic, Spirit*, 177.
89. Nietzsche, *Will to Power*, 17: 15.
90. Friedrich Nietzsche, *Beyond Good and Evil*, trans. R. J. Hollingdale (England: Penguin Books, 2003), sec. 186.
91. Dienstag, *Pessimism: Philosophy, Ethic, Spirit*, 178.
92. Nietzsche, *Will to Power*, 12: 13.
93. Friedrich Nietzsche, *The Twilight of the Idols*, trans. Judith Norman (Cambridge: Cambridge University Press, 2005), 8: 182. See, in particular, "The Four Great Errors."
94. Ibid.
95. Dienstag, *Pessimism: Philosophy, Ethic, Spirit*, 176.
96. Nietzsche, *Will to Power*, 13: 14.
97. Ibid. 14: 14.
98. Simone De Beauvoir, *The Ethics of Ambiguity*, trans. Bernard Frechtman (United States: Citadel Press, 1962), 52.
99. Nietzsche, *Will to Power*, 14: 14.
100. Nietzsche, *Will to Power*, 12: 13.
101. Ibid. 15: 14–15.
102. Ibid. 585: 318.
103. "Kant considered the hypothesis of 'intelligible freedom' necessary on order to acquit the *ens perfectum* of responsibility of the world's being such-and-such—in short, to account for evil and ills: a scandalous bit of logic for a philosopher." Ibid. 17: 16.
104. Nietzsche, *Beyond Good and Evil*, Sec. 203.

105. Dienstag, *Pessimism: Philosophy, Ethic, Spirit*, 181.
106. Ibid. 182.
107. Nietzsche, *Zarathustra*, 3: 277.
108. Williston, "Complete Nihilism," 361.
109. Ibid. 365.
110. See, Giles Deleuze, "Active and Reactive," in *The New Nietzsche*, ed. Davis B. Allison (Cambridge: MIT Press, 1985), 81.
111. Williston, "Complete Nihilism," 362.
112. Ibid. 365.
113. Ibid. 361.
114. Ibid.
115. Ibid.
116. On this view Kant can be viewed as an instance of the last (European) "Man" and Schopenhauer can be viewed as an instance of the higher (European) "Man," who collapsed back into pessimism, and became stuck, or a weak nihilist who grew weary. Williston helps explain, "The hope expressed in the initial distinction between the two types is abandoned as Nietzsche subjects his contemporaries to a blanket condemnation." Ibid. 362.
117. Ibid. 365.
118. Deleuze, "Active and Reactive," 99.
119. Williston, "Complete Nihilism," 366.
120. Nietzsche, *Zarathustra*, "The Three Metamorphoses, 1: 22.
121. Dienstag, *Pessimism: Philosophy, Ethic, Spirit*, 182–183.
122. "If the world may be thought of as a certain definite quantity of force and as a certain definite number of centres of force—and every other representation remains indefinite and therefore useless—it follows that, in the great dice game of existence, it must pass through a calculable number of combinations. In infinite time, every possible combination would at some time or another be realized; more: it would be realized an infinite number of times. And since between every combination and it's next recurrence all other possible combinations would have to take place, and each of these combinations conditions the entire sequence of combinations in the same series, a circular movement of absolutely identical series is thus demonstrated: the world as a circular movement that has already repeated itself infinitely often and plays its game *in infinitum*."

Nietzsche, *Will to Power*, 1066: 549.

123. Ibid. 1060: 546.
124. Ibid. 1059: 545.
125. Ibid. 1041: 536–537.
126. Ibid. 1054: 544.
127. Ibid. 953: 500.

Chapter 3

White Nihilism and Antiblack Racism

> All the values by means of which we have tried so far to render the world estimable for ourselves and which then proved inapplicable and therefore devalued the world—all these values are, psychologically considered, the results of certain perspectives of utility, designed to maintain and increase human constructs of domination and they have been falsely projected into the essence of things. What we find here is still the *hyperbolic* naiveté of man: positing himself as the meaning and measure of the value of things.[1]

Underneath every cultural way of life is an ordering of philosophical conditions enabling that reality. The availability of discursive resources within cultural ways of life tends to delimit possibilities for creating meaning within that reality. The reality of antiblack racism in Western cultural life is historically rooted in weak philosophical ideals of (European) "Man." I have heard enough, privately admitted, in order to conclude that antiblack racism is philosophically structured according to the weak nihilistic needs of (European) "Man," who traditionally only chooses to fallaciously appear to me as strong optimistic (European) "Man" with a bag of false idealisms. The original and continued rationalizations for antiblack racism and its failures to often display even the barest elements of human decency, empathy, and mutual self-recognition for others; its overall despicableness and utter disregard for the well-being of any other but itself; and its gruesome histories are all a result of modern European existential needs, weaknesses, continuing to prefigure our current reality.

Antiblack racism as a form of weak nihilism because it attempts to arrest human development by destroying the possibility of producing values beyond the imagined metaphysical affirmations of ideals supporting antiblack racist conceptions of whiteness. Modern antiblack racism is part and parcel of the historical value systems of (European) "Man," who imagined all phenomenal activity, but especially rational cognition, through restrictive conceptions of Humanity as racially white. He imagined himself as the only human existing in a physical world of nature, animals, and Brutes, only there to be mastered.[2]

The traditional philosophies of (European) "Man" interpreted the geopolitical practices of Western colonialism, slavery, genocide, and antiblack racism, within a constellation of metaphysically affirmed ideals that imagined such atrocities as good, moral, necessary, and in the most historical and epistemological sense, "true," of the progress of Humanity in this world. Modern European cultural expansion relied on rational idealism, claiming scientific knowledge of the nature of the universe, including ultimate values for human life. Concomitant with these "truths" were the brutalities of Western colonialism, antiblack racism, and the sedimentation of a weak nihilistic valuation of "Man."

Modern antiblack racism is traditionally justified according to the idealist view that only racially white people possess rationality and, therefore, Humanity. This is a form of weak nihilism. For example, criticizing Descartes's attempt to develop a singular rationalistic human perspective, Nietzsche wrote as follows:

> It is in the nature of thinking that it thinks of and invents the unconditioned as an adjunct to the conditioned; Just as it thought of and invented the "ego" as an adjunct to the multiplicity of its processes; It measures the world according to magnitudes posited by itself—such fundamental fictions as "the unconditional," "ends and means," "things," "substances," logical laws, numbers in forms. There would be nothing that could be called knowledge if thought did not first re-form the world in this way into "things," into what is self-identical. Only because there is thought is there untruth. Thought cannot be derived, anymore than sensations can be; but that does not mean that its primordiality or "being-in-itself" has been proved! All that is established is that we cannot get beyond it, because we *have* (Emphasis in original) nothing but thought and sensation.[3]

Traditional modern Western philosophy fuses the "unconditioned" weight of metaphysical affirmations onto the "conditioned" historical existence of its antiblack racist values. Antiblack racism is based upon weak nihilism, which might not be a problem in a private context. But, in this society, the entire affair of antiblack racism can be condemned in terms of political and public insistence on policies ultimately dependent upon metaphysically affirmed values. Nietzsche's words support my theorization that the political absurdities of antiblack racist policies are reflective of the weak nihilistic constitutions of their proponents, which they must insist upon, sort of like an "emergency measure."

> To assert the existence as a whole of things of which we know nothing whatever [universal reality], precisely because there is an advantage in not being able to know anything of them, was a piece of naiveté of Kant, resulting from needs, mainly moral-metaphysical.[4]

He further wrote as follows:

> The idea of the "true world" or of "God" as absolutely immaterial, spiritual, good, is an emergency measure necessary while the opposite instincts are still all-powerful.—
> The degree of Moderation and humanity attained is exactly reflected in the humanization of the gods: the Greeks of the strongest epoch, who were not afraid of themselves but rejoiced in themselves, brought their gods close to all their own affects—.
> The spiritualization of the idea of God is therefore far from being a sign of progress.[5]

Antiblack racist societies are nothing more than an "adapted world which [they] feel to be real."[6] It relies upon values that violently enforce the (un)reality of antiblack racist values onto the world's black people. That "real world" of antiblack racism is completely condemnable. Nietzsche criticized *and* confessed the need for (European) "Man" to have such a "real world," when he wrote, "Our particular case is interesting enough: we have produced a conception in order to be able to live in a world, in order to perceive just enough to endure it."[7] The modern Western world is a world constructed according to weak nihilistic desires. On my view, the opposite of the modern European worldview is not another, "real," "real world," but the "formless unformulable world of the chaos of sensations—*another* (Emphasis in original) kind phenomenal world, a 'unknowable' to us."[8] There is a performative contradiction involved in pointing out the unreality of a world by referring to the realness of that unreality, which amounts to pointing out "the really real." The point is there are stronger ways of valuing human existence that go beyond European nihilism.

Modern European nihilism is a foundational element of antiblack racism. Nietzsche's analysis, perhaps inadvertently, helps explain European attitudes as a pretext for black experiences of existential invisibility within antiblack racist worlds. Traditional conceptions of (European) "Man" entail antiblack racist conceptions of black people, and only make sense when considered from weak nihilistic perspectives of European humanity. Accordingly, strong nihilistic conceptions of black humanity may be the key to understanding the other "kind of phenomenal world," that Nietzsche claimed, remains "unknowable." Black perspectives are not "unknowable," antiblack racism belies certain needs to deny them, make them unknowable, in order to render one's own existence valuable. Nietzsche's internal critique of modern (European) "Man" exposes this weak nihilistic solipsism, which I argue is at the heart of antiblack racism:

> [The question] what things "in-themselves" may be like, apart from our sense receptivity and the activity of our understanding, must be rebutted with the question: how could we know that things exist? "Thingness" was first created by us. The question is whether there could not be many other ways of creating such an apparent world—and whether this creating, logicizing, Adapting, falsifying is not itself the best-guaranteed reality; In short, whether that which "posits things" is not the sole reality; and whether the "effect of the external world upon us" is not also only the result of such active subjects—The other "entities" act upon us; our adapted apparent world is an adaptation an overpowering of their actions: a kind of defensive measure. the subject alone is demonstrable; hypothesis that only subjects exist—that "object" is only a kind of effect produced by a subject upon a subject—*a modus of the subject* (Emphasis in original).[9]

Modern European philosophy situates a weak nihilistic notion of (European) "Man," as that which fixes the meaning of "things."

Traditional Western reality has proceeded according to weak nihilistic values, including the ideal that racially white people exclusively possess the human capacity to produce values, such as "truth." For this reason, weak nihilism and antiblack racism permeate traditional discourses on human understanding. For instance, after Descartes introduced *Rules for the Direction of the Mind* (1628), European society began producing mass volumes of texts espousing rationalistic knowledge of the human condition. In addition to Descartes's *Meditations on First Philosophy* (1641), there were John Locke's *An Essay Concerning Human Understanding* (1690), George Berkeley's *A Treatise Concerning the Principles of Human Knowledge* (1710), David Hume's *An Enquiry Concerning Human Understanding* (1748), and of course, Immanuel Kant's *On the Different Races of Man* (1775) and *Critique of Pure Reason* (1781), to list several. Weak nihilism and antiblack racism are theoretically implicit to many, if not most, modern European philosophical ruminations about "Man." A brief sketch of some key Enlightenment thinkers demonstrates weak nihilistic commitments through implicit appeals to antiblack racist conceptions of "whiteness," or what I call "white nihilism."

European philosophies were produced by allegedly "value free subjects . . . observing, comparing, ordering and measuring in order to arrive at evidence sufficient to make valid inferences, confirm speculative hypotheses, deduce error-proof conclusions, and verify true representations of reality."[10] The bases of Western life, therefore, involves antiblack racist legacies of situating traditional viewpoints as the only philosophical perspectives from which to legitimately inquire about reality, or the only perspective from which "truth" can be validated. Whiteness was viewed as prerequisite for philosophical inquiry, which ought to result in presumed value-free, rational, projections. Whiteness *is* "Humanity," and (European) "Man" is white. Given Nietzsche's criticism of idealist conceptions of humanity, then, this form of "whiteness" is also weak nihilistic; it is the value of chosen "appearance," masquerading as "true" reality:

> Appearance is an arranged and simplified world, at which our practical instincts have been at work; It is perfectly true for *us* (Emphasis in original); that is to say, we live, we are able to live in it: proof of its truth for us—the world, apart from our condition of living in it, the world that we have not reduced to our being, our logic and psychological prejudices, does not exist as a world "in-itself"; it is essentially a world of relationships; under certain conditions it has a differing aspect from every point; its being is essentially different from every point; It presses upon every point, every point resists it—and the sum of these is in every case quite incongruent.[11]

Nietzsche admitted that the world of (European) "Man" is merely a world of relative appearances, (European) "Man's" nihilistic proclivity for distancing himself from his value projections, which is indicative of weakness. The weak nihilism demanding the antiblack racist world can be further observed through antiblack racist's continued willing that there never, ever, ever, ever be another world of value beyond whiteness. Thus, black life in antiblack racist contexts is situated by white nihilism and antiblack racism, and this causes grievous occasions for pessimism and nihilism by black people facing the, alleged, universal nature of "whiteness," which demands *our* suffering.

Modern European understandings of the human category traditionally rendered black humanity as nonexistent, or existentially invisible, which means, only comprehensible in relation to the white nihilistic ideals of (European) "Man."[12] Some modern European thinkers even claimed Europeans had an entirely different evolutionary ancestry from Africans.[13] Others claimed that a purely rationalistic basis for ordering and ranking the various anthropological data of "other" cultures was possible. Still, others argued that an explanation of the inferiority of black cultures could be understood as a result of black underdevelopments of phenomenal capacities.

Some early modern European thinkers suggested, perhaps, a distant anthropological relative existed between white and black people, but resulted in antithetical qualities inhering between the divergent races.[14] In *Voyages de*

François Bernier (1670), in an essay entitled "A New Division of the Earth According to the Different Species or Races of Men Who Inhabit It," Bernier argued that geographically identifiable physical differences in human groups are anthropologically and aesthetically important.[15] In the process, Bernier simply asserted the normative status of "generally all Europe" in human anthropology. He praised "a small part of [northern] Africa . . . [and] a good part of Asia," where, "although the Egyptians . . . and the Indians are very Black, or rather copper-colored, that color is only an accident in them, and is because they are constantly exposed to the sun."[16] The accidental nature of Egyptian blackness, for Bernier, meant they were not "a species apart," as he put it.[17]

Modern Western Humanism was founded according to such inherent distinctions of superiority and inferiority residing within racial difference. The biological and anthropological arguments of Bernier, Voltaire, J. G. von Herder, and J. F. Blumenbach, to name a few, helped establish a white-normative sensibility of modern European thought concerning the human category, which included Galton's eugenic claim that the health of the human race depended upon conquering and eliminating "degenerative" races.[18] Kant furthered the biological-anthropological sentiment by supplying a philosophical correlate to models of white superiority, producing texts concluding that only certain races of human beings possessed the rational, moral, and political capacities. He understood antiblack racist conceptions of anthropology to be the empirical analogue for the philosophy of (European) "Man."[19] In "The Different Races of Mankind" (1775), Kant provided a detailed racial taxonomy suggesting the inferiority of black people as a natural result of misuse and/or lowered intellectual capacities. "When a people does not perfect itself in any way over the space of centuries, so it may be assumed that there exists a certain natural predisposition that the people cannot transcend."[20] He argued that African peoples failed to transcend primitivism because of a lack of intellectual aptitude and/or autonomy of the will. Such beings, he thought, demonstrated capacities typical of the black body, wherein "every man should let his talents rust and should be bent on devoting his life solely to idleness, indulgence, procreation, and, in a word, to enjoyment."[21]

In another essay, "Perpetual Peace" (1795), Kant wrote as follows:

> The negro countries, the spice islands, the Cape [of Good Hope] etc. were, on being discovered, looked upon as countries which belonged to nobody; for the native inhabitants were reckoned as nothing. . . . Oppression of the natives followed, famine, insurrection, perfidy and all the rest of the litany of evils which can afflict mankind.[22]

Here, black people are literally described as nonentities, invisible, "nothing," or "nobody," for whom human rights of autonomy apply. In *Anthropology from a Pragmatic Point of View* (1798), in, "On How to Discern Man's Inner Self from His Exterior," Kant directly argued that global domination of black people is best for all humanity.[23] According to this view, blacks are incapable of anything more than a "slave culture," and the advancement of humanity is and ought to be centered in Europe.[24] Black people have been traditionally viewed from such antiblack racist perspectives as lacking intellectual capacities for human development, as invisible nonbeings there only to be mastered by (white) Human beings.

Antiblack racist expositions of value were produced in line with metaphysical affirmations of varying forms of idealism by modern (European) "Man." Traditional European philosophy exhibits an attempt to universalize white nihilistic conceptualizations of the human being. For example, at the dawn of the nineteenth century, Hegel's "A Geographical Basis for a World History," from his *Lectures on the Philosophy of History* (1837), captured the legacy of European nihilism and antiblack racism:[25]

> Africa proper. . . . The characteristic part of the whole continent as such . . . the consciousness of the inhabitants has not yet reached an awareness of any substantial and objective existence. Under the heading of substantial objectivity, we must include God, the eternal, justice, nature, and all natural things. When the spirit [rational phenomenal capacities] enters into relations with substantial things such as these, it knows that it is dependent upon them; but it realizes at the same time that it is a value in itself in so far as it is capable of such relationships. But the Africans have not yet attained this recognition of the universal . . . what we call religion, the state, that which exists in and for itself and possesses absolute validity—all this is not yet present to them. . . . The characteristic feature of the negroes is that their consciousness has not yet reached an awareness of any substantial objectivity—for example, of God or the law—in which the will of man could participate and in which he could become aware of his own being. The African . . . has not yet succeeded in making this distinction between himself as an individual and his essential universality . . . has not progressed beyond his immediate existence. . . . The Negro is an example of animal man in all his savagery and lawlessness, and if we wish to understand him at all, we must put aside all our European attitudes. We must not think of a spiritual God or of moral laws. . . . For this very reason, we cannot properly feel ourselves into his nature, no more than into that of a dog, or of a Greek as he kneels before the statue of Zeus. . . . The condition in which they live is incapable of any development of culture, and their present existence is the same as it has always been.[26]

Modern European understanding of human life fundamentally gestured at weak nihilistic rejections of the idea of black humanity. Hegel counted black people as having only attained "immediate existence," or a pure sentience lacking capacities for subjective reflection beyond sensation. Immediate existence is contrasted with phenomenal existence, wherein the subjective capacity for reflection separates human from animal consciousness. Human consciousness experiences itself as a phenomenal being. For Hegel, black humanity was the opposite of human consciousness, it was marked by an inability to experience itself; black humanity, for Hegel, is "animal man."

Whereas Descartes and Kant relied purely on analytic approaches, Hegel emphasized imagination as fundamental to philosophy. In *The Phenomenology of Spirit* (1807), he creatively subjected traditional European philosophy to cultural historicizing, while simultaneously developing a rationalistic metaphysical narrative for humanity with a particularly white nihilistic end.[27] Modern European philosophy, from Descartes through Hegel, at least, depended on transcendentalist notions of human consciousness. Descartes articulated the transcendental dimensions of human consciousness in the form of the thinking ego, Kant developed it in the form of its synthetic a priori capacities, and Hegel articulated it in terms of a metaphysical teleology of phenomenal spirit. Implicit within each of these foundational moments for Western philosophy was a gestural dependence upon weak nihilistic understanding of whiteness in justifying human life in antiblack racist terms. In other words, at least all of the traditional philosophers of Europe that I have listed are "white nihilists." "White nihilism" refers to values supporting realities negatively delimiting "theoretical alternatives and strategic options regarding the idea of white supremacy."[28] In other words, white nihilism refers to anyone who values in such a way as to make "the implicit notion of white supremacy unavoidable if one wishes to have any hope for knowledge formation and understandings of reality."[29]

Weak nihilistic valuations of whiteness have functioned as an existential basis for justifying reality in my society, the United States, since its beginning. For example, the eighteenth-century antislavery advocate, Benjamin Rush, could only conceive of rejecting the chattel enslavement of black people by arguing they ought to be cured of the disease causing their mistreatment: black skin.[30] It was simply considered a pre-given truth that black skin marks deviance from what is normative about human being. Even President Abraham Lincoln, the famous Emancipator, metaphysically affirmed the value of whiteness as axiomatic for Humanity.[31] What is crucial is how the president that emancipated black people in America from slavery proclaimed, nevertheless, that there *must* be a "superior" and "inferior," and asserted of the value of whiteness as that which any (European) "Man" would prefer.

In the watershed American Supreme Court case, *Dred Scott V. Sandford* (1856), which politically sanctioned black inferiority as a legal precedent, Chief Justice Roger B. Taney further espoused white nihilistic metaphysical affirmations.

[Black people] had for more than a century before been regarded as beings of an inferior order, and all together unfit to associate with the white race, either in social or political relations; and so far inferior, that they had no rights which the white man was bound to respect; and that the negro might justly and lawfully be reduced to slavery for his benefit. He was bought and sold and treated as an ordinary article of merchandise and traffic, whenever a profit could be made by it. The opinion was at that time fixed and universal in the civilized portion of the white race.[32]

Thomas Jefferson, an original drafter of America's Constitution, argued that according to history, science, and philosophy, black people are inferior and ought to be enslaved, if not removed, "beyond the point of mixture." "Advance it therefore as a suspicion only," he said, "that the blacks, whether originally a distinct race, or made distinct by time and circumstances, are inferior to the whites in the endowments both of body and mind."[33]

White nihilism continues to motivate antiblack racism in twenty-first-century America. There has been a prolonged playing out of deeply rooted existential commitments to white nihilistic desires developed and held over centuries. Nihilism, weakness, exhaustion, and fear are the existential leitmotifs driving antiblack racism.

In his final analysis of (European) "Man," Nietzsche coldly displayed a weak nihilism rooted in fear. Concerning the psychology of modern (European) "Man," and fear, he wrote as follows:

> That which has been most feared, the cause of the most powerful suffering (lust to rule, sex, etc.), has been treated by men with the greatest amount of hostility and eliminated from the "true" world. Thus, they have eliminated the affects one by one—posited God as the antithesis of evil, that is, placed reality in the negation of desires and affects (i.e., in *nothingness*) (Emphasis in original).
>
> In the same way, they have hated the irrational, the arbitrary, the accidental (as the causes of the measurable physical suffering). As a consequence, they negated this element in being-in-itself and purposiveness.
>
> In the same way, they have feared change, transitoriness: this expresses a straitened soul, full of mistrust and evil experiences.[34]

Pessimistic lack of meaning for (white) Humanity is "that which has been most feared" and is "the cause of the greatest suffering." (European) "Man" unleashed a cauldron of pent-up weakness, impotence, anxiety, fear, and repression, onto the non-white peoples of the world, through antiblack racist and white supremacist colonial projects, as a means to keep the "irrational," arbitrary, and evil away, which their children continue to deflect, or rather, sublimate, onto the "hated" black body.

I have finally got what I came for. I left the backroom of modern European doubt. There were many conversations, too many of which I found boring, stuffy, presumptuous, haughty, verbose, elitist, full of themselves, detached from the everyday world; they were also stinking of the weaknesses of antiblack racism. Why, then, have I subjected you, the reader, to this stench? Because I am made to start from an absurd beginning.

Economic mountains of debt, psychological, and emotional costs notwithstanding, simply to peer into the hallowed halls of white nihilism tunneling underneath the philosophical foundations of my society, I have waded through seemingly endless rivers of absurdity, boredom, and shit, to hear them in their own words. It wasn't confirmation of the weaknesses of whiteness that I sought; I have always known that only feebleminded people could possibly believe in racial superiority. Instead, I sought their own words to use against them. What potentially justifies this effort are hopes that documenting the sources of white nihilism undergirding antiblack racism, which I have uncovered by putting myself at risk, as a bugged, clandestine observer, a sort of "spook who sat by the door," peeping the entire Western "Human" affair, might be useful for establishing a need to no longer prioritize the fragilities of antiblack racist's chosen disposition.

I have seen and heard enough to confirm an awful truth that I have known all along: black humanity is the antithesis of weak nihilistic conceptions of (white) Humanity, or white nihilism; I am feared, denied, hunted, and erased, because my existence denigrates the core of that which holds white meaninglessness at bay. They persecute me in order to avoid their own suffering. Weak nihilistic whites seek to erase blacks in order to make white life valuable, bearable, good. Wicked.

Black humanity threatens that which holds white existential life together. Without blackness to deny as a nonexistence against which to positively project meaning, without blackness removed as a source of value in human affairs, blackness erased, reproduced for eternal repetition of infernal white nihilistic value cycles demanding antiblack racist worlds, whiteness is left alone, irrelevant, feeling nothing more for itself than pain, suffering, exhaustion, boredom, and drives toward suicide. When Nietzsche admitted that the world, apart from the fact of (white) psychological prejudices, did not exist as an in-itself, but as essentially a world of relations, he implicitly confessed that the antiblack racist world is philosophically dependent on nothing more than an enforcement of relations. There is no meaning in the world that is not the product of human interrelations. He conceded that under certain circumstances, reality presents different aspects from every different point at which it is seen. There exists not only other ways and possibilities for conceiving reality but also multiple perspectives from which reality can be viewed; thus, no particular perspective can be deemed "real" or "unreal," and (European)

"Man" *knows* this. Thus, all human realities are equally "unreal." Yet, in my society, there are too many who are committed to antiblack racism as a weak nihilistic form of "reality."

Antiblack racism is motivated in significant part, then, by modern European philosophical attempts to deny the pessimistic truth of the human condition, and partially by a fear of facing the prospect that we live in a world of others with whom meaning is nihilistically forged. Depending on weak nihilistic conceptions whiteness a means for valuing life completely abnegates the dynamism and freedom of human existence. Thus, "white nihilism" is a philosophical denial of black humanity that evidences its own failures, a flight from the pessimistic truth of the human condition, a condition wherein the *truth* lurking behind whiteness is an abysmal nothingness of meaning. This horrifying meaninglessness of existence is what (European) "Man," in his whiteness, denies, or rather, refuses to face; so, he faces me.

I see clearly, now, the traditional attitudes of white nihilism and antiblack racism that (European) "Man" has taken for himself: weakness, fear, flight, distortion, illusion. Now, my question is, "What attitude should I take toward this man who faces me by refusing to see me, who also tries to prevent me from seeing beyond him, who only faces me through implicit and explicit, subtle and not so subtle, conjuring of values that destroy my humanity?"

Insisting on the value of my black phenomenal existence, for no other reason than the fact of its existence, is the most direct affront to the unilateral imposition of metaphysically affirmed white nihilistic values imposed by antiblack racism. Blackness insisting upon the value of itself inherently militates against the white nihilistic bases of the antiblack racist world, which potentially causes white suffering and doubt. Antiblack racist's direct hostility toward that which jeopardizes the "reality" of their desperately chosen white nihilistic "unreality." Thus, when Nietzsche said that "creatures" act upon them, that their adjusted world of appearance was an arrangement and overpowering of others, a sort of defense measure, he implicitly confessed the logic of antiblack racism, a deluded act of white retaliatory resentment in pursuit of self-preservation through weak nihilistic self-aggrandizement. Any activity of the black, on this view, is devalued by the adjusted reality of white culture, and is perceived as threatening. Any values projected opposed to whiteness causes fear, calling attention to the irrelevance they seek to avoid. The white nihilism of antiblack racism, then, is an existential and philosophical disposition of weakness seeking to avoid the pessimistic truth of the human condition by producing values only made valuable by denying the existence of the phenomenal perspectives of black people.

Antiblack racism, today, continues to reflect ideals of modern European cultural desires to remove the "irrational," and "evil," causes of suffering from their world. Those rendered invisible from a white nihilistic perspective are viewed as antitheses of humanity. Black humanity is feared, dreaded, loathed, and assaulted, when and wherever it makes its humanity known. My society is built on an ontological basis wherein I am absent; I am rendered invisible, simply, because my humanity presents a threat to the value of whiteness. Existing from the space of blackness means living one's humanity in the face of demands against living, against valuing, and against *being* human. To be black in my society means having to defend the legitimacy of my phenomenal existence against weak nihilistic avowals of humanity denouncing it. In other words, if I say, strongly, "Black lives matter!" Antiblack racists weak nihilistically reply, "All lives matter." Black people are demanded to struggle against a legacy of philosophical absurdities grounded in (European) "Man's" weak nihilistic Humanism, which erases us.

Nietzsche's analysis of (European) "Man" revealed motivating belief structures underlying antiblack racism. "Nihilism" is the situation of struggling against meaninglessness, where the pessimistic truth is that there are no universal truths. "White nihilism" further describes traditional Western Humanism. Nihilism in black America, or what I call "Black Nihilism," then, responds to existential conditions precipitated by white nihilistic renderings of human reality. Similar to Schopenhauer's weak nihilistic attempt to produce an end to human suffering, antiblack racism is a white nihilistic attempt to produce an end to human valuing. By way of conclusion, it may be worth mentioning that although Nietzsche intended his analyses to be useful, I am sure he never intended for them to be used this way. Nietzsche was a horrible racist, and the fact is, I don't find anything about his life redeemable except the import of his philosophy on nihilism when it comes to understanding the inner turmoil of (European) "Man." As far as I am concerned, Nietzsche was a rat; he just didn't know that this black fly was listening. In the interests of maintaining the myths around traditional whiteness, he talked too much. In the interest of divulging everything I needed to know, he says just enough. He was useful. He was a proponent of strong nihilism, *and* he was an unapologetic antiblack racist. Nietzsche's particular style of antiblack racism is moot. The point is antiblack racists continue to accomplish their goals by constructing social and political worlds that attach metaphysically affirmed values to the definition of whiteness, that is, white nihilism.

In some ways, Nietzsche's antiblack racism may actually be more nefarious than traditional antiblack racism. How much more difficult would it be to understand the continued willing of antiblack racist ideals in the world today, if the morality of African chattel slavery, for instance, were never argued to be morally justified in the first place? Typically, antiblack racists, like Schopenhauer, display an implicit moralistic, although misguided, desire to be "good," and, similar to Schopenhauer's desire to make human meaninglessness bearable by subduing will through an implicitly resentful judgment against the universe, whiteness and blackness become symbolic poles in European war between (white) Human will and (Black) eternal nothingness.

As a result of white nihilistic attempts to socially and politically order the meaning of reality, antiblack racism seeks to annihilate my black phenomenal perspective, or at least bring it to the point of inconsolable pessimism, as a means of aiding white people, men, women, boys, and girls, in avoiding the ultimate meaninglessness of their lives. Blackness is traditionally represented as wild, chaotic, animal being, which the whiteness of human rationality keeps in order. Unless the human world is to "degenerate" in Gobineau's sense, fall prey to evil and immorality in Jacobi's sense, become unjustified in its phenomenological movements in Hegel's sense, or be lost to the "brutes" in Kant's sense, the values of (white) "Man" must be superimposed onto the irrational chaos of blackness, according to these views. White nihilism situates the axiomatic structures upon which traditional meanings of whiteness and blackness in the antiblack racist world have been built. What are some of the traditional constellations of meanings generated by black people in response to this world? Exploring this question may help decide what attitudes might be worth assuming, ultimately, in response to antiblack racism.

NOTES

1. Friedrich Nietzsche, *The Will to Power*, trans. Walter Kaufmann (New York: Vintage Books, 1967), 12: 13. Originally published (posthumously) in 1901.

2. We have recognized the "real world" as a "false world" and morality as a form of immorality. We do not say: "the stronger is wrong." We have grasped what it was that determined Supreme value and why it became master over the opposing valuation—: it was stronger numerically period now let us purify the opposite valuation of the infection and half-measures of the degeneration characteristic of the form in which it is known to us.

Nietzsche, *The Will to Power*, 401: 217–218.

3. Ibid. 574: 309.
4. Ibid. 571: 307.
5. Ibid. 573: 308.
6. Ibid. 569: 306–307.
7. Ibid. 568: 306.
8. Ibid. 569: 307.
9. Ibid.
10. Cornel West, *Prophesy Deliverance!* (Louisville: Westminster John Knox Press: 1982), 53.
11. Nietzsche, *Will to Power*, 568: 306.

12. For instance, modern European thought first described black humanity in purely physical, biological, and anthropological terms of inferiority, that is, François Bernier and François-Marie Arouet (Voltaire), before evolving into philosophical-anthropological condemnations of black consciousness, that is, Immanuel Kant; eugenic assaults on black existence, that is, Arthur de Gobineau and Francis Galton; and existential and phenomenological denials of black perspectives, that is, G. W. F. Hegel, to list a few important traditional moments.

13. Allegations of African ape ancestry were scholarly popular in the 1750s where modern European conceptions of humanity were taking shape. West, *Prophesy!* 56.

14. Georges-Louis Leclerc Comte de Buffon, *Natural History of Man, the Globe, and of Quadrupeds, Vol. 1* (United States: Fb&c Limited, 2018). Originally published in 1788. Buffon argued that black skin was an epidermal result of hot climate, and that Africans possessed only the "seeds" of human virtue.

15. François Bernier, "A New Division of the Earth According to the Different Species or Races of Men Who Inhabit It," in *The Idea of Race*, eds. Robert Bernasconi and Tommy L. Lott (Cambridge: Hackett Publishing, 2000), 1–4. See also, François Bernier's, *Travels in the Mogul Empire Bernier* (United States: Ross & Perry, 2001). Originally published (anonymously) in 1670. The text was a compilation of his travel recordings through Egypt, India, and Persia. He cited five "species" of humans as relevant for proper geographical understanding of humanity.

16. Lott, *The Idea of Race*, 2.

17. "What induces me to make a different species of the Africans are . . . their hair, which is not properly hair, but a species of wool, which comes near the hair of some of our dogs." Ibid.

18. Francis Galton, "Eugenics: Its Definition, Scope and Aims," in *The Idea of Race*, eds. Robert Bernasconi and Tommy L. Lott (Cambridge: Hackett Publishing, 2000), 79–83.

19. Mathew R. Hachee, "Kant, Race, and Reason," Hachee's Michigan State University website, accessed May 24, 2014, https://www.msu.edu/~hacheema/kant2.htm.

20. Hachee, "Kant, Race, and Reason."

21. Ibid.

22. Immanuel Kant, *Perpetual Peace*, trans. M. Campbell Smith (New York: Garland Publishing, 1972), 139–142.

23. Immanuel Kant, *Anthropology from a Pragmatic Point of View* (Cambridge, Cambridge University Press, 2006), 183–238.

24. Ibid.

25. Georg Wilhelm Friedrich Hegel, "A Geographical Basis for a World History," Appendix A, in *Lectures on the Philosophy of History* (Cambridge: Cambridge University Press, 1980), 173–190. This text is a collection of lectures given by Hegel at the University of Berlin, between 1821 and 1831. The collection was originally published as a text in 1837.

26. Hegel, "A Geographical Basis for a World History," 174–175.

27. George Wilhelm Friedrich Hegel, *The Phenomenology of Mind*, trans. J.B. Baillie (New York: Dover Publications, 2012). Originally published in 1807.

28. West, *Prophesy!* 59.
29. Ibid.
30. Ibid. 61.
31. Albert P. Blaustein and Robert L. Zangrando, eds., *Civil Rights and African Americans* (Evanston: Northwestern University Press, 1968), 171–174.
32. Roger B. Taney, "Dred Scott v. Sandford: Court Opinion," in *Civil Rights and African Americans*, eds. Albert P. Blaustein and Robert L. Zangrando (Evanston: Northwestern University Press, 1968), 162.
33. Thomas Jefferson, *Notes on the State of Virginia* (London: Burlington House, 2002), 14: 270. Originally published in 1787.
34. Nietzsche, *Will to Power*, 576: 309.

Chapter 4

Traditional Black Nihilism
Bell's Pessimism and West's Optimism

> Up above, Heaven with its promises of an afterlife, down below [antiblack racists] with their firm promises of jail, beatings and executions. Inevitably, you stumble up against yourself.[1]

Antiblack racism conditions black pessimism and black nihilism in ways that militate strongly against the force of Nietzsche's (and by extension Schopenhauer's) conclusions concerning possibilities for overcoming these phenomena. For instance, if the production or the apprehension of aesthetic value, especially music and tragic poetry, achieve the best means for making the unbearable bearable, then both the esteem with which Nietzsche endows the human condition, and the asceticism which Schopenhauer uses to disavow it, themselves become unbearable. But, if it is true that nihilism is inevitable during periods of social decay, the canary in the coal mine ultimately signaling the impending death of white nihilism might be black nihilism. The conditions that have historically made life bearable for white people are becoming harder for them to maintain, and these conditions are precisely the same conditions that have historically made life almost impossible for black people. As such, black nihilism signals hell for the antiblack racist and a potential hope for the black nihilist.

As the previous chapter explains, the dehumanizing circumstances of antiblack racism are consequent of cultural engagements with nihilistic circumstances by modern European society. The issue is one of values, value production, and (European) "Man's" attempt to blockade blackness from alternative forms of valuing. Many Africana thinkers have taken up questions concerning black value production in the face of antiblack racist values. From Alaine Locke's theorizing of an axiological basis for alternative value production in the face of a decadent antiblack American culture, to W. E. B. Du Bois's socio-philosophical engagements with the meaning of the human question and traditional antiblack racist methodologies of inquiry, to Charles W. Mills's thought on the necessity of nonideal theory and the prospects for cosmopolitanism in the face of expansive contractual relations premised upon the devaluation of black people, to name a few, the question of how to alternatively value humanity beyond antiblack racism is not a new one.

In antiblack racist worlds, the primordial universe gets replaced by white nihilistic renditions of reality purportedly grounded on that which is objectively good, and this becomes the backdrop of black nihilistic reality. The assertion and insistence of sincerity at all costs regarding the goodness of white nihilistic values by antiblack racist systems provides the occasion for grievous turmoil and angst as black people struggle to value against bewildering feelings of failure, and rejection, associated with attempts to live the ethos of whiteness in good faith. Black nihilism is a philosophical framework that highlights critique of antiblack racist values by elucidating forms of life and value constructions emanating from the perspectives of subjugated, historically colonized, viewpoints.[2] Two theoretical poles for understanding traditional black values in response to antiblack racism are Derrick Bell's "black pessimism" and Cornel West's "black optimism."

The thought of Derrick Bell on black pessimism serves as an excellent starting point for considering black nihilistic responses to antiblack racism. Bell exercised a practical wisdom by acknowledging the historical permanence of racism in America; he suggested *treating* antiblack racist values as though they might remain such in order to avoid discouragement in defying them. From my perspective, this move reflects a form of black pessimism that undertakes necessary steps toward nihilistically valuing beyond antiblack racism. His pessimism, unlike Schopenhauer's asceticism, resists the charge of resignation. Bell's pessimism "avoided discouragement and defeat because at the point that [one is] determined to resist her oppression, she was triumphant."[3] Bell's pessimism is an ironic form of victory, and in this important way is contrary to the motivations behind Schopenhauer's resignation. The simple fact is "slavery refuses to fade, along with the deeply embedded personal attitudes and public policy assumptions that supported it for so long."[4] Bell provided statistical data demonstrating that America remained uncommitted to addressing antiblack racism in the decades following the signing of American Civil Rights legislation.[5] The numbers, as it were, continue to illustrate the persistence of antiblack racist oppression in today's world. I recently read a news article with the following headline, "Healthy US Economy Failed to Narrow Racial Gap," which struck me as consistent with every other phenomena antiblack racism and whiteness. "Health," for them, demands a "racial gap."[6] Or, as Bell worded it, "The general use of so-called neutral standards to continue exclusionary practices reduces the effectiveness of Civil Rights law."[7]

Bell's pessimism is substantiated by transdisciplinary evidence in literature, case law, history, and science fiction, reflecting the historical reality, and seeming permanence, of antiblack racism. Reading Bell, one experiences a sinking fatalism, which potentially leads to a defiant upsurge. His philosophies call to mind the kind of dread imagined when Arthur Schopenhauer miserably attempted to comprehend the metaphysical universe, but Bell attempted to value beyond the predicament. Bell argued that late twentieth-century Civil Rights policies have led to a continuation of racism, particularly in the name of modern color blindness, or what can also be called "colorblind racism." Today, antiblack racists either explicitly deride blackness or camouflage themselves by advocating for a color blindness that inherently destroys the terms of black existence and struggle.[8] There has not been progress, according to Bell, but there has been an evolution of antiblack racism:

> Today, because bias is masked in unofficial practices and "neutral standards", we must wrestle with the question whether race or some individual failing has cost us the job, denied us the promotion, or prompted our being rejected. . . . When whites perceive that it will be profitable or at least cost-free to serve, hire, admit, or otherwise deal with blacks on a non-discriminatory basis, they do so. When they fear—accurately or not—that there may be a loss, inconvenience, or upset to themselves or other whites, discriminatory conduct usually follows. Selections and rejections reflect preference as much as prejudice. A preference for whites makes it harder to prove the discriminating outlawed by civil rights laws.[9]

Antiblack racism is a totalizing experiential reality that has historically struck, murdered, subordinated, imprisoned, humiliated, brutalized, terrorized, and dehumanized black people, causing the mental, spiritual, and existential breakdowns, and sufferings, of billions of these human beings. Antiblack racism seeks to erase black humanity through a semiotic linking of "blackness" with absence or erasure from Human life according to white nihilistic conceptions of the value of (European) "Man." Modern Western philosophical engagements with questions concerning the category of the Human being, as (European) "Man," from the perspective of black humanity, fail and lose legitimacy. There is, as Frantz Fanon famously observed, a "zone of non-being," from which black people are forced to manifest their humanity. Will, force, power, subordination, and suffering; the struggle of the subordinated against the powerful; liberation, freedom, and responsibility, these are the leitmotifs of black nihilistic struggles. In Nietzsche's nihilism, I have found phenomenal willing desired for the sake of power, ultimately, perhaps as a vehicle toward health, nobility, and individuation, resting in ambitions of distinction, rule, subordination, and mastery.

Derrick Bell was an insurrectionist aimed at material change. Theoretically, he employed a distinct creativity in response to antiblack racism, exemplifying Nietzsche's point that certain forms of radical invention are only brought about under nihilistic circumstances. Bell illustrated how black existence struggles in what sometimes seems like futility against a contradictory and self-justified white will that erases blackness and makes itself known through a complete encapsulation, or representation, of the human social, political, moral, and aesthetic world, but through which blackness can nevertheless insist upon itself. Like Schopenhauer, Bell responded to a profound sense of valuelessness meliorated by failed attempts at universalistic reconciliations; yet, unlike Schopenhauer, he remained defiant. Bell searched for ways to create circumstances in which black suffering could be ameliorated. He tried to conceive the highest level of black life possible given what he considered to be the immutability of a vastness of pessimistic conditions.

Does Bell's attempt at aligning theories of justice with the permanence of antiblack racism belie a forfeiture similar to that which Nietzsche openly accused Schopenhauer in *The Twilight of the Idols*?[10] I don't think so. Bell urged us not to retreat, but to be defiant in the face of the immutable. His discussion seeks to defy the "universe" of values essential to antiblack racism and whiteness.[11] In this sense Bell's pessimism functions as a form of black nihilism. Black nihilism inherently defies the values of white nihilism as a backdrop against which one engages the prospect of producing values supporting black life in an antiblack racist society:

> Black people will never gain full equality in this country. Even those Herculean efforts we hail as successful will produce no more than temporary "peaks of progress," short lived victories that slide into irrelevance as racist patterns adapt in ways that maintain white dominance. This is a hard fact to accept that all history verifies. We must acknowledge it, not as a sign of submission, but as an act of ultimate defiance. . . . African Americans must confront and conquer the otherwise deadening reality of our permanent subordinate status. Only in this way can we prevent ourselves from being dragged down by society's racial hostility. Beyond survival lies the potential to perceive more clearly both a reason and the means for further struggle.[12]

Black pessimism is a form of black nihilism because it seeks to find meaning in continued struggle against the permanence of antiblack racism. On this view, antiblack racism presents an eternal recurrence of ironic opportunities for triumph through struggle. In this way, black pessimism can be seen as an attempt to elicit a nihilistic response to antiblack racism, one that also buffers against what may be inevitable failure.

Bell developed several public policy scenarios that creatively demonstrated nihilistic approaches to the permanence of racism. For instance, a "Racial Preference Licensing Act" would balance reparations for past injustices against antiblack racist preferences to interact only with whites.[13] Social establishments would need an expensive Racial Preference License to practice antiblack racist preferences. Proceeds from the License would support better living conditions for black Americans, that is, no-interest mortgage loans and college scholarships, and so on. The point is to demonstrate Bell's creative sociopolitical imagination and the kind of radical thinking required to make black life meaningful in spite of pessimistic knowledge of antiblack racism's status as "real." My theorization of black nihilism finds support in Bell's suggestion that we investigate "every racial policy, including those that seem most hostile to blacks, and determine whether there is unintended potential African Americans can exploit."[14] Black pessimism can encourage nihilistic ways of exploiting antiblack racist policies, symbols, and languages to make black life meaningful; however, it is empirically the case that American society has never been nationally committed to opposing antiblack racism, and it is a matter of deduction that one ought not expect it to. American sociopolitical institutions have had a perfect historical record of failing to seriously criticize the conception of humanity underlying its original ideals. One faces overpowering obstacles impeding the ability to construct meaningful and significant values for human life outside of whiteness. In pessimism, it is not that one cannot value human life, but rather that one faces the project of valuing against the immutability of an anti-valuing force. Be it Schopenhauer's metaphysical cosmos or the white nihilistic value constellations of antiblack racism, the instability of the human valuing project is revealed in and through pessimism. Bell's pessimism appears as a potential-filled stage in the black nihilistic process. As such, however, it runs the risk of being weak nihilistic, in Schopenhauer's sense, because it involves potentially determining that certain values, for instance, valuing a complete devaluation of white nihilistic values, are ineffective against anti-valuing forces, which in this case would be antiblack racist institutions. Black pessimism can lead to a debilitating form of weak nihilism, but it does not necessarily need to. What is necessary in struggling against antiblack racism is acknowledgment of the ways in which racists construct their values. Thus, Bell's pessimism is not wrong in its diagnoses of the antiblack racist situation, although it does not develop a prognostic correlate for valuing beyond black pessimism.

One point is clear: Bell's black pessimism is opposed to the traditional religious narratives central to West's black optimism. Bell did not focus on questions of the teleological inevitability of black liberation from suffering, instead he focused on the inevitability of black suffering. Schopenhauer argued that human values ought to value adapting to the immutability of the universe's usurping power; black pessimism, on the other hand, values running counter to the oppressive will of antiblack racism. Valuing in deference to that which usurps value can lead to *ressentiment*, and one could argue that Bell's pessimism demonstrates a form of *ressentiment* in relation to antiblack racism. But is this a bad thing? Not necessarily; however, it may involve valuing a form of impotence as good, necessary, or at least intelligent, in the short run; one must be careful, here, to observe the difference in valuing weakness and valuing sustained resistance in the face of power. According to Nietzsche, moral judgments necessarily demonstrate weakness, which he calls, "bad conscience."[15] "Bad conscience" entails an inability to pursue the instincts of freedom. On Bell's picture, the instincts of black freedom are pursued nevertheless, but given a predetermined antiblack racist human reality against which to understand the meaning of its pursuits, and this situates a potentially perpetual black struggle against antiblack racist reality. How does one move beyond this pessimistic phase of black nihilistic resistance to antiblack racism? How should we understand the potential involved in this incomplete stage of black nihilism? Bell's black pessimism affirms the ironic value of victory through struggles in defeat. Black life can be made valuable by permanently struggling against the seeming permanence of antiblack racism. In other words, no matter how many times I get knocked down, I am never beaten so long as I continue to get up. In this way, Bell's philosophy provides, at least, a foreground for black nihilistic responses to antiblack racism.

The weak nihilism that is inherent in antiblack racism is white nihilism, and there are weak black nihilistic ways of responding that rely on metaphysically affirmed ideals for affirming blackness. I call this "weak black nihilism." Perhaps all forms of weak nihilism, that is, metaphysically affirmed ideals, including some used in black struggles against antiblack racism, which I have labeled "black optimism," deserve interrogation. Cornel West's black optimism is one of the most well-known critiques on black nihilism and can be viewed as a correlate to Bell's pessimism, through which further discussion of the category of black nihilism may be had.

It became popular among certain scholars at the end of the twentieth century to write about nihilism among "black people" living in "America." Cornel West produced the most popular analysis and I first encountered it as a high school student. By the first chapter of the text, I couldn't help but feel personally misunderstood. Like many of my peers, I had a profound sense of defiance and utter rejection of traditional American societal ideals as well as religious narratives, moral norms, and ethical rules. I was already well into my own processes of black pessimistic devaluation, which amounted to much, if not all, of the practices and behaviors that West laments. I read his description and prescription for what he called "black nihilism in America":[16]

> Nihilism . . . understood here not as a philosophic doctrine that there are no rational grounds for legitimate standards or authority; it is far more, the lived experience of coping with a life of horrifying meaninglessness, hopelessness, and (most importantly) lovelessness. . . . The major enemy of black survival in America is neither oppression nor exploitation but rather the nihilistic threat—that is, loss of hope and absence of meaning. . . . The monumental eclipse of hope, the unprecedented collapse of meaning, the incredible disregard for human (especially black) life and property in much of black America. . . . A numbing detachment from others and a self-destructive disposition toward the world . . . a coldhearted, mean spirited outlook that destroys both the individual and others . . . angst resembling a kind of collective clinical depression in significant pockets of black America . . . like Alcoholism or drug addiction, nihilism is a disease of the soul.[17]

West was correct that there is a form of response to antiblack racism that chooses in despair a form of nonresponse, and yet he was only partially correct in labeling such responses as black nihilism. He has identified one form of black pessimism that may be committed to a particularly weak response to antiblack racism. That form of pessimism is concerned with hedonistic pleasure and acquisition. However, while it is true that black nihilism results partly from failures of American social and political institutions to address sufficiently the economic needs of black Americans, the debilitating effects of black nihilism are first precipitated by the existential dimensions of antiblack racist assaults on black humanity. This is not a point that is lost on West; in fact, in *Prophesy Deliverance!* (1982), he argued that antiblack racism is an inevitable feature of American philosophical life.[18] America is historically predicated on modern European Enlightenment constructions of human reality out of which its social and political lives was born:

> It is important to note that the idea of white supremacy not only was accepted by . . . Montesquieu and Voltaire of the French Enlightenment, Hume and Jefferson of the Scotch and American Enlightenment, and Kant of the German Enlightenment. . . . [They] not merely held racist views; they also uncritically—during the age of criticism—believed that that the authority for these views rested in the domain of naturalists, anthropologists, physiognomists, and phrenologists.[19]

Black struggles in America began with chattel slavery because most black people in this period (the sixteenth century to the early nineteenth century) were introduced into American society as enslaved chattel. American cultural attitudes toward black people traditionally denied black humanity and proceeded entirely as if human cognition, intellect, and consciousness did not exist within black bodies. Since most black people from this period came into America as chattel slaves stripped of all indigenous cultural realities, most were forced to depend on appropriating European discourses to articulate their realities. One traditional articulation of black American reality was religious and produced masses of black people confessing their devotion to the Christian faith. Historically, the black American Christian tradition has been the most dominant spiritual, social, and political tradition of resistance and struggle against antiblack racism in America.

The fact that black people in America have been forced to live antiblack racism as if it were a permanent feature of universal reality cannot be overstated. It is not difficult to understand why Christianity's emphases on salvation for the individual soul were so appealing for black people in America. It was among the first public, though secret, sites of affirmation for black consciousness. Black American Christian beliefs created value systems that erected a cultural barrier between the realities of black invisibility and the value of the individual black soul. The Christian theodicy assuring a triumph of universal goodness and God's will over earthly ills was made applicable to the evils of antiblack racism. According to West, "[Most] black [American] people became Christians for intellectual, existential, and political reasons." Ironically, he channeled Nietzsche when describing Christianity as "a religion especially fitted to the oppressed."[20] This is so because "Christianity also is first and foremost a theodicy, a triumphant account of good over evil."[21] The historical appeal of Christianity for black Americans remains its rejection of the value of nothingness conferred onto black life, and its promises of liberation and rebirth. It allowed many black Americans to emerge into Western reality as persons, if only in the sight of God. Moreover, it reinforced black existence as valuable, supremely favored, and blessed according to the highest standard for metaphysical affirmation, God's will. West offered a critique of traditional black Christian inability to "talk specifically about the way in which the existing system of production and the social structure relate to black oppression and exploitation."[22] In *Prophesy Deliverance!*, he combined elements of Marxist analyses with black American Christian critiques of American racism and socioeconomic oppression; the result was an "Afro-American Revolutionary Christianity," which I, simply, call "black Christianity."[23] The focus of black Christianity is "on praxis against suffering, not reflection upon it" according to West.[24] The primary goal is to provide positive meaning for black life.

Black American Christianity has traditionally been Baptist and/or Protestant. These forms of Christianity enabled black people to be actional in seeking out their conversion, whereas Catholicism, for example, does not require individual consent for conversion.[25] The sense of "self" involved in Protestant forms of Baptist and Methodist Christian conversion were particularly enticing for early black Americans.

> The black church was a communal response to an existential and political situation in which no ultimate reasons suffice to make any kind of sense or give any type of meaning to the personal circumstances and collective condition of Afro-Americans.[26]

The religious polity is where the first sites of political and social self-organizations of black Americans were formed, and where black optimistic values have traditionally served as the axiological context for political struggle.[27]

Black Christianity ultimately places the power to effect political transformation in God's will. It advances a notion of universal truth outside of human history. God, and/or Christ, functions as "The Truth," which is a conception that cannot be intellectually demonstrated, but can be appropriated and made conducive for black struggles.[28] Black American Christianity relies on metaphysically affirmed values aimed at warding against the black pessimism accompanying antiblack racism. It seeks to emulate, according to West, "as close as is humanly possible the precious values of individuality and democracy" with prophetic faith in earthly struggles until or "as soon as God's will be done."[29] The black Christian tradition is a profoundly optimistic response to antiblack racism and black invisibility intended to fortify black political struggles.

The optimism from which black Christian traditions, for example, make sense of black suffering and struggles involves affirming the metaphysical value of a symbolic linkage between the crucifixion and spiritual resurrection of Jesus Christ and the historical overcoming of black suffering.[30] "[Black people have] transformed a prevailing absurd situation into a persistent and present tragic one, a kind of 'Good Friday' state of existence in which one is seemingly forever on the cross."[31] Furthermore, according to West:

> Ultimately, triumph indeed depends on the almighty power of a transcendent God who proleptically acts in history, but who also withholds the final, promised negation and transformation of history until an unknown future. In the interim, imperfect human negations and transformations must persist.[32]

God is the ultimate author of human history and meaning and his transcendent will is what promises black victory. Through this view, an ethic of "subversive patience" is necessary for sustaining the value of black life through its struggles.[33] God promises liberation, which has already "occurred but was not yet consummated, with evil conquered but not yet abolished," in the interim, social and political struggle and the need for resilient Christian faith continues.[34]

Black Christianity has traditionally dignified black Americans with a sense of "sombodiness in a situation that denies one's humanity."[35] These are not "logical or reasonable" reasons for valuing blackness; however, as West explained, "Such belief is requisite for one's sanity."[36] Black optimism is a "hope-laden articulation of the tragic quality of everyday life."[37] On this view, black nihilistic philosophies signal "suicide for the downtrodden."[38] Here, black nihilism "discourages purposeful struggle, especially communal and collective struggle."[39] Pessimistic philosophy, in particular, expresses "the ironic consciousness of the declining petit bourgeois," which produces "profound insights," but means "suicide for the downtrodden."[40] Traditional black optimistic responses to antiblack racism in the form of black American Christianity, it seems, finds no value in philosophies of pessimism and nihilism.[41] They do not seek to gain "contemplative knowledge" from suffering.[42] Instead, they affirm that, "ultimately, with the aid of divine intervention, suffering is overcome."[43]

Reminiscent of Søren Kierkegaard, black nihilism is viewed as suffering from a lack of religious faith. However, unlike Kierkegaard, who argued that nihilism may be required to forge authentic believers, optimistic responses to antiblack racism tend to view black nihilism as having no redeeming qualities. I do not think that is correct. Strong values can come from nihilistic circumstances, but only provided one suspends metaphysically affirmed bases for valuing. Black optimism, on the other hand, unabashedly promotes metaphysical affirmations of black selfhood. Perhaps, this is why the traditions of black American Christianity, for example, fail to find any redeemable value in black nihilism.[44] It is in light of these tenets of black Christianity that West understands black nihilism as a sick, unhealthy, and counterproductive response to antiblack racism. His diagnosis of black nihilism drew on language from Kierkegaard, wherein he also considered nihilism a form of sickness driven by "despair."[45] Despair is a profound sense of meaninglessness one feels is attached to their life. Kierkegaard argued that despair was an implicit element of the human existential experience and could only be overcome by producing Christian values. The main difference between West's and Kierkegaard's prognoses is that, for Kierkegaard, nihilism and despair are necessary preconditions for authentic Christian faith; whereas, for West, despair only means closing oneself off from Christian faith. In *Sickness unto Death* (1849), Kierkegaard argued that since God's consciousness precedes the consciousness of humankind, human consciousness is only authentic, or "itself to itself," in relation to a metaphysical idea of divine consciousness, or God.[46] Grounding identity in God is the ultimate form of existential health, on this view.⁴⁷ Sickness results from a failure to relate to God.⁴⁸ Despair, in other words, is a form of pessimism concerning the value of human existence in the absence of Christian ideals. Kierkegaard called this situation "despair," precisely because human value, for him, could only be justified through metaphysically affirmed terms. In the absence of God's presence, human life is left devoid of meaning and left to despair over its lack of value. Hence, despair, on this view, is any understanding of the "self" outside of Christian frameworks; it is an alienation from the grounds of one's existence, or "a sickness of the spirit, of the self."⁴⁹ However, it also has a redemptive quality for Kierkegaard; it is "man's advantage over the beast."⁵⁰

Despair, on Kierkegaard's view, is a necessary but ironic condition for choosing authentic Christian personhood. Nihilism is seen as an affirmative choice to remain in despair, which is considered "sin."⁵¹ Nihilism becomes "sickness unto death," on this view, because one chooses sin. According to Kierkegaard, this self-imposed sickness involves an awareness of God's existence and either a refusal or inability to "relate." The inability to value God's existence is called "wanting in despair to be oneself"; its refusal is called "in despair not wanting to be one self."⁵² "Self" is defined here as an a priori "relation which relates to itself, or that in the relation which is its relating to itself," or in a less confusing way, a relation between God's metaphysical reality and human phenomenal experiences of itself; human consciousness is not an entity that envisions God, but an identity relationship between God's existence and human experiences of consciousness.⁵³ Nihilism is sin because it involves questioning, potentially devaluing, the metaphysically affirmed value of God's existence. In other words, human life, for both West and Kierkegaard, overcomes being tempted by the sin of nihilism by grounding itself in its original source—God. In *Fear and Trembling* (1843), Kierkegaard argued that Christian faith required processes of despair in resignation of human will through absolute deference to the infinite will of God.⁵⁴ He argued that it is through bitter trials of despair that true Christian faith is molded.

Traditional black Christian understandings of black nihilism are almost identical to West's and Kierkegaard's philosophies of nihilism; both agree that nihilism is a form of despair over lack of meaning in life, which functions as a simultaneous estrangement from God and self. Nihilism, for both West and Kierkegaard, is an especially nefarious and unhealthy response to despair because it amounts to atheism on their view, which is a death knell. Kierkegaard's conception of despair and nihilism is what West ultimately identified as black nihilism in *Race Matters*, although the latter is specific to black humanity and the former is articulated as a possibility for (European) "Man." The Kierkegaardian thread of West's black Christianity views black nihilistic people as in need of a "true" sense of self that can only be achieved through absorption in black Christian ideals.

Understanding black needs to completely immerse within metaphysically affirmed ideals involves delving into "the cultural depths of black everyday life," which suffers from an "unrelenting assault on black humanity," and which produces the "fundamental condition of black culture—that of black invisibility and namelessness."[55] Consider West's critique that W. E. B. Du Bois's famous "talented tenth" argument failed to appreciate this dimension of black cultural life. West called Du Bois's program an attempt to "boost his flagging spirit" through European rationalism but criticized it for mistaking Enlightenment sensibilities for an effective way of spiritually countering black invisibility.[56] West criticized Du Bois for employing "Victorian strategies in order to realize an American optimism."[57] His central criticism of Du Bois was, ironically, of the latter's optimism regarding the role of rationality and education in combating racism. Du Bois did not feel the lived reality of black invisibility "in his bones deeply enough, nor was he intellectually open enough to position himself alongside the sorrowful, suffering, yet striving ordinary black folk" according to West.[58] Du Bois intended "to scatter civilization among a people whose ignorance was not simply of letters, but of life itself."[59] The role of the talented tenth was to civilize and refine black Americans by selecting the best among them to serve as conduits for the rest toward "knowledge of life." For Du Bois, according to West, "the ultimate evil was stupidity. The cure for it was knowledge based on scientific investigation."[60] West called this Du Bois's "Enlightenment naiveté."[61] Du Bois's responses to the problems of black life, however, were attempts to draw existential sustenance from rationalistic tropes of European modernity and Victorian culture, which may have been the best available to the education afforded him at the time. Nevertheless, West considered young Du Bois's rationalism as an attempt to keep "the deep despair that lurks around the corner . . . at arm's length."[62]

West argued that spiritual programs, that is, black Christianity, and not rationalism, are required to sustain suffering black people. In an essay entitled, "Nietzsche's Pre-figuration of Postmodern American Philosophy," he cited Nietzsche's position that nihilism would be the debilitating result of Western philosophical praxes unless decadent ideals of modern Enlightenment philosophy were sufficiently replaced.[63] As previously discussed, Nietzsche forewarned that modern Enlightenment philosophy, and transcendental idealism in particular, falsely pretended to regulate an unpredictable world of human becoming; Nietzsche called this phenomenon "European nihilism."[64] European nihilism is a way of understanding modern philosophy's assuredness of its idealist methodologies in producing universal value and order in human life. West criticized Du Bois' rationalism for failing to construct alternative ways of valuing. As such, West's criticism of Du Bois drew on Nietzsche's critique of modern Western philosophical ideals.

Nietzsche expressed abhorrence for value-free, objectively grounded interpretations of truth and reality.

> The "real world"—an idea no longer of any use, not even a duty any longer—an idea grown useless, superfluous, consequently a refuted idea: let us abolish it.... We have abolished the real world: what world is left? The apparent world perhaps?[65]

In *The Will to Power*, he further wrote as follows: Against positivism, which halts at phenomena—"there are only facts"—I would say: No, facts are precisely what there is not, only interpretations. We cannot establish any fact "in itself," perhaps it is folly to want to do such a thing.[66] "Facts" of reality are inherently fallacious, on his view. "There are no facts, everything is in flux, incomprehensible, elusive; what is relatively most enduring is—our opinions."[67] Furthermore, there is "no limit to the ways in which the world can be interpreted; every interpretation is a symptom of growth or decline."[68] Truth in human life is a matter of positing and achieving certain goals within the frameworks of one's value systems.

West's criticism is that Du Bois was weak nihilistic in Nietzsche's sense of the term for overly relying on rationalistic discourses for combating black suffering and not fully immersing himself in the cultural frameworks of black American values. In effect, West claimed that Du Bois did not feel black invisibility or, at least, some of its debilitating effects deeply enough. His "fundamental problem with Dubois [sic] is his inadequate grasp of the tragicomic sense of life—a refusal candidly to confront the sheer absurdity of the human condition."[69] For early Du Bois, the best framework for coping with and understanding black reality was a rational and scientific Enlightenment approach to race.[70] For this reason, West argued, Du Bois failed to understand, perhaps out of fear, the "tragic prerequisite of America itself."[71] According to West, Du Bois's famous opposition to Garvey's Black Nationalism was motivated by fear of confrontation with despair.

> Dubois [sic] feared that if [Black Nationalists] were right, he would be left in a state of paralyzing despair that results not only when all credible options for black freedom are closed, but also when the very framework needed to understand and cope with that despair is shattered.[72]

As West put it, Du Bois thought, "The cure for [black suffering] was knowledge."[73] West's counter is that the answer for black coping in America is not rationality, but black Christianity motivated by Black Nationalism.

The upshot of Black Nationalism, for West, was its acknowledgment of the pessimistic circumstances facing black Americans. West described the pessimistic dimensions of black struggles against antiblack racism in terms of "existential levels of what to do about 'what is' or when 'what ought to be done' seems undoable."[74] He claimed that Black Nationalism gets it descriptively right concerning the "dark night" of the black American soul, "that gray twilight between 'nothing to be done' and 'I can't go on like this.'"[75] Black Nationalism's "cultural efforts to express the truth of modern tragic existence and build on the ruins of modern absurd experiences at the core of American culture" suggests better processes for overcoming the "tragedies and absurdities" of black life. In effect, West argued that Du Bois missed important elements of "black strivings" through nihilistic circumstances, which caused his overestimation of rationalism as an effective response.[76]

"Black strivings are the creative and complex products of the terrifying encounter with the absurd in America—and the absurd as America."[77] The aim of black strivings is to construct positive meaning for black life in the face of these absurdities. "The specificity of black culture," argued West, lies in black people's "attempts to sustain their mental sanity and spiritual health."[78] Hence, black strivings are primarily about spiritual, or existential, sustenance. These "strivings," argued West, "occur within the whirlwind of white supremacy . . . the vicious attacks of black beauty, black intelligence, black moral character, black capability, and black possibility."[79] Black strivings are made within a tumultuous, metastable world of whiteness. According to West, "The basic predicament exists on at least four levels—existential, social, political, and economical."[80] Here, the lived dimension of antiblack racism becomes the most relevant because it is most explicitly concerned with "what it means to be a person."[81] Black humanity in America faces "the sheer absurdity of being a black human being whose black body is viewed as an abomination," that is, a negation of all that is normatively human. According to West, "On the crucial existential level relating to black invisibility and namelessness, the first difficult challenge . . . is to ward off madness and discredit suicide."[82] Here, warding off black madness and suicide involves "confronting candidly the ontological wounds, psychic scars, and existential bruises of black people while fending off insanity and self-annihilation."[83] The fundamental task of black striving is to construct healthy ways of being black in America without succumbing to pessimism and despair. "Black striving resides primarily in movement and motion, resilience and resistance against the paralysis of madness and the stillness of death."[84] The black American Christian tradition, on this view, embodies a "life-preserving content of black style," providing sustenance for black life.[85] Black Christianity, according to West, exemplifies a "shift from a mournful brooding to a joyful praising," a courageous effort to "look life's abyss in the face and keep 'keepin' on.'"[86]

West's analysis offers instructive discourse on traditional black American Christian values, which have traditionally gained their place in struggles against antiblack racism by creating "ritual art and communal bonds out of black invisibility and namelessness."[87] West's criticism is that Du Bois produced a weak nihilistic appeal to rationality in response to antiblack racism, because he did not feel deeply enough the despair black striving can entail, and the sustenance religious values can provide. West was right to be suspicious of the utility of rationalistic ideals for alleviating the problems of black misery; but the question remains, "Is black Christianity any less of a fearful attempt at keeping despair at arm's length?"

My reading of West's Kierkegaardian and Nietzschean critique of Du Bois highlights a tension between Kierkegaard's and Nietzsche's conceptualizations of "nihilism," which needs to be resolved. Kierkegaard viewed nihilism in exclusively negative terms, Nietzsche explored the phenomenon's positive dimensions. West correctly identified how Nietzsche's conceptualization of nihilism would negatively read Du Bois's appeals to Victorian rationalism, but West argued for the utility of black Christian ideals to replace them; thus, the question remains, "How might Nietzsche's conceptualization of Nihilism read West's black Christian response to antiblack racism?" The previous chapter's discussion attempted to make clear Nietzsche's rejection of metaphysically affirmed values. Yet, West views black nihilism in a Kierkegaardian way, which relies on metaphysically affirmed ideals in order to refer to nihilism as a spiritual sickness where "black self-hatred and hatred of others" serves to parallel "all human beings, who must gain some sense of themselves and the world."[88] A critique of West's optimism as a form of weak nihilism is, therefore, warranted.

A nonidealistic conception of humanity and freedom can be constructed beyond antiblack racism and traditionally optimistic Christian narratives; one that does not depend upon metaphysical affirmations in public and political affairs, although individuals, of course, are always free to establish personal and private meanings for themselves in whatever way they choose. Jean-Paul Sartre's philosophy, for example, supports commitments to producing values that do not depend on metaphysically affirmed ideals. As Christina Howells articulated in "Sartre and the Language of Literature," Sartre conceived of commitments to thought, freedom, and language as "dialectically interdependent; thought comes into being through language; language clarifies and defines thought."[89] On this view, the value of human freedom entails an actional commitment to producing languages that promote responsibility while valuing in relation to others. That form of willing which potentially crushes and destroys our will toward life, and in this case involves valuing values that are themselves antithetical to the situation of human valuing, is "weak nihilism." Anguish, despair, forlornness, nihilism, each describe enduring the task of having to create meanings for which we are responsible within a world that is ultimately meaningless. We can attempt to flee this absurdity of the human condition by denying the paradoxes of freedom and responsibility involved in the situation of human valuing.

"Weak nihilism" designates human desires to deny inherent freedoms and responsibilities while producing values. In other words, such moves repeat the error, discussed in the previous chapter, committed by Schopenhauer, the paradoxical will of willing a non-willing for others, which requires a performative contradiction. Here, one attempts to fill vacuous voids of meaning in human life with values which one wishes to deny freedom and responsibility in having produced. This is the goal of weak nihilism. Sartre described this as a form of "dishonesty," or, "obviously a falsehood because it belies the complete freedom of involvement. On the same grounds, I maintain that there is dishonesty if I choose to state that certain values exist prior to me."[90]

Strong nihilism, on the other hand promotes human freedom in projecting meaning onto the world in a way that embraces our responsibility. My theorization of strong nihilism finds support in Simone De Beauvoir's *The Ethics of Ambiguity* (1947), where she argued that human freedom cannot be realized in the abstract, but "requires the realization of concrete ends, or particular projects."[91] She advanced the view that "human freedom is the ultimate, the unique end to which man should destine himself," calling it the "universal, absolute end." Echoing De Beauvoir, Sartre explained "anguish" and attempts to escape our "original relation" to valuing:[92]

> There is . . . anguish when I consider myself in original relation to my values. Values in actuality are demands which lay claims to a foundation. But this foundation can in no way be being. For every value which would base its ideal nature on its being would thereby cease even to be a value and would realize the heteronomy of my will. Value derives its being from its exigency and not its exigency from its being. It does not deliver itself to a contemplative intuition which would apprehend it as being value and thereby would remove it from its right over my freedom. On the contrary, it can be revealed only to an active freedom which makes it exist as a value by the sole fact of recognizing it as such. It follows that my freedom is the unique foundation of values, and that nothing, absolutely nothing, justifies me in adopting this or that particular value, this or that particular scale of values. As a being by whom values exist, I am unjustifiable. My freedom is anguished at being the foundation of values while itself being without foundation. It is anguished in addition because values, due to the fact that they are essentially revealed to a freedom, can not disclose themselves without being at the same time "put into question," for the possibility of

overturning the scale of values appears complimentarily as my possibility. It is anguish before values which is the recognition of the ideality of values.[93]

Pessimism and nihilism are descriptions of the anguished processes of recognizing the ideality of traditional values. Conceptualizing reality as an ideal form of being is weak nihilism. Such moves are criticized by Sartre and De Beauvoir because they treat values as if they are transcribed from the universe and not choices for which we are responsible. From this perspective, we can see why traditional black Christian value systems view black pessimism and nihilism pejoratively, because of their commitment to God's will as the foundation for valuing black life. Thus, traditional black Christianity demonstrates weak nihilism by locating the ultimate value of all values, including white nihilism, which they reject, as being outside the scope of human affairs. However, human life can be viewed as necessarily being anguished by virtue of its nature, that is, for having to perpetually face responsibility for values production. Anguish gets exacerbated by white nihilism and antiblack racist impositions against free black valuing. Therefore, black pessimism does not result solely from a lack of religious faith; it also results from a confrontation between black phenomenal freedom facing antiblack racist limitations. Likewise, black nihilism does not result solely from a lack of "sombodiness"; it also results from a confrontation between strong black beings fighting to devalue and transvalue the values of whiteness opposing their free and responsible value production.

Values and their persistence across generations are based on freedoms of choice; human beings are the creators of values:

> To say that we invent values means nothing else but this: life has no meaning *a priori*. Before you come alive, life is nothing; it's up to you to give it a meaning, and value is nothing else but the meaning that you choose.[94]

The question becomes whether or not one's chosen values reflect the realities surrounding their existence; this can take the form of the question of whether one's values promote the value of freedom for the existence of other human beings, or whether one needs to challenge the existence of others in order to value life. Black nihilism is not about accepting or avoiding anguish in human life, it is about addressing and responding to a certain form of anguish and despair precipitated by white nihilistic denials.

There is an important distinction between traditional Christian despair and existentialist despair.[95] Despair, anguish, and forlornness, from the existential viewpoint, are descriptions of the human condition, not moral responses to it. Strong nihilists seek to respond healthily to the absurdity of the human condition by valuing freedom and responsibility in value production. "I'm quite vexed that that's the way it is; but if I've discarded God the father, there has to be someone to invent values."⁹⁶ Precisely for this reason, optimistic programs depict philosophies of pessimism and nihilism as "disenabling," but from the strong black nihilistic perspective, "existentialism is optimistic, a doctrine of action."⁹⁷ Contrary to West, black pessimism and nihilism can lead to mature action, and invention of newer values.

Human consciousness lives a tenuous existence between its freedoms and limitations, or its, "transcendence" and "facticity":⁹⁸

> It is a certain art of forming contradictory concepts which unite in themselves both an idea and the negation of that idea. The basic concept which is thus engendered utilizes the double property of the human being, who is at once facticity and transcendence. These two aspects of human reality are and ought to be capable of a valid coordination. But bad faith does not wish either to coordinate them or to surmount them in a synthesis. Bad faith seeks to affirm their identity while preserving their differences. It must affirm facticity as being transcendence and transcendence as being facticity.⁹⁹

Weak nihilistic values rely on denials of the original human condition by conflating its constitutive elements. The factical, or "factual condition of man, beyond the psychological," are conflated with the transcendent, which reference our capacities to project values beyond immediate experiences. It is bad faith to regard oneself as pure transcendence, as a detached producer of objective value, because human beings are always in a relationship with our transcendent capacities *and* our factual limitations. It is weak nihilism to deny the relative contextualization of all human values. For example, Sartre wrote as follows:

> When we say that a man is responsible for himself, we do not only mean that he is responsible for his own individuality, but that he is responsible for all men.... In fact, in creating the man that we want to be, there is not a single one of our acts which does not at the same time create an image of men as we think he ought to be. To choose to be this or that is to affirm at the same time the value of what we choose.¹⁰⁰

Furthermore, "there is no universe other than a human universe, the universe of human subjectivity."¹⁰¹ However, this is precisely what white nihilists and antiblack racists deny. They insist upon a universe of white-normative values. In order to do so, they collapse the category of human transcendence into the category of racial "whiteness," such that white people alone function as transcendence, or "mind," and black people are forced to function as facticity, or "body." In this way anything, everything, whites desire is purported to be objectively valuable. In Sartre's words, weak nihilistic whiteness assumes "a plane where no reproach can touch me since what I really am is my transcendence."[102] He further wrote, "[Believing that] our transcendence changed into facticity [sic] is the source of an infinity of excuses for our failures of weakness."[103]

Healthily valuing in a world filled with others entails embracing the inherent intersubjectivity of the human world. White nihilistic ideals are not only distortions of the human world that one may personally value; in an antiblack racist society, they are also political and public attempts to impose distortion on others:

> [Although] this metastable concept of "transcendence-facticity" is one of the most basic instruments of bad faith, it is not the only one of its kind. . . . [There] is another kind of duplicity derived from human reality which we will express roughly by saying that its being-for-itself implies complimentarily a being-for-others. Upon anyone of my conducts it is always possible to converge two looks, mine and that of the Other. The conduct will not present exactly the same structure in each case. . . . [As] each look perceives it, there is between these two aspects of my being no difference between appearance and being—as if I were to myself the truth of myself and as if the Other possessed only a deformed image of me. The equal dignity of being possessed by my being-for-others and by my being-for-myself, permits a perpetually disintegrating synthesis and a perpetual game of escape from the for-itself to the for-others and from the for-others to the for-itself.[104]

"Bad faith," in other words, is a denial of the relationship between facticity and transcendence inherent within the subjectivity of individual human consciousnesses on the intersubjective level of worlds with others. Weak nihilism, then, is a form of bad faith because it implies a denial of the relationship between the meaning one attaches to their own reality and that which "Others" could potentially attach to it.

Human freedom is necessarily bound up with the existence of others and functions on at least two levels. On one level, "man is freedom," man is transcendence and is phenomenally responsible for the values individually produced; but on another level, since there is "involvement" in terms of living in a world with others, freedom and responsibility in value production demands acknowledgment of Other's freedom. That is, responsible human beings value values that inherently acknowledge the interdependence of self and other in creating reality. Man is a freedom that creates realities for which he is responsible. As a result, Human reality consists of multiple interconnective projects constructing matrices of meaning between our realities and that of others. Those that deny this responsibility to and for others, that human reality is not dependent on such interconnectivity, are "cowards"; they are weak nihilists who must deny themselves and others in order to value life. "Those who hide their complete freedom from themselves out of the spirit of seriousness or by means of deterministic excuses, I shall call cowards."[105] Antiblack racists are "cowards" who commit to bad faith and weak nihilistic evaluations of human life by conflating their values with universal reality, and then deny having done so. They are "stinkers," who deceive regarding the true value and actual necessity of their productions, including the meaning of "freedom," when in fact all human values are premised upon the same "contingency of man's appearance on earth."[106]

The responsibility all human beings have for giving life meaning is the only objective, universal, fact of our existence.[107] On this view, the human condition is neither subjective, nor objective, but an interplay between the two:

> Historical situations vary . . . what does not vary is the necessity for [man] to exist in the world, to be at work there, to be there in the midst of other people, and to be mortal there. The limits are neither subjective nor objective, or, rather, they have an objective and subjective side. Objective because they are to be found everywhere; subjective because they are lived and are nothing if man does not live them, that is, freely determine his existence with reference to them. And though the configurations may differ, at least none of them are completely strange to me, because they all appear as attempts either to pass beyond these limits or recede from them or deny them or adapt to them. Consequently, every configuration, however individual it may be, has a universal value.[108]

Human freedom and responsibility in valuing are universal but individual responses may assume any number of attitudes in relation to this fact. On this view, the self is "nothing," which ironically finds its being through the activity of perpetual becoming through choice. Consciousness is freedom living the situation of choice in relation to possible futures. Consciousness, understood as a freedom of nothingness choosing possibilities of becoming, carries the potential for bad faith and weak nihilism. The act of interpreting oneself in exclusive or reductive terms does so by eliding the situation of "continued choice." Lewis Gordon describes the anxiety of consciousness facing its freedoms of continued choice in terms of constantly having to face possibility and never being able to "settle down":

> As a freedom, I seem to have nowhere to settle down. Wherever I land is always posed as an object to me and is therefore not identical with what I am . . . like a figure attempting to stay afloat on the Arctic Ocean by hopping from ice cap to

ice cap—always facing the possibility of sinking and never facing the condition of standing still.[109]

Human consciousness is a form of being that demands choice at each instance of being. The situation of perpetual freedom and continued choice causes anguish. Consequently, human life requires constant productions of value. Each production brings with it a perpetuity of subsequent choices, and further responsibility. To attempt valuing without this anguish is weak nihilism. It is an attempt to exist as a being whose essence is treated as a fixed object rather than a freedom.

Human consciousness is identified by an awareness of our inability to be identical with the objects of our value projections. Thus, the freedom inherent to human valuing has limitations, or parameters. How one chooses to give themselves meaning is, at the phenomenal level, entirely one's own choice. In anguish, human beings realize, as Gordon put it, "we are the ones who must make choices that constitute ourselves."[110] The problem is that the meaning of our existence is necessarily indeterminable. The stability of each value projection is undermined by the necessity of continued projections. Every moment of choice entails a future choice to be made. We experience ourselves at each instance as freedom, facing responsibility for how we choose to be, as well as how we chose to have been. Choosing to not have choices, however, or choosing to choose without the anguish of responsibility, is out of the question. It is a delusion achievable only by distorting human reality.

Weak nihilism is a form of bad faith. Both attempt to avoid responsibility for value productions through denials of the "original choice" of valuing.[111] Since anguish is a reflective apprehension of freedom facing itself, my theorization of weak black nihilism finds support in Sartre's analysis that bad faith is an attempt to flee from the anguish of the human existential situation. Weak nihilism seeks to avoid the responsibility entailed by human freedom; it is a decision to escape the anguish of choice and responsibility by paradoxically choosing to deny responsibility for choice. Or, in Sartre's words:

> If I am anguish in order to flee it, that presupposes that I can de-center myself in relation to what I am, that I can be anguish in the form of "not being it," that I can dispose of a nihilating power at the heart of anguish itself. This nihilating power nihilates anguish in so far as I flee it and nihilates itself in so far as I am anguish in order to flee it. This attitude is what we call bad faith.[112]

Bad faith inherently presupposes the weak nihilistic constitution of the actor; it is an attempt to "nihilate" the negating dimensions of human existence by pretending to be a transcendence whose meaning is fixed, complete, and outside the bounds of intersubjectivity, that is, God, and in this case, God is white.[113] Valuing white nihilism and antiblack racism involves producing values that deny the human condition of valuing. White nihilism and antiblack racism demand black invisibility in order to function as absolute value, wherein black people are forced to respond to the meaning of whiteness as being on par with the metaphysical universe.

In light of white nihilism's presumptions of the positive and negative values of white and black people, respectively, black optimism denies the value of whiteness, but does so by affirming a metaphysical ideal for the value of blackness. Acknowledging the fallaciousness of whiteness as a metaphysical standard for valuing human life is correct; replacing white nihilism with a metaphysically affirmed system for valuing black humanity is weak. It paradoxically responds to the weakness of white nihilism with weak black nihilism. If antiblack racism depends on weak nihilism, then it might follow that black liberation will depend on strong black nihilism. Freedom for black people in America demands transcending "the being or ontological limitation of human reality in an antiblack world."[114] Thus, black existentialism, and perhaps a philosophy of black nihilism, is a preferred methodology for studying such processes of transcendence because, as a discipline, it begins by focusing on indubitable truths about the human experience, and not the presumptions of metaphysically affirmed ideals.

Cornel West's engagement with black nihilism is instructive and gets much work done, but it overestimates the optimism of its black Christian program for the purposes of what he deems is a necessary counteracting of black nihilism. West writes that when people

> conclude that "the way of the world is closed to me" . . . this conclusion yields two options—nihilism and hedonism. . . . This nihilism leads to lives of drift, lives in which any pleasure, especially instant gratification, is the primary means of feeling alive.[115]

Licentiousness, debauchery, and hedonism are his primary tropes for describing black nihilism. He concludes that providing love for the love-less through reconstructing black sites of community organization, primarily through the Christian church, under the direction of "quality, race-transcending, prophetic" leadership can provide the grounds for dignity, moral righteousness, and self-love in the fight against black nihilism. His analysis correctly identifies a momentous increase in the intensity of degenerative forms of nihilistic values commensurate with an increased involvement and exposure within capitalist culture, and pathological obsessions with material accumulation, spontaneous violence, murder, excessive drug indulgence, promiscuous sex, and so on. However, one must not confuse the persistence of decadent, or perhaps weak nihilistic, values in a given population with absences of value. Black Nihilism elucidates a linkage of failure in black life with construction of certain forms of value in the face of impositions of power and erasure. Black nihilists, for instance, might affirm much of the values, practices, and behaviors traditionally denounced. One can argue that constructing values embracing the human realities of fleetingness and death could also be the occasion for magnificent forms of human expression. However, that groundlessness can also serve as an occasion for decay.

West's philosophy for combating antiblack racism delves into the cultural depths of black everyday life and attempts to provide a program for filling the void of pessimistic meaning implicit to black nihilism. Providing existential sustenance for black struggles against antiblack racism while attempting not to succumb to despair is the traditional role of black American Christianity. In sum, West's black optimism accounts for black nihilism by referring to tenets of Kierkegaard's Christian metaphysical ontology. My critique of West's black optimism notwithstanding, his analysis sheds light on the role of "White supremacy," in precipitating the phenomenon, which he rightly concludes "makes this human struggle for mature black selfhood even more difficult."[116] Black Americans live the contradictions of America's lauding of liberty and freedom while sustaining structures of degradation and stratification that impede black attempts to lead free and healthy lives.

There have been some well-known critics of West's analysis of black nihilism. Floyd Hayes, III, argued that West added fodder for neoconservative perspectives on black poverty. Lewis Gordon suggested a fuller analysis of the phenomenon of nihilism could be developed. With the exception of Hayes and Gordon, most commentators neither did bother to challenge West's philosophical conceptions of nihilism nor did attempt to resolve the tensions between his Kierkegaardian and Nietzschean dimensions. Instead, most critics wrote about the political efficacy, utility, or implications of his analysis. For instance, Stephen Steinberg argued that West failed to provide real or practical solutions for a "politics of conversion." David Gabbard, in *Democracy Matters* (2004), discussed West's conception of "political nihilism" while uncritically accepting it as a purely negative and destructive phenomenon.[117] Gabbard uncritically deployed West's conception of nihilism. "Nihilists, after all, deny all meaning."[118] He used nihilism to argue against political frameworks rooted in "unprincipled" schemas of valuing.[119] In doing so, he collapsed the meaning of nihilism into *simply* the production of arbitrarily formed values having nothing to do with processes of transvaluation, responsibility, or freedom, which can obviously be concluded as deplorable political philosophy.

Certain critics produced views that served as a precursor to my own. In "Gangster Rap and Nihilism in Black America: Some Questions of Life and Death," Nick De Genova used Richard Wright's literature to argue that nihilism was "modern American racism's most significant contribution to black culture."[120] He objected that West painted a pathological picture of black nihilists, whose "disease of the soul is a greater threat to their well-being and survival than any objective structures of exploitation and oppression."[121] He referred to West's claim, "The major enemy of black survival in America . . . is neither oppression nor exploitation but rather the nihilistic threat—that is, loss of hope and absence of meaning."[122] On his view, West treated nihilism too much as a self-imposed disease and not enough as a disease situated by experiences of antiblack racism in America, that there was too much emphasis placed on black people for alleviating their condition. However, perhaps De Genova's criticisms of West could be attenuated in light of the abovementioned West's writings in *Prophesy*, where he makes explicit connections between the absurdities of black life and ideals of modern European philosophy. Yet, De Genova is correct, in light of West's Kierkegaardian commitments, that there is a problem with situating nihilism exclusively as a negative phenomenon that must be overcome.

In "Black Dada Nihilismus: Phillis Wheatley, Malcolm X, and the Traumatic Politics of Conversion," Kimberly Benston suggested the "function of violence and negativity" associated with nihilism is necessary for black projects of liberation.[123] According to Benston, the subtext of West's chapter on black nihilism in *Race Matters* admits of a positive articulation of the role for violence, trauma, and perhaps nihilism, despite his explicit disavowals. She argues there may be revolutionary potential for experiences of "negativity and violence" in black nihilistic populations; it could be a negative antecedent with potentially positive consequences. Needless to say, I think Benston is right about this.

Floyd Hayes, III, also used Richard Wright's work to elaborate black nihilism. Hayes argues that Wright's character, Damon Cross, in *The Outsider*, represented the quintessence of black nihilism. For Hayes, "Wright's Outsider provided a context in which we can consider the effects of social and historical factors on this self-constitutive process as it operates for black people."[124] He further wrote, "Wright hints at a conceptualization of the multiple, fragmented black self in the postmodern age of nihilism—modern Western culture in ruins."[125] On this view, Damon represents the black nihilist who "found no absolute standard by which to appraise his actions," which included four murders and impregnating a minor.[126] With a conviction that "life means nothing in particular," Damon undertook a quest for self-identity.[127] Although he had to struggle against the absurdities of antiblack racism and its stereotypes, there remained a possibility of using "these situations to his advantage."[128] "Familiar with the literature of the irrational—Nietzsche, Heidegger, Dostoyevsky, and Kierkegaard—Damon holds the view that all men are free to create their own meaning.

Consequently, Damon is his own God."[129] Furthermore, Damon's nihilistic perspective puts him in an advantaged epistemic location. He becomes positioned to see the "double lies" of the "Communist Party nihilists,'" and determines that their will to power is weak.[130] In other words, according to Hayes, the black nihilist is led through the absurdities of black invisibility to a doubled vision of Human meaning, wherein the pessimistic truth of each person being radically responsible for producing value conflicts with the idealist languages of certain political and religious programs. Hayes cited Damon's rejection of the Communist Party as a prime instance of the epistemic and ontological potential for nihilistic power. "I'm propaganda-proof. Communism has two truths, two faces. . . . You use idealistic words as your smoke screen, but behind that screen you rule . . . It's a question of power."[131] In other words, black nihilists reject the philosophical idealism of antiblack racism but also any form of weak nihilistic idealism in response.

"The existential-nihilist perspective," on this view, situates one "within the historical transition between modernity and postmodernity," that is, between idealist and nonidealist renderings of value.[132] The nihilist suspects all forms of idealism as concealing wills for power behind a "smokescreen." In "Cornel West and Afro-Nihilism," Hayes challenged West's description of black nihilism by arguing that it could serve as a critique of the foundations of Western life.[133] Hayes's is a natural predecessor of my theorization of Black nihilism. He argued that the nihilist was, in the words of Albert Camus, "not one who believes in nothing, but one who does not believe in what exists."[134] An important distinction. In other words, Hayes correctly points out that "the nihilist rejects as absurd the values and laws articulated by the dominant culture, which itself devalues its own values and breaks its own laws."[135] The black nihilist, in particular, expresses profound doubt about traditional cultural formulations of human life in antiblack racist societies. "The nihilist is a rebel," explains Hayes, filled with resentment that can lead to rebellion against the absurdity of certain values.[136]

Ressentiment, in Nietzsche's sense, is a profound philosophical repulsion from an existing state of affairs, which involves inverting or attempting augmentation of traditional value systems. Hayes's analysis stopped short of adopting *ressentiment* and opted for, "resentment" in depicting black nihilism. Resentment entails an implicit acknowledgment of impotence in directly changing one's condition. In the case of black life, white nihilistic values supporting antiblack racist desires for black invisibility are resented because they impose, idealistically situated as permanent, repulsive values experienced by black people as horrifically false. Nevertheless, Hayes may be implicitly relying upon Max Scheler's definition of *Ressentiment* in explaining black resentment as a reactive, long-lasting desire for redress of prior attack or injury:[137]

> The long standing and ever-present impulse of resentment can give way to rebellion. At times, the feelings of hatred, anger, and revenge are unleashed against the oppressor, transforming individuals experiencing resentment into persons who decide to embody a sense of freedom by resisting the injustice of a racist culture.[138]

Hayes claimed that "Afro nihilism" is not "an appeal to ideal resentment; rather, it is ordinary or general. . . . Resentment is not a necessary or universal response to racist oppression. Resentment is not essential to black identity."[139] He suggested ordinary resentment, not *ressentiment*, could produce revolutionary activity; however, he did not further investigate the connection between what he called "ideal resentment," or *ressentiment*, and the ideality of modern Western philosophies. In this way, my theoretical approach to the problem to black nihilism is distinct from Hayes's "Afro Nihilism." "Black nihilism" describes responses to racism; but it is also designates a philosophical framework that can explain "ideal resentment," prefiguring categories of whiteness and blackness in antiblack racist societies, that is, white nihilism.

Another philosopher, Charles Ephraim, produced a criticism of the idealist nature of antiblack racist values as "symptomatic of a uniquely European disease, namely, *ressentiment*."[140] In *The Pathology of Eurocentrism* (2003), Ephraim described *ressentiment* as a European repulsion to the human condition of there being no objective standards by which to affirm the value of life. He offered an analysis of Eurocentrism that articulated its antiblack racist dimensions as dependent upon pathological needs for self-aggrandizement.[141] Ephraim's work supports my theorization that antiblack racism is motivated by European desires for revenge against the absurdity of human existence, which it plays out on black bodies.[142] His theory that antiblack racism is the result of weak European psychological dispositions inspires what I call "white nihilism"; although, unlike Ephraim, my analysis does not focus on the role of phallic symbology in colonial domination.

Finally, Lewis Gordon in *Her Majesty's Other Children* (1997) provides illumination for studies of nihilism and antiblack racism.[143] According to his view, black American struggles against antiblack racism seek to force American institutions to face the "theodicean problem of legitimacy. . . . How can it legitimate its conquest without depending on conquest itself as its source of its legitimation?"[144] In other words, Gordon argued that antiblack racist values can only appear to be valuable by discounting, erasing, and/or making invisible black consciousnesses. Therefore, he concluded, black perspectives function as "anomalies, the sites of contradictions," against the antiblack racist world, which attempts to demonstrate itself as "pure . . . good, in the midst of its contradictions" by making black perspectives supposedly extraneous.[145] According to Gordon, black people in antiblack racist worlds are charged with the paradoxical task of struggling against injustices that function as justice, which involves responsive struggles for justice that appear as injustice. The tragedy, so to speak, is the social demonization of black struggles challenging unjust systems. For example, consider Gordon's analysis of "Tragic Revolutionary Violence," where he writes as follows:

> In other words, regardless of the characters' point of view, the world must be placed back into a certain order. The tragedy in tragedies is that the "innocence" of the characters who occupy a wrongful place in the drama is ultimately irrelevant. Thus, the tragic protagonist finds himself guilty by virtue of deed and circumstance, not intent, and finds himself suffering, ironically, for the sake of justice.[146]

"Justice" is being used here in a classic Aristotelian sense, whereby it is a seeking of virtue and balance in relation to one's self and others. Aristotle understood justice as a virtuous application of virtues to others.[147] For this reason, he thought the highest science was political science because it is concerned with justice in relation to the polis. Yet, in an antiblack racist society, the antagonist fighting against antiblack racism is set to face the despair, pessimism, and nihilism of one who is perceived to be guilty, and punished as socially immoral, for insisting on the full freedoms of their human existence. The result is a condemnation for simply existing attenuated by a deep intuition of one's right to exist. In other words, the black fighter against antiblack racism in America is charged as guilty, and who among us is not? While feeling deeply the sentiment of Damon, *The Outsider*, "In my heart . . . I'm . . . I felt . . . I'm innocent. . . . That's what made the horror."[148]

Gordon's critique of West warned us that black existential freedom should avoid furthering the weak nihilism it seeks to escape. Gordon was calling to mind the abovementioned discussions when he ultimately concluded of West's theory of nihilism as follows:

> Even if the equality sought by West were achieved, the irony is that, if Nietzsche is right, the problem of nihilism will be intensified. . . . A black person who desires to be equal to whites is, in the end . . . pathetic. The damage achieved by racism is such that even equality may not be enough.[149]

Gordon's critique of West's theory of black nihilism employs a Nietzschean understanding of nihilism and raises the problem of assessing values in an antiblack racist world. As Gordon put it, "The fact that decay pervades American society leaves no room for an optimism that is not paradoxically a nihilism."[150]

Black people have fought to tear through the veils of whiteness enshrouding white antiblack racism; it is now revealed that the hideous face behind the veil is pale, white nihilism blocking blackness from the universe. Struggles for the vitality of black life carry with them necessarily tragic circumstances of fighting against values presumed universally and objectively "good." Thus, what would appear in congruence with antiblack racist values as normal and healthy in the antiblack racist world may be weak and sick, and what would appear as contemptible, destructive, sinful, and nihilistic may be, as Gordon suggests, an "active nihilism . . . a response to racism/passive nihilism."[151] I call the possibility for this type of active nihilistic response to antiblack racism "strong black nihilism."

In conclusion, West's optimism and Bell's pessimism are theoretical poles useful for understanding traditional black American responses to the absurdities of antiblack racism. Bell's philosophy was a profound pessimism that sought the inversion of white supremacist and antiblack racist values but stopped short of prescribing ways for strong nihilistically valuing beyond pessimistic responses to antiblack racism. West's philosophy was a brilliant description of debilitating aspects of the black invisibility attenuating black nihilistic experiences but stopped short of exploring the strong dimensions of black nihilism. Thus, Bell's analysis of black pessimism and West's "optimistic" analysis of black nihilism can each be further developed in strong nihilistic terms. Given an understanding of white nihilism as the root of the problems of black nihilism, surviving the naked truths of (European) "Man," his desires, will, force, and suffering, unleashed from behind the veil of antiblack racism, may require the cultivation of a radically fearless strong black nihilistic disposition in response. I suggest that, having gone through the traditional stages of black optimism and black pessimism constituting weak black nihilism, strong black nihilism reveals itself as the appropriate response to white nihilism and antiblack racism, or at least one worth considering carefully.

NOTES

1. Frantz Fanon, *The Wretched of the Earth*, trans. Richard Philcox (New York: Grove Press, 2004), 232. Originally published in 1963.

2. Although the societal context for this study has been the United States, the term could apply as a philosophical framework for understanding productions of and responses to antiblack racism in more global contexts. As a convenience, I refer to the United States as simply, "America." In similar kind, in agreement with George Cotkin's *Existential America* (Baltimore: Johns Hopkins University Press, 2003), my approach to existentialism will be premised upon its already situated history in the American context.

3. Derrick Bell, *Faces at the Bottom of the Well: The Permanence of Racism* (New York: Basic Books, 1992). vii.

4. Ibid. 3.

5. For example, between 1970 and 1990, black Americans saw their socioeconomic situation steadily deteriorate. Unemployment rates remained more than double that of white Americans, black per capita income remained less than two-thirds of whites, and black people were three times more likely to live below the poverty line according to the American Census Bureau. Ibid. 3–5.

6. [The] median wealth for white families in 2019 was still much higher, at $188,200, compared with $24,100 for black families and $36,200 for Hispanics. Economic research has found that differences in inheritances are a major factor behind the racial wealth gap. A separate Fed Note released Monday found that 30% of white families report receiving an inheritance three times the corresponding proportion of black families and four times that of Hispanic families.

Christopher Rugaber, "Healthy US Economy Failed to Narrow Racial Gap . . .," AP News, September 28, 2020, https://apnews.com/article/virus-outbreak-race-and-ethnicity-health-united-states-hispanics-d575192ae495ac0415f587f02b79bae0.

7. Bell, *Faces*, 6.

8. Our country has changed. While any discrimination in voting is too much, congress must ensure that the legislation it passes to remedy that problem speaks to current conditions. . . . Today . . . towns are governed by African American mayors. Problems remain in these states and others, but there is no denying that, due to the voting rights act, our nation has made great strides. These words were uttered by Chief Justice John G. Roberts, Jr., in 2013, when the U.S. Supreme Court struck down key portions of the 1965 Voting Rights Act, which reinforced black suffrage, granted by the Fifteenth Amendment, a century earlier in 1870. Adam Liptack, "Justices Void Oversight Of States, Issue At Heart Of Voting Rights Act," *The New York Times*, June 26, 2013, A1.

9. Bell, *Faces*, 6–7.

10. "Schopenhauer . . . a mendacious attempt of genius to marshal, in aid of a nihilistic total devaluation of life, the very counter-instances, the great self-affirmations of the 'will to live,' the exuberant forms of life . . ." Friedrich Nietzsche, *Twilight of the Idols and the Anti-Christ*, trans. R. J. Hollingdale (Harmondsworth: Penguin, 1990), 79–80.

11. The development of "White Nihilism" out of "European Nihilism" in conjunction with the rise of modern Western antiblack racism is explained in chapter 3.

12. Bell, *Faces*, 12.

13. Ibid. 47–64.

14. Ibid. 60.

15. "[Bad] conscience is nothing other than the instinct of freedom forced to become latent, driven underground, and forced to vent its energy upon itself." Friedrich Nietzsche, *The Genealogy of Morals*, trans. Francis Golffing (New York: Anchor Books: 1956), XVII: 220.

16. Cornel West, *Race Matters* (Boston: Beacon Press, 1993), 17–31.

17. Ibid. 22–29.

18. Cornel West, *Prophesy Deliverance!* (Louisville: Westminster John Knox Press: 1982).
19. West, *Prophesy Deliverance!* 61.
20. Ibid. 35.
21. Ibid.
22. Ibid. 109–111.
23. West, *Prophesy Deliverance!* See, especially, chapter five, "Afro-American Revolutionary Christianity."
24. Cornel West, ed., *The Cornel West Reader* (New York: Basic *Civitas* Books, 1999), 438.
25. For example, in Catholicism, babies could be "converted" or baptized without the subjective act of personal conversion on their part. Catholicism, Greek or Russian Orthodoxy, Coptic Christianity, or Abyssinian Christianity are not traditional "African American" religious responses to the existential and political situation of blackness.
26. Cornel West, "Prophetic Christian as Organic Intellectual: Martin Luther King, Jr.," in *The Cornel West Reader*, ed. Cornel West (New York: Basic *Civitas* Books, 1999), 427.
27. West, *Prophesy Deliverance!* 35.
28. Ibid. 96–97.
29. Ibid. 146.
30. Ibid. 109.
31. West, "Prophetic Christian as Organic Intellectual,"427.
32. Cornel West, "Black Strivings in a Twilight Civilization," in *The Cornel West Reader*, ed. Cornel West (New York: Basic *Civitas* Books, 1999), 96.
33. Cornel West, "Subversive Joy and Revolutionary Patience in Black Christianity," in *The Cornel West Reader*, 435–439.
34. West, "Prophetic Christian as Organic Intellectual," 427.
35. Cornel West, "Subversive Joy," 436.
36. Ibid.
37. Ibid. 437.
38. Ibid. 438.
39. Ibid.
40. Ibid.
41. The purpose of suffering is rendered problematic and the knowledge resulting from suffering is suspect. The very notion of a moral order is called into question and displaced by a preoccupation with the consciousness occupying the suffering, the details of the context in which the suffering occurs and the ways in which suffering is evaded or tolerated. This viewpoint has little persuasive power for black Christianity in that its rejection of any end or aim of human existence discourages purposeful struggle . . . it is disenabling for degraded and oppressed peoples. The tragic sense of life in black Christian eschatology views suffering as a stepping-stone to liberation. Yet liberation does not eradicate the suffering in itself. Therefore, suffering is understood only as a reality to resist, an actuality to oppose. It can neither be submitted

to in order to gain contemplative knowledge nor reified into an object of ironic attention. Rather, it is a concrete state of affairs that produces discernible hurt and pain, hence requiring action of some sort. Black Christian eschatology focuses on praxis against suffering, not reflection upon it.

Ibid.

42. Ibid.
43. Ibid.
44. "[Black Christianity] linked God's plan of salvation to black liberation—inseparable, though not identical—and bestowed upon black people a divine source for self-identify—for example, as children of God—that stood in stark contrast to the cultural perceptions and social roles imposed upon them by a racist American society". Ibid.
45. "The formula for that state in which there is no despair at all: in relating itself to itself and in wanting to be itself, the self is grounded transparently in the power which established it." Søren Kierkegaard, *The Sickness unto Death* (London: Penguin Books, 2004), 165. Originally published in 1849.
46. Ibid. 109.
47. Where then does despair come from? From the relation in which the synthesis relates to itself, from the fact that god, who made man this relation, as it were let's go of it; that is, from the relation's relating to itself. Ibid. 46.
48. Ibid. 47–51.
49. Ibid. 43.
50. "[The] possibility of this sickness is man's advantage over the beast; to be aware of this sickness [as a sickness, one might add] is the Christian's advantage over natural man; to be cured of this sickness is the Christian's blessedness." Ibid. 45.
51. Ibid. 109–120.
52. Ibid. 109.
53. Ibid. 43.
54. Søren Kierkegaard, *Fear and Trembling* (Cambridge: Cambridge University Press, 2006).
55. West, "Black Strivings," 88–101.
56. Ibid. 93.
57. Ibid. 89.
58. Ibid. 90.
59. Ibid.
60. Ibid. 91.
61. Ibid.
62. Ibid. 93.
63. Cornel West, "Nietzsche's Pre-figuration of Postmodern American Philosophy," in *The Cornel West Reader*, ed. Cornel West (New York: Basic *Civitas* Books, 1999), 188–210.
64. Friedrich Nietzsche, *The Will to Power*, trans. Walter Kaufman (New York: Vintage Books, 1967). Originally published in 1901.
65. West, "Nietzsche's Pre-figuration," 195.

66. Ibid.
67. Ibid.
68. Ibid. 196.
69. West, "Black Strivings," 89.
70. The "mature" Du Bois renounced his earlier optimism in America. See, W. E. B. Du Bois, *The Autobiography of W.E.B. Du Bois: A Soliloquy on Viewing My Life from the Last Decade of Its First Century* (New York: International Publishers, 1968).
71. West, "Black Strivings," 98.
72. Ibid.
73. Ibid. 91.
74. Ibid. 98.
75. Ibid.
76. Ibid. 101–115.
77. Ibid. 101.
78. Ibid.
79. Ibid.
80. Ibid.
81. Ibid.
82. Ibid. 102.
83. Ibid.
84. Ibid. 103.
85. Ibid. 102.
86. Ibid. 103.
87. Ibid. 112.
88. Ibid. 109.
89. Christina M. Howells, "Sartre and the Language of Literature," in *The Modern Language Review* 74, no. 3 (July 1979): 572–579. Here, it is explained that language and literature can also alienate human beings from existential freedom. Sartre was critical of this capacity in the first volume of his *Critique of Dialectical Reason* (1960).
90. Jean-Paul Sartre, *Existentialism and Human Emotions* (New York: Philosophical Library, 1957), 45.
91. Simone De Beauvoir, *The Ethics of Ambiguity* (New York: Philosophical Library, 1948).
92. Jean-Paul Sartre, *Being and Nothingness* (New York: Washington Square Press, 1957), 76.
93. Sartre, *Being and Nothingness*, ibid.
94. Sartre, *Existentialism and Human Emotions*, 49.
95. Existentialism is nothing else than an attempt to draw all the consequences of a coherent atheistic position. It isn't trying to plunge man [further] into despair at all. But, if one calls every attitude of unbelief despair, like the Christians, then the word is not being used in its original sense . . . not that we believe God exists, but we think that the problem of His existence is not the issue . . . it is plain dishonesty for Christians to

make no distinction between their own despair and ours and then to call us despairing.

Sartre, *Existentialism*, 51.

96. Ibid. 49.
97. Ibid. 51.
98. Sartre, *Being and Nothingness*, 98.
99. Ibid.
100. Sartre, *Existentialism and Human Emotions*, 16–17.
101. Ibid. 50.
102. Sartre, *Being and Nothingness*, 99.
103. Ibid.
104. Ibid. 100.
105. Sartre, *Existentialism and Human Emotions*, 46.
106. Ibid.
107. "It is impossible to find in every man some universal essence which would be human nature, yet there does exist a universal human condition . . . the a priori limits which outline man's fundamental situation in the universe." Sartre, *Existentialism and Human Emotions*, 38.
108. Ibid. 38–39.
109. Lewis Gordon, *Bad Faith and Antiblack Racism* (New York: Humanity Books), 9.
110. Gordon, *Bad Faith and Antiblack Racism*, 13.
111. Sartre, *Existentialism and Human Emotions*, 71.
112. Sartre, *Being and Nothingness*, 83.
113. Sartre, *Existentialism*, 60–67.
114. Gordon, *Bad Faith and Antiblack Racism*, 1.
115. West, "Black Strivings," 111–112.
116. Ibid. 109.
117. Cornel West, *Democracy Matters* (New York: Penguin, 2004).
118. David Gabbard, "Meaning Matters: Education and the Nihilism of the Neocons," *The Journal of Thought* 41, no. 3 (Fall, 2006): 39.
119. Gabbard, "Meaning Matters," 39–44.
120. Nick De Genova, "Gangster Rap and Nihilism in Black America: Some Questions of Life and Death," *Social Text* 43 (Autumn, 1995): 91. De Genova is quoting Paul Gilroy's description of Richard Wright.
121. De Genova, "Gangster Rap and Nihilism," 92.
122. Ibid.
123. Kimberle Benston, "Black Dada Nihilismus: Phyllis Wheatley, Malcolm X, and the Traumatic Politics of Conversion," *The Journal of Power and Ethics* 2, no. 3 (2001): 149–185.
124. Floyd Hayes, III, "The Concept of Double Vision in Richard Wright's The Outsider," in *Existence in Black*, ed., Lewis Gordon (New York: Routledge, 1997), 174.

125. Hayes, III, "The Concept of Double Vision," ibid.
126. Ibid. 175.
127. Ibid.
128. Ibid. 177.
129. Ibid. 179.
130. Ibid.
131. Ibid. 180. See, Also, Richard Wright, *The Outsider* (New York: Random House, 2021).
132. Hayes, III, "The Concept of Double Vision," 182.
133. Floyd W. Hayes, III, "Cornel West and Afro-Nihilism: A Reconsideration," in *Cornel West: A Critical Reader*, ed. George Yancy (New York: Wiley Press, 1999), 245–260.
134. Hayes, III, "Cornel West and Afro-Nihilism," 249. See, also, Albert Camus, *The Rebel: An Essay on Man in Revolt*, trans. Anthony Bower (New York: vintage books, 1991), 69.
135. Ibid.
136. Ibid.
137. For instance, Scheler wrote, "Revenge tends to be transformed into resentment the more it is directed against long standing situations which are felt to be 'injurious' beyond one's control—in other words, the more injury is experienced as a destiny." Ibid. 250. See, especially, footnote 17.
138. Ibid. 255.
139. Ibid. 251.
140. Charles Wm. Ephraim, *The Pathology of Eurocentrism: The Burden and Responsibilities of Being Black* (New Jersey: Africa World Press, 2003), 36.
141. This obsessive need for self-aggrandizement has given rise to a host of problems constituting the so-called "pathology of black life conditions." The "peculiar institution" of slavery, the disempowerment of indigenous peoples by imperialism and colonialism, as well as the infamous Jim Crow laws, and the prevailing system, of anti-black discrimination, have all been consequences of the white obsession with self-aggrandizement. Among the manifold ways of its expression . . . resentment entails elements of xenophobia and misanthropy. . . . The white passion for self-aggrandizement, which necessitated the myth of black inferiority, has been the greatest obstacle to black liberation.

Ephraim, *The Pathology*, 2–3.

142. Ephraim, *The Pathology*, 67–140.
143. Lewis R. Gordon, *Her Majesty's Other Children* (Lanham, MD: Rowman and Littlefield Publishers, 1997), 165–177.
144. Ibid. 166.
145. Ibid.
146. Lewis Gordon, *Fanon and the Crisis of European Man* (New York: Routledge, 1995), 75

147. Aristotle, *Nicomachean Ethics*, 3rd Edition, Translated, Terence Irwin (Cambridge: Hackett Publishing Company, 2019), 79–99.

148. Hayes, III, "The Concept of Double Vision," 175.

149. See, Lewis Gordon, "The Unacknowledged Fourth Tradition: An Essay on Nihilism, Decadence, and the Black Intellectual Tradition in the Existential Pragmatic Thought of Cornel West," in *Cornel West: A Critical Reader*, ed. George Yancy (United Kingdom: Wiley Press, 1999), 44.

150. Gordon, "The Unacknowledged Fourth Tradition," 45.

151. Ibid. 44.

Chapter 5

Strong Black Nihilism

> For these patients there is no just cause. A tortured cause is a weak cause. The first thing to do is to increase one's power and not pose the question of the merits of a cause. Power is the only thing that counts.[1]

Antiblack racism confronts black people with a "nihilistic threat," a consequence of which is the notion that human life is valuable only for those who, today, count as racially "white."[2] Antiblack racism embodies a form of weak nihilism dependent upon philosophical ideals of white normativity, which I call "white nihilism," or "whiteness," in order to justify itself. As the previous chapter explains, since antiblack racism depends on forms of nihilism making the subjectivity of black people invisible, then, sometimes, black responses lead to conclusions that the overall meaning of life, especially black life, is meaningless, that is, black pessimism and black nihilism. Derrick Bell argued that black pessimism was an intelligent response to the permanency of antiblack racism.[3] Cornel West, on the other hand, argued that black pessimism and nihilism evidences a "disease of the soul," and prescribed black Christianity as an optimistic response.[4] Those responses can be used to establish a traditional binary between black optimism and black pessimism. My analysis of black nihilism, however, contends, in the spirit of Frantz Fanon and Lewis Gordon, that what is needed in response to antiblack racism "is not reformation but a different civilization."[5] We need alternative frameworks for evaluating Human values, especially those of blackness and whiteness, and neither a revitalization of traditional optimism nor a resignation to pessimism quite fits the bill.

Black nihilism undertakes the project of value creation through the additive experience of black existential invisibility. Black invisibility is the phenomenon of experiencing one's being through a reality that coalesces around presumptions of one's nonexistence. "A feeling of inferiority; no, a feeling of nonexistence."[6] The black nihilistic situation involves valuing against value structures of whiteness which render black values inherently meaningless. Black pessimistic devaluation of white nihilistic values is a first step toward producing strong black values. Black pessimism creates an opportunity for strong black nihilistic value projections, by rejecting not only white nihilism but all metaphysically affirmed ideals in public and political affairs. Seeking to establish political realities based upon values justified solely in terms of each human's freedom and responsibility for constructing Human reality is the goal. The Promethean endeavor to transvalue white nihilistic humanity from the existential space of black invisibility is an utterly nihilistic task, and, indeed, the weak perish of it.[7]

Frantz Fanon's work provides a descriptive account of black consciousness living through invisibility, experienced as a denial of human freedom, against people who refuse responsibility for the values they produce. Fanon's thought deepened Sartre's elucidation of human existentialism by analyzing the additive absurdity of the lived situation of blackness within an antiblack racist world. Fanon advocated for what I call a "strong nihilistic" response to antiblack racism. He announced the nihilistic strength of his position when he proclaimed, "I do not come with timeless truths. My consciousness is not illuminated with ultimate radiances. Nevertheless, in complete composure, I think it would be good if certain things were said."[8]

Fanon announcing that he does not come with "timeless truths" was a direct shot at the philosophies of (European) "Man." The entire affair of modern European philosophy, from this perspective, is seen to be a smoke screen covering up colonial lusts for domination, rape, and murder, while being concerned with how to best hide these forms of pessimism and nihilism behind weak facades of universalism. When Fanon said, "My consciousness is not illuminated with ultimate radiances," he signaled the earthly contextualization of his critical engagements with whiteness. When he said, "Nevertheless . . . I think it would be good if certain things were said," he inverted the axiological schemas rendering such perspectives as valueless. By invoking the term "good" he announced himself as a determiner of value outside of modern (white) Human traditions. Fanon announced his strong black nihilism; then he offered a narrative that can be read as foretelling of the pitfalls encountered while maturing into this perspective. I will explicitly address this point in the final chapter. Here, we will cite Fanon in support of my general theorization that strong black nihilism is a healthy means for transvaluing the white nihilism underlying antiblack racism.

Fanon's thought provides a healthy alternative to the options of black optimism and black pessimism as a response to antiblack racism. He would have been compelled to reject the "ultimate radiances" of West's response to black invisibility, and perhaps would have challenged the strategic utility of Bell's pessimism regarding the values of antiblackness. If antiblack racism depends upon unsubstantiated claims of God being on the side of whites, how long can unsubstantiated claims of God being on the side of blacks remain motivating? On the other hand, can treating antiblack racist values as permanent be a useful means for eradicating them, even if that strategy might allow for some relief? Fanon's thought helps to identify strong black nihilism as an appropriate response to antiblack racism. His analyses insist upon a transvaluation of white nihilistic values through a strong black nihilistic response. He proposed nothing short of "the liberation of the man of color from himself," for which, he said, "There are two camps: the white and the black."[9]

The liberation of Humanity from white nihilistic ideals of antiblack racism is the goal of strong black nihilism. Fanon's thought supports this mission. He employed a black existential understanding of human freedom in analyzing the lived situation of blackness. According to this approach, the existence of human consciousness is understood to precede its essence. Human essence is fundamentally indeterminable, or nonexistent, precisely because consciousness exists prior to experiencing questions concerning the meaning of itself.[10] The essence of human being, so to speak, is to lack a predetermined meaning outside of freedom and nothingness through which it constructs value. Thus, there is nothing we may know a priori about the meaning of human existence aside from the fact of its freedoms in producing value. We simply found ourselves existing with others at some long-ago point; then, we came to question our meaning while constructing reality. Antiblack racism, however, is a direct injunction against the participation of black people in constructing reality. Existence precedes essence in the human world, but essence precedes existence in the antiblack racist world. In the antiblack racist world, Human reality is a construction, and so it is not unlike Paley's clock. However, the intuition behind Paley's analogy is that God must be the author of reality; the intuition behind antiblack racism is that whiteness must be the author of reality.[11] Through weak nihilistic, bad faith conceptions of themselves, whites desire to be God, or at least godlike in relation to black people. White nihilism and antiblack racism introduce metaphysical ideals partitioning human existential spaces along racially somatic and semiotic lines indicating the presence or absence of full humanity. A complete rejection of antiblack racism, therefore, requires rejecting weak nihilistic conceptions of race and developing strong ones. Yet, nihilists have been regarded as scourges, the wretches of civilization, going as far back as Jacobi's criticism of Fichte, precisely because they are perfectly willing to be viewed as "wrong," in light of traditional values. This is why, as Nietzsche warned, the weak tend to perish of it. Strong nihilism requires valuing in the face of traditional values, normatively held and metaphysically affirmed. It means, sometimes, battling people who claim to have God, and the truths of the universe, on their side.

Blackness in an antiblack racist world is a peculiar space of nonexistence, within a universe of whiteness, that situates black subjectivities. The objectivity of the category of blackness, in antiblack racist worlds, contextualizes the subjectivity of each phenomenal black perspective. Blackness is thus, at first, not a choice but a predicament concerning how one will choose to live their life; it is a situation against which, and through which, people live and attempt to make their lives valuable. W. E. B. Du Bois, in *The Souls of Black Folk* (1903), wrote about black people in America living through denials of humanity, which he described as a "peculiar sensation":[12]

> It is a peculiar sensation, this double consciousness, this sense of always looking at one's self through the eyes of others, of measuring one's soul by the tape of a world that looks on in amused contempt and pity. One ever feels his twoness— an American, a Negro; two souls, two thoughts, two un-reconciled strivings; two warring ideals in one dark body, whose dogged strength alone keeps it from being torn asunder.[13]

What Du Bois described was an inability to function as the source of legitimacy for the value of his own being. Du Bois's notion of "double consciousness" ultimately implies white denials of black phenomenal existence. Fanon addressed black invisibility on a similar level, where the meaning of one's existence becomes uncertain because it is not simply being determined through the eyes of others but being demanded by the other to not exist. "Colonialism forces the colonized to constantly ask the question, 'Who am I in reality?'"[14]

It is as a form of nonexistence that black humanity functions as an antithetical "No," according to Fanon, in relation to the positive thesis of white humanity. But rather than become a "man of resentment," a pessimist who treats antiblack racist values as immutable, or perhaps, a black optimist that requires belief in God's benevolence to fight, Fanon attempts to live blackness as a "yes," on the sole grounds that *he* insists upon himself. This is what I call "strong black nihilism":

> Man is a yes that vibrates to cosmic harmonies. Uprooted, baffled, doomed to watch the dissolution of the truths he has worked out for himself one after another, he has to give up projecting onto the world an antinomy that coexists with him.[15]

He further wrote, "Man is not merely a possibility of recapture or of negation. If it is true that consciousness is a process of transcendence, we have to see too that this transcendence is haunted by the problems of love and understanding."[16] Man exists through a situation where he is constantly uprooted from the stability of each moment of choice by an eternal recurrence of phenomenal moments of choosing. Thus, on this view, man is fated to watch the dissolution of the truths he has worked out for himself one after another.

Fanon's strong black nihilism can be further observed in his critique of Georg Wilhelm Friedrich Hegel's master-slave dialectic.[17] Hegel's phenomenology ascribed a telos to the dialectical processes of human becoming in terms of an ultimate resolution of the particular into the universal. However, as Valentine Moulard-Leonard demonstrates in "Revolutionary Becomings: Negritude's Anti-Humanist Humanism," Fanon proposed his own version of the dialectic of liberation, which finds its resolution in ways that encourage black freedom in valuing (white) Humanity anew. On Fanon's view, conflict based upon strong, violent, black determinations, insistent on the value of its own existence, is required to move forward. As Moulard-Leonard points out, "The West cannot engage in such self-examination as long as it does not fundamentally put into question the very metaphysics of recognition on which all its values are built."[18] Hegel argued that human phenomenal life entails the ability to posit universal reality through considerations of one's phenomenal being:

> [Consciousness] enters into relations with substantial things . . . it knows that it is dependent upon them; but it realizes at the same time that it is a value in itself in so far as it is capable of such relationships.[19]

In other words, consciousness, which is abstract, is inseparable from the concrete world in which it plays out its potential.

Hegel's use of the master-slave dialectic is an early moment in the process of consciousness aspiring to absolute knowledge. Consciousness finds itself with self-certainty but lacking truth since it has mastery over only inanimate objects. It has certainty of itself, on Hegel's view, through the process of satisfying its desires. But when an "other" appears, it desires recognition from this other, and concludes it must "master" the other in order to attain the "truth" of self-certainty. Attempts at mastery fail since mastery over others doesn't grant recognition of an equal but of an inferior. Analogous to mastery over objects in the world, mastery over the slave initially appears as being insufficient to grant the truth of self-certainty sought. The slave, on the other hand, attains the truth by generating an inner life, since restricted, and externalizing his inner life through work. In other words, "the master is an independent self-consciousness whose essence is to be for-itself by excluding everything else from-itself (negation)."[20] The slave exists outside of truth and self-certainty, which on this view, it can only attain through the

Master. Ironically, Hegel claims, this causes a reversal where the truth of the master then becomes "the servile consciousness of the bondsman."[21] Here, the slave is not aware that "it does in fact contain within itself the truth of pure negativity."[22] The slave discovers its consciousness through mixing with the inanimate objects on which it works at the master's behest. He discovers what he truly is by putting his subjective life at stake through the objective activities of labor. The particularities of the subjective are enabled in this way to potentially lose themselves in the universal, generating moments of abstraction "necessary for attaining universal consciousness (negation of the negation)."[23] On Hegel's view, the emergence of the slave's consciousness suspends that of the master's, causing an abstract equilibrium of recognition wherein each sees themselves, mutually, as particular and universal. But is mutual recognition what antiblack racist slave masters ultimately desire from black people?

Human reality, for Fanon, is comprised of interdependently constituted perspectives creating and recreating cultural worlds through complex matrices of meaning. Here, the antiblack racist world is seen as a gross perversion of the original human condition. According to Fanon's reading of Hegel, "natural reality," or consciousness outside of engagement with others, becomes "human reality," only when realizing that "the other has to perform the same operation."[24] A dialectic between self and other emerges in establishing values, even when represented through the relationship between master and slave. Hegel conceded that "action from one side only would be useless" and both must "recognize themselves as mutually recognizing each other."[25] However, as shown in the previous chapter, Hegel explicitly endorsed antiblack racist tropes of (European) "Man." From that vantage point, the consciousness of black people disappears as black people were meant to be perpetually enslaved, and their progeny occupants of spaces of black invisibility. What then of the mutual forms of existential recognition that Hegel described as fundamental to *all* humanity?

Fanon fundamentally challenged the nature of the "truth" accomplished by the master and the slave in Hegel's dialectic. The primordial flaw is the master's presumptions of consciousness not existing in black people. Hegel believed there was absolutely no phenomenal consciousness to be found in black bodies whatsoever. The white nihilistic attitudes that drove antiblack racist institutions of slavery in the West have no theoretical room for mutual recognition. We can say that black people, on this view, do not discover their own humanity through enslavement, they are forced into a black nihilistic encounter with white nihilistic Humanity. There are two conceptions of humanity facing each other, one of which entails a denial of black phenomenal existence. Strongly insisting upon the value of black consciousness, language, and expression threatens the nihilism underwriting antiblack racist valuations of (white) Human life, and means risking being viewed, and enforced upon, as nefarious. If one begins with the original affirmation that black people are human beings, then strong nihilistic rejections of white nihilism and antiblack racism become unavoidable. Unlike the slave in Hegel's dialectic, the black slave must entirely, of his own will, "make himself recognized," as one who perhaps has been shattered by the (white) Humanity of antiblack racist enslavement, but not constituted by it.[26] In other words, the black slave is tasked to respond to more than the political ethicality of involuntary servitude; he must respond to white nihilistic ideals originally situating black humanity as nonexistent.

Black nihilism involves conflict between the strength of black wills versus the weakness of white wills in the same way that human existence requires tension between phenomenal willing and the givenness of the cosmos; insisting on black will means going against the entirety of the (white) metaphysical world. There is a Manichean relationship between these two competing forms of humanism. White people in antiblack racist worlds neither need nor desire black participation and recognition for their "truth." For them, "truth" depends upon avoiding our gaze; they depend on denying our points of view in order to make their world valuable. They do not seek to make themselves known to black people; rather, they work to keep themselves concealed from black people. As Fanon put it, "What [the master] wants from the slave is not recognition but work."[27] It is from this space that black humanity confronts the master, who is bewildered, violently, abrasively, and suddenly removed. Any form of black liberation that does not aim to obliterate the philosophical conditions enabling black invisibility, to kill the white nihilism on which antiblack racists depend, misses the mark. White nihilism and antiblack racism do not admit of any mutual recognition between whites and blacks because of their paradigmatic dependence upon assaults, erasures, and denials of black consciousness. There is no middle ground for respect and dignity under these circumstances; there are no calm conversational working out of issues to be had. As Oladipo Fashina demonstrates, in "Frantz Fanon and the Ethical Justification of Anti-Colonial Violence," for black people, "respect and dignity do not come from freedom unless freedom also results from conflict and risk of one's life. Thus, in order to win genuine respect and dignity, the colonized must force the settler's recognition through physical violence."[28] He went on to explain, for example, we shouldn't misunderstand what Fanon meant when writing in *Black Skin; White Mask* as follows:

> Man is human only to the extent to which he tries to impose his existence on another man in order to be recognized by him. As long as he has not been affectively recognized by the other, that other will remain the theme of his actions. It

is on that being, on recognition by that other being, that his own human worth and reality depend.[29]

According to Fashina, we should consider the above quote in terms of another, which Fanon provided in *The Wretched of the Earth*: "On the logical plane, the Manicheism of the colonists produces a Manicheism of the colonized. The theory of the 'absolute evil of the colonist' is in response to the theory of the 'absolute evil of the native.'"[30] Fashina's explanation of the connection between the two passages supports my theorization that the recognition achieved through strong black nihilistic struggles for black liberation does not come from a shared conception of humanity between antiblack racists and black people.[31] Strong black nihilists are neither, nor do they desire to be, "equally" human with white nihilistic conceptions of humanity. Black humanity precedes the impositions of antiblack racism.

We do not share a common conception of humanity with antiblack racists; rather, we insist upon the value of our humanity in spite of white desires to eviscerate it. There are no shared values between antiblack racist whites and black people. Here, there are opposing conceptions of humanity facing each other:

> If we look carefully at Fanon's own major writings on violence, the view that he called the colonized to violence in the name of human dignity is incorrect. Appeal to human dignity presupposes some general conception of humanity. But Fanon claimed that the colonized possessed no evidence of the existence of a common (general) humanity. Even if the colonized is concerned about dignity, for him this is not a concern about human beings in general. It was Fanon's view that the colonized did not define their own humanity in the same way as the settlers defined theirs. This is because the settlers' idea of humanity is embedded in values which the colonized reject, "mock at," "insult" and "vomit up." The only option to the colonized is to define his own humanity negatively, as the complete denial of all the values that characterized the settlers.[32]

On this view, it is absurd for black people to seek, or value, recognition from whiteness. No; the aim of Fanon as a strong black nihilist, for example, was to completely, utterly, coldly, and callously, categorically, dismiss the value of whiteness. Sartre acknowledged this in the preface to *The Wretched of the Earth*:

> And if you mumble, sniggering awkwardly: "He's really got it in for us!" you have missed the true nature of the scandal, for Fanon has got nothing "in for you" at all; his book, which is such a hot issue for others, leaves you out in the cold. It often talks about you, but never to you.[33]

Sartre continued, "For the fathers, we were the only interlocutors; For the sons, we no longer count: We are the object of their discourse."[34] Fashina demonstrated what can be called Fanon's strong black nihilistic dialectic of liberation:

> Since [The colonized] only defines his own humanity negatively (relative to the settler's), it follows that the colonized will discover his own humanity only when he rejects the values of the settler. We may even suppose that he will discover his humanity, whatever that is, in his relationship with the settler. But none of these implies that the discovery of his humanity (or sense of self-worth) requires the settler's recognition of him as human. It may be thought that violence will force a change of conception: it will force the settler to recognize that the colonized is human in the same way as the settler is. But it is more plausible, given the logic of Manicheism, that this recognition is unimportant to the colonized. Fanon seemed to be saying to the colonized: "You are, and you believe that you are human. But the settler denies that you are. Free yourselves from colonial rule and the process of social reconstruction that follows will show you how right you are about yourself."[35]

Fashina's work helps to identify Fanon's distrust of Western discursive appeals to humanity as strong black nihilistic rejections of white nihilistic presumptions of the ahistorical nature of (European) "Man." Fashina demonstrates a way in which acceptance of white nihilistic values entails acceptance of "an internal human nature," which "forces us to mistake the dominant image of human nature—an image which is historically restricted, for eternal."[36] Fanon rejects the forms of universalism inherent in Hegel's master-slave dialectic, in other words, and supplants it with a strong black nihilistic dialectic of liberation. Fanon's point is that strong black nihilistic awareness of one's life as valuable by virtue of the sheer fact of its existence offers a propellant to positive violent actions within antiblack racist worlds. Being propelled to violence by insisting upon one's humanity is not the same as accomplishing one's humanity through violence, which is how it goes according to Hegel's schema. Rather, as Fashina explains, Fanon implies that "the colonized possesses a sense of his own humanity which precedes and is a causal factor of anti-colonial violence."[37]

Blackness in America is born of struggles to affirm the value of blackness from a space of black invisibility. In antiblack racist societies, black subjectivities are forced to exist as nonbeings, as Lewis Gordon writes, living "in conscious realization of denied insides."[38] This is why in antiblack racist master-slave conflicts, black humanity can only be violently inserted into the relationship through a sudden suspension, devaluation, and replacement of white nihilistic conceptions of Humanity, and not through a shared humanism mutually developed by the master and the slave. In antiblack racist relationships, whites desire to eradicate, to never have to face, the perspectives of blacks. In order for blackness to emerge as a "yes," and not as a "don't," black people must produce strong nihilistic values, languages, and expressions. There must be a sudden replacement of one form of humanity for another:

> The end of race prejudice begins with a sudden incomprehension. The occupant's spasmed and rigid culture, now liberated, opens at last to the culture of people who have really become brothers. The two cultures can affront each other, enrich each other . . . universality resides in this decision to recognize and accept the reciprocal relativism of different cultures, once the colonial status is irreversibly excluded.[39]

Only under conditions of intersubjective, reciprocal, recognition based on strong, free, and responsible conceptions of Humanity can worlds be constructed where "colonial" understandings of Humanity are "irreversibly excluded." As Fanon put it, "I demand that notice be taken of my negating activity, insofar as I pursue something other than life; insofar as I do battle for the creation of a human world—that is, of a world of reciprocal recognitions."[40]

Strong black nihilism imposes a confrontation with white nihilistic values and forces recognition of blackness as a source of values. Upon emancipation, in America, black people were not necessarily regarded as equal to their former masters. White nihilism and antiblack racism remain the case. Phenomenal consciousness implicit to human existence continues to be treated as secondary qualities benevolently bestowed from some whites onto blacks. The "freedom" so accorded to black people entails a form of humanity whereby blacks are simply allowed to be as weak nihilistically situated as traditional whites. In this way, antiblack racism continues to situate blackness outside the self-other dialectic by essentially locking black people into a reality where we function as beings without perspectives, or original points of departure from which to insist upon and fight for. What does the requirement of fighting for one's humanity mean under such circumstances? How does one accomplish one's humanity? There is no legitimate form of inclusion on this view. One cannot go from (black) chattel slave to free (black) subject without theoretically questioning the conditions of (white) Humanity that demand enslavement in the first place.

Black existential freedom requires nihilistic struggles against traditional (white) human values. It requires producing languages, meanings, traditions, ways of being that push beyond traditional boundaries defining the antiblack world. The experiences of human freedom, those fleeting series of seemingly infinite moments experienced within the vicissitudes of each phenomenal spirit, for many black people, remain a tragic tight rope balanced between felt potential and the foreboding facts of antiblackness. Fanon encouraged producing an "authentic upheaval." He described the effects of what I call, white nihilism, constructing the spaces of black existential invisibility, creating the situation of what I call black nihilism, which, in Fanon's terms, amounts to a "zone of nonbeing," or, an "utterly naked declivity," where, nevertheless, "an authentic upheaval can be born."[41] On this view, black upheavals against antiblack racism entail rejecting white nihilistic valuations of humanity. For instance, once, when a white woman remarked of how handsome Fanon, "the negro," was, he retorted, "Then come and fuck the handsome Negro, Madame!"[42] Strong black attitudes can and do emerge through the lived fact of blackness, and they often cause even the most liberal white racists to flush with the embarrassment of having been recognized.

Black humanity comes into the antiblack racist world "imbued with a will" to find a meaning in things, but instead finds that it is "an object in the midst of other objects."[43] It goes from being totally erased through slavery, to being a self that is "put together again by another self," through emancipation.[44] In antiblack racist societies, as Fanon demonstrated, the humanity of black people arrives on the scene, far too late. The human world already exists, and is "anticipated, thought out, demonstrated, made the most of."[45] What options remain outside of a sudden and violent insisting upon one form of humanity for another? In, *Towards the African Revolution* (1964), in an essay entitled "Racism and Culture," Fanon argued, "In order to achieve liberation," the inferiorized man brings "all his resources into play, all his acquisitions, the old and the new, his own and those of the occupant."[46] Yet, he warned against a "mummification of individual thinking" which tends to produce decadent values.[47] In Fanon's terms, white nihilistic values seek the "destruction of [black] cultural values, of ways of life." Here, "lines of force, having crumbled, no longer give direction. In their stead a new system of values is imposed, not proposed but affirmed, by the heavy weight of cannons and sabers."[48] Black humanity is induced under "the heavy weight of cannons and sabers" toward weak nihilistic, including black optimistic, responses to antiblack racism. Black people are inundated with commands to retain appeals to "humanity," "love," and respect for "supreme values," which in this case, means being induced into committing the mistake of "forgetting racism as a consequence" that "obeys a flawless logic," and not necessarily a lack of "love."[49] Antiblack racists do not have a pathological disposition against loving and respecting; clearly, they love and respect one another. It is when it comes to loving and respecting those who are not white, the black, that "the white man remains intractable."[50] The attitude of antiblack racism is not "a constant of the human spirit," on Fanon's view; it is "a disposition fitting into a well-defined system."[51] Understanding the dispositions involved require understanding the systematic production of white values. By collapsing black phenomenal perspectives into an object of nonexistence, antiblack racism accomplishes "enslavement, in the strictest sense," enabling white people to live in a reality where they function as Gods, authors of universal value, or masters of the universe.[52] Antiblack racism demands that black strength, freedom, and being for-it-self collapses into a weak thing-in-itself; it attempts to stop all black phenomenal systems from self-referencing outside of whiteness. As a result, the entire social panorama of black existential life is "destructured," and values are, as Fanon said, "flaunted, crushed, emptied."[53]

Under these circumstances, black people in an antiblack world may, at first, discover "dignity" as a form of optimism, as if "having discovered a spontaneous truth," where "the inferiorized rediscovers a style that had once been devalorized."[54] One could interpret black Christian responses to antiblack racism in this way; it is a "traditionalism," according to Fanon, which is a hallmark of weak nihilism.[55] On this view, having rediscovered their freedoms in terms of powers to alternatively interpret white nihilistic Christian narratives, the traditional black Christian utilizes his spontaneous truth, and "goes into ecstasies over each rediscovery . . . formerly inferiorized, [they are] now in a state of grace."[56] But, at this point, Fanon offers a warning:

> The culture of the enslaved people is sclerosed, dying. No life any longer circulates in it. Or more precisely, the only existing life is dissimulated. The population that normally assumes here and there a few fragments of life, which continues to attach dynamic meanings to institutions . . . in a colonial system these are the traditionalists.[57]

One must resist attaching certain "dynamic meanings" to antiblack racist institutions, which I interpret to mean avoiding what I call "weak black nihilism." Nodding at the ways black optimists strive to preserve "a few fragments of life," one is ultimately forced to criticize the underdevelopment of thought, or "mummification" of human freedom entailed by such approaches to black struggle.

The strong black nihilist, for example, might read the optimism of traditional black Christianity as "a passion-charged mechanism making it possible to escape the sting of paradox."[58] That is, it may be viewed as a paradoxical appeal to illogic that seeks to escape the burdens of not only black suffering, but human existential freedom altogether. In the previous chapter we saw Cornel West admit this approach is not primarily concerned with logic but with preserving black "sanity." Catharsis becomes necessary. "Sanity" struggling, more or less, to keep itself intact, ultimately must desire to become actional. "Rediscovering tradition . . . as a symbol of purity . . . leaves the impression that the mediation takes vengeance by substantializing itself."[59] That is, appealing to metaphysically affirmed traditions may provide, perhaps, necessary moments of emotional catharsis, but such responses alone are not sufficiently active in the sense of developing "elaborate methods" of response. They run the risk of valuing a form of weak nihilism that believes that "the mediation takes vengeance [simply] by substantiating itself." As Fanon summed it up, "Falling back on archaic positions having no relation to technical development is paradoxical. The institutions thus valorized no longer correspond to the elaborate methods of action already mastered."[60]

When responding to antiblack racism, falling back upon traditional values is the most direct way to further weak nihilism. Such responses respond to decadent values with the decadence of values that have already decayed. "The culture put into capsules, which has vegetated since the foreign domination, is revalorized. It is not reconceived, grasped anew, dynamized from within. It is shouted. And this head long, unstructured, verbal revalorization conceals paradoxical attitudes."[61] Strong black nihilism suggests responding to antiblack racism by devaluing and transvaluing metaphysically affirmed modes of valuing in attempts to move beyond "verbal revalorization" of traditions.

Fanon was a strong nihilist whose thought fostered demands for intellectual integrity in conformity with what is undeniably the case about the human condition. His descriptive unveiling of antiblack racist attitudes and responses allows for conceptualization of "black existential freedom." If the fundamental question of existential phenomenology is, "In what ways does consciousness experience being?", one answer could be, "Black consciousness is made to experience its being through white nihilistic ideals of European humanity." Yet, the parameters of meaning for human consciousness are socially generated phenomena, established through interactive, subjective-objective, self-other, human dialectics. It is precisely these conditions of mutual recognition in constructing Human reality that are denied to black people. Black people are made to exist as human beings whose subjectivity is not only unreciprocated but denied and forced to manifest itself from a space of nonexistence, which constitutes the inhumanity of the lived fact of blackness. And, if I am correct, the entire affair can be understood as a project of black nihilism, one where black people are forced to respond to white nihilism. Healthy responses to antiblack racism and white nihilism, then, not only reject the concrete elements of antiblack racist oppression, they also reject their philosophical preconditions.

New forms of valuing humanity are required to move beyond the decadent parameters of the antiblack racist world. Fanon's work provides support for my theorization that strong black nihilism, as he wrote in the opening pages of *Black Skin; White Masks*, may be a potential way forward, "toward a new humanism."[62] He suggested, in the closing sentences of that text, the goal of a new humanism is to adopt an open disposition toward Humanity. "I want the world to recognize, with me, the open door of every consciousness."[63]

Black nihilistic struggles against antiblack racism make visible that which the (white) Human world desires not to see. Black nihilistic humanity emerges as a blemish, a counterclaim menacing against the allegedly universal value of whiteness. Black nihilism involves facing a situation where there is no way to insist upon one's "original relations to value," without appearing violent and pathological of the normative order of (white) Humanity. If black existential life involves struggling for meaning from the space of non-meaning, then struggles of back humanity against antiblack racism necessarily involve fighting a nihilistic war. White nihilism and black nihilism are the two camps in the war for human existential freedom. White nihilism distorts the Human world by destroying the significance of black life. Strong black nihilism insists on the value of all human phenomenal perspectives, provided they do not "stink." The following quote from Frantz Fanon captures the strong black nihilistic spirit:

> I said in my introduction that man is a yes. I will never stop reiterating that. Yes to life. Yes to love. Yes to generosity. But man is also a no. No to degradation of man. No to exploitation of man. No to the butchery of what is most human in man: freedom. Man's behavior is not only reactional. And there is always resentment in reaction. Nietzsche had already pointed that out in *The Will to Power*. To educate man to be actional, preserving in all his relations his respect for the basic values that constitute a human world, is the prime task of him who, having taken thought, prepares to act.[64]

BLACK NIHILISM AND THE AFROPESSIMISM DEBATE

The question of whether black people ought to view their future prospects in struggling against antiblack racism optimistically or pessimistically is an old one. Several contemporary philosophers have begun writing on multiple elements constituting what I call "black nihilism," although, they tend to limit the discussion between what I call "black optimism" and "black pessimism." The previous chapter demonstrates connections between the thought of Derrick Bell and black pessimism, and Cornel West and black optimism, which can be understood as theoretical precursors to the contemporary positions of Afropessimism and Afro-optimism. The main exemplars of the contemporary debate are Frank Wilderson, III, and Jared Sexton. However, I will also consider the contributions of several other interlocutors. Afro-optimists, as previously demonstrated, ultimately seek intervention from "beyond." For

Afropessimists, as previously explained, the world is hopelessly filled with immutable ideals of white nihilism. And, where the removal of white nihilistic ideals may be unachievable, the pessimistic goal is to seek the disarmament of antiblack racist institutions. In other words, as already explained, both positions suffer from potential forms of weak black nihilism. I will conclude this chapter by sketching several positions from the Afropessimism debate and contextualizing them within my larger framework for black nihilism.

Frank Wilderson's "Biko and the Problematic of Presence" describes black pessimism, but offers an example of weak black nihilism in response that should be avoided.[65] According to Wilderson,

> What we learn from Fanon and others is that the world is unethical due to its subsumption by the slave relation. The slave relation, then, relegates the [Marxist] capital relation (the irreconcilability between the position of the worker and the position of the capitalist) to a conflict, and not the antagonism that Marx perceived it to be.[66]

Here, the sufferings of capitalist oppression are contextualized by the relationship between master and slave. Drawing on Orlando Patterson's *Slavery and Social Death*, Wilderson argued that the economic features of the master-slave relationship is not a constituent element of slavery, but an incidental (though commonplace) experience of the slave. Patterson's corrective involves seeing slavery, first and foremost, as a structuring relation that constitutes the paradigm of human interaction.[67] In *Red, White, & Black: Cinema and the Structure of United States of America Antagonisms* (2010), Wilderson argues antiblack racism is dependent upon black death, which "connotes an ontological status" of existential invisibility for blackness.[68] "White, Human ... exists ontologically as a position of life in relation to the black/slave position, one of death."[69] Wilderson's work highlights black invisibility as a result of weak nihilistic ideals situating (white) Humanity. Whiteness depends upon the existential erasure, or "social death," of blackness:

> In short, political ontology, as imagined through Humanism, can only produce discourse that has as its foundation alienation and exploitation as a grammar of suffering, when what was needed (for the black, who is always already a slave) is an ensemble of ontological questions that has as its foundation accumulation and fungibility as a grammar of suffering.[70]

Wilderson demonstrates ways white life is made valuable through the weak nihilistic cost of antiblack racism. He describes the black pessimistic situation of having to value against the seemingly immutable force of white Humanity. For example, when he argues that whiteness functions in terms of a denial that "can grasp its own capacity, be present to itself, coherent, by its unavailability to the a priori violence of . . . Black accumulation and fungibility," he illustrates its weak nihilism, its need for epistemological guarantees of security:[71]

> Settler ontology is guaranteed by way of a negative knowledge of what it is not, rather than by of its positive claims of what it is. Ontological whiteness is secured not through its cultural, economic, or gendered identities; but by the fact that it cannot be known (positioned) by genocide (or by Accumulation and Fungibility).[72]

Wilderson proceeds to argue that "it is impossible to disentangle both blackness and Africanness from the constituent elements of slavery since their emergence and legitimacy are inextricably bound with the centuries of process through which subjects were turned into objects."[73] He claims that "empowerment predicated on Black Consciousness can only impact/liberate the Black at the level of preconscious interests and at the level of unconscious identifications; but not at the level of structural positionality."[74] This is not incorrect; black consciousness and black political activity are distinct but related subjects. Yet, Wilderson treats black consciousness as distinct from political consciousness. This is because he is convinced that "antiblackness is a structural necessity and a paradigmatic constant" of the contemporary Human political world. He is a black pessimist who believes that "Black Consciousness cannot restore the Black to a world predicated on his/her absence. No matter what blacks do (fight in the realm of preconscious interest or heal disalienation in the realm of unconscious desire), Blackness cannot attain relationality."[75] After describing black pessimism, Wilderson stops. He collapses, like Schopenhauer, into phenomenal resignation. Wilderson seems to suggest a form of valuing nonblack valuing. This, to me, seems eerily close to valuing white nihilism. He appears, simply, to capitulate to the fact of black pessimism.

Wilderson displays weakness in the face of black nihilism; he describes black pessimism but collapses before seeing how it can become active and strong, or occasion newer ways of being that *can* lead to free political realities. Wilderson's Afropessimism is a form of weak black nihilism. Rather than considering how strong black nihilistic perspectives can help pave the way, enabling the emergence of black political demands, out of which healthy political arrangements can be fought for, and won, Wilderson laments black invisibility. He appears inconsolably forlorn about black preclusion from white worlds. But why lament so deeply black inability to join the antiblack world? Why should anyone want to join *that* world?

Perhaps it is the job of the black pessimist to complete the task of black nihilism, strongly, that is, to create newer worlds. What is needed is not a reformed civilization, but a new Humanity, newer ways of valuing the "human," beyond the decayed rubble, and rubbish, of the pessimistically hammered ideals of the antiblack racist world. Wilderson used the hammer of black pessimism to destroy white nihilistic values, but he did not have the strength to wield it to build. He demonstrated weak black nihilism when he wrote, "My gaze, my black gaze, cannot restore me to a paradigm whose coherence—that is the integrity of Humanity at every scale; the national, the civic, the domestic, the corporeal—is predicated on the production and reproduction of my non-being."[76] But, what is needed is not restoration within this civilization, what is needed is a new humanity. The strong black nihilist does not lament a black gaze that cannot restore it to a white world; my gaze has never belonged to such a world, and I can't miss what I have never had. Furthermore, if I am right, the black gaze should not aim to restore black people to the antiblack world. Black disconnection from the white world is not a "failure," in the same sense that the colonial construction of the (white) Human world is not an "achievement." Gordon echoes this point "*an* antiblack world" is not identical with "*the world is antiblack.*" Rather, "such a world is an antiblack racist *project*. It is not *the* historical *achievement*. Its limitations emerge from a basic fact: Black people and other opponents of such a project fought and continue to fight."[77] In other words, the strong black nihilistic gaze should aim to shoot, pierce through, and go beyond the antiblack racist world, toward an existentially free world, and not seek restoration within this nihilistically weak one.

Black pessimism, as I have defined it, is a fundamental recognition of the weak nihilistic, decadent, nature of antiblack racist ideals; it involves an espousal of the structure of race antagonisms situating blackness as invisible. The problem with this version of black pessimism is its potentially inherent weak black nihilistic response to antiblack racism. Black pessimism, from my perspective, ought to be viewed as a stage conditioning further choices to be made between strong and weak nihilism. In the same way that Schopenhauer's pessimism collapsed into weak phenomenal resignation, which was a contradictory and self-defeating use of will, Wilderson laments black invisibility, producing weak nihilistic proclamations of its political futility. When considering the possibilities for the "black gaze," Wilderson, it appears, is blinded and cannot see beyond the metaphysical rays of whiteness. Black pessimism, however, can be a precursor to strong black nihilism, not merely a death sentence. The limited scope of Wilderson's view enabled a false dichotomy to emerge between Afropessimism and Afro-optimism. However, as Stephen Marshall suggested, in "The political Life of Fungibility," there are important points of overlap between the binary positions that should be considered:

> Despite their quarrel, there are three crucial moments of convergence between Afropessimism and Afro-optimism. Both positions affirm black vulnerability

as an effect of fungibility. Each claim that vulnerability and fungibility are achievements won through the reconstitution of slave law. And, both positions strive to formulate, in theoretical terms, the subjective and intersubjective dimensions of fungibility as a structure of political antagonism.[78]

That is, there is convergence on the general nature of the problems of blackness whereby one is demanded to face what I call, the black nihilistic situation, of having to value beyond the suffocating confines of white nihilism and antiblack racism.

Fred Moten is associated with Afro-optimism. In "The Case of Blackness," Moten treats blackness as a pathogen blocking the way toward a more humane sense of humanity.[79] His reading of Frantz Fanon suggested that the "Black" is a man haunted by ambivalence:

> It could be said that Fanon moves within an economy of annihilation even though, at the same time, he mourns his own intentional comportment toward a hermeneutics of thingliness. Is blackness brought to light in Fanon's ambivalence? Is blackness given a hearing—or, more precisely, does blackness give itself to a hearing—in his phenomenological description (which is not but nothing other than a representation) of it? Studying the case of blackness is inseparable from the case blackness makes for itself in spite and by way of every interdiction. In any case, it will have been as if one has come down with a case of blackness.[80]

Moten understood Fanon as paradoxically struggling against the categories of terms needed to articulate himself. However, I argue, Moten misunderstood the strong black nihilism inherent in Fanon's thought. Neither did Fanon seek to relieve black people of the "case of blackness" nor did he consider blackness a disease to be alleviated; he did, however, consider antiblack racist values to be an eradicable disease infecting humanity and causing the underdevelopment of its possibilities. Fanon did not seek to restore his blackness within a (white) Human world that cannot justify its original exclusion of blackness. By "restoring *them* to the world," Fanon meant to liberate *all* humanity from weak nihilistic conceptions of itself, which in its modern sense, is most fundamentally overdetermined in terms of racial whiteness and blackness.

In the face of social death, the strong black nihilist is at once both a pessimist and a nihilist; he is a destroyer and a builder that creates, and forges anew. Jared Sexton put it as follows:

> Black optimism is not the negation of the negation that is Afropessimism, just as black social life does not negate black social death by inhabiting it and vitalizing it. A living death is as much a death as it is a living. Nothing in Afropessimism

suggests that there is no black (social) life, only black life is not social life in the universe formed by the codes of state and civil society ... the modern world system. Black life is not lived in the world that the world lives in, but it is lived underground.[81]

The error by Wilderson, for example, is that he is conflating "the modern world system" with the (white) modern world system. This is why, in my opinion, Afropessimism, would be better off developing and occupying a space of black pessimism, similar to Fanon's version of negritude. There, at least, negritude only implicitly accepts reason, and not the entire world, as "white." Black nihilistic life is forged underground, at first, beneath and in spite of the antiblack racist world. It is forced to develop itself as far removed as possible from the pale, weak nihilistic, light of white-normative ideals. This life, and persisting through it, involves living through a state of exception between life and death. "Double emphasis, on the lived and on death. That's the whole point of the enterprise at some level."[82] The fact of white nihilism is the starting point for Afropessimism and Afro-optimism.

Support for my theorization that the choice between Afropessimism and Afro-optimism is a false dichotomy can be further found in Sexton's defense of some of the features of Wilderson's pessimism. Afropessimism entails the erasure of neither black phenomenal capacities nor the agency of black performance, as Wilderson claims, but rather simply highlights the facts of black invisibility within antiblack racist societies. Wilderson points out the fact that "black social death is black social life."[83] Sexton responds to both Moten and Wilderson when arguing that "Afro pessimism is 'not but nothing other than' black optimism." Perhaps, the point of contention is that the dichotomization misses the question of strong versus weak black nihilism in response to antiblack racism. Blackness is lived through a logic of "improvisational immanence," in other words, the "permanence is a pedestrian sense that something 'lasts or remains without essential change.'"[84] The contention arises over "what it means to inhabit this permanence."[85] Regarding what I call Wilderson's weak black nihilistic claim that the "performance" of black consciousness cannot change the ontological situatedness of Western political reality, Sexton is charitable:

> Does Afropessimism fail to hear the resonance of black optimism? Or might something else be at work. Of course, when Wilderson writes that "performance meets ontology," he is saying quite a bit more than that. Though he is attempting to think the two registers together—the performative and the ontological—he is indicating not so much that ontology is not performative, but rather more so that performativity does not, in fact, have disruptive power at the level or/in the way that it has been theorized to date. More radically still, he is suggesting that this theorization remains insufficiently elaborated.[86]

One can perhaps be satisfied with Sexton's reading of Wilderson as simply doubting theorizations of black performativity leading to political change. At any rate, black pessimism and black optimism, as features of the processes of black nihilism, remain crucial lenses for theorizing existential needs of black life in contemporary America, calling to attention some of the most hidden, denied, aspects of the problems associated with antiblack racism.

Sexton's work can be used to further illuminate black nihilism. In "People-of-Color-Blindness: Notes on the Afterlife of Slavery," Sexton discusses how contemporary political ideals of color blindness paradoxically rely on simultaneous acknowledgment and denial of black invisibility.[87] Sexton argues that the phenomenon of color blindness by those claiming to be allies in struggles against antiblack racism, sometimes, renders invisible the lived realities of black people and thereby exacerbates our condition. For example, he wrote, "Black existence does not represent the totality of the racial formation—it is not the beginning and the end of the story—but it does relate to the totality; it indicates the (repressed) truth of the political and economic system." The repressed truth undergirding antiblack racist political and economic systems refers to what I call "white nihilism," which situates even "colorblind" values within a structure of weak nihilistic frameworks. The phenomenon of there being other oppressed groups referred to, sometimes, as "new blacks," or oppressed groups that claim equivalence between black struggles and that of their own, demonstrate the malleability of white nihilism. Firstly, blackness, as a nonexistence, situates the value of whiteness and relates to the "totality" of racism. Thus, "new blacks" can say whatever they want; "old blacks" are still catching hell. Secondly, the ability of black existential struggles to be analogized, while simultaneously silenced, perpetuates white-normative vacuums in which "black noise" remains unheard and deemed incomprehensible. Sexton explores the relationship between antiblack racist censures of black inquiry and the tendency of certain, nonblack, peoples-of-color toward recurrent analogizing of black suffering:

> They bear a common refusal to admit to significant differences of structural position born of discrepant histories between blacks and their political allies, actual or potential. We might finally name this refusal "people-of-color-blindness," a form of colorblindness inherent in the concept of "people of color" to the precise extent that it misunderstands the specificity of blackness and presumes or insists upon the monolithic character of victimization under white supremacy—thinking (the afterlife) of slavery as a form of exploitation or colonization or a species of racial oppression among others.[88]

While it remains theoretically possible to allegorize Western slavery, or the black experience, "the hemispheric black struggle against actually existing slavery and its afterlife cannot authorize itself literally in those same terms."[89] An ironic feature of black nihilism, today, is the general unavailability of legitimate political discourses by which to articulate black grievances against antiblack racism, and the supplanting of that possibility with a loose ability to analogize, but never speak literally, and plainly, about the very real issues continuing to affect black life in antiblack racist societies.

In "The Avant-Garde of White Supremacy," Jared Sexton and Steve Martinot elaborated ways in which what I call white nihilistic ideals continue to pervade Leftist and Liberal attempts at radical critique of American political life.[90] Marxism, for example, subordinates race to class struggles, while liberalism subordinates the issues of racism to "the presumed potentialities of individual development."[91] There is a chasm between the metaphysical constellations of traditional (white) Human morality, for example, and the facts of black nihilism living underneath it. The resulting incommensurability between these competing ethics transcends the dialectical, "indeed, that ignorability becomes the condition of possibility for the ethical coherence of the inside."[92] The black nihilist suffers as one whose moral and ethical concerns are forced to remain on the plane of the ignoble.

Achille Mbembe, Saidiya Hartman, and Stephen Best are some other interlocutors whose thoughts are compatible with my theorization of black nihilism. Achille Mbembe identified "sovereignty" as a driving desire of whiteness. In "Necropolitics," he articulated whiteness in part through a desire to dictate life and death for black subjects. He developed Michel Foucault's conception of "biopower," wherein sovereignty entails the strength to "exercise control over morality and to define life as the deployment and manifestation of power."[93] Mbembe describes antiblack racist political reality as a form of war. He investigates the role of death, life, and the human body, in constructing conceptions of antiblack racist "power." As a result of the "sovereign" status whites seek in relation to black people, blacks are forced into what Mbembe calls a "state of exception," or what I call black pessimistic and nihilistic spaces. These are existential spaces where black life and death meet their limits in terms of incomplete realizations of each other.[94] As a result, the "state of exception," acquires a spatial arrangement that locates it "outside the normal state of law."[95]

Antiblack racism's arrangement of black spaces beyond the scope of morality justice, and law, has both a geographical and an existential landscape. Mbembe's thought sheds light on the black nihilistic terrain of the "state of exception," revealing the white-normative structuring of the "sovereign" subject around which antiblack racist political institutions are built. He argued that Western notions of justice are predicated upon modern European philosophical categories and white-normative conceptions of "pure reason." He countered, "Instead of considering reason as the truth of the subject, we can look to other foundational categories that are less abstract and more tactile, such as life and death."⁹⁶ He exposed white nihilistic dimensions of antiblack racist notions of sovereignty when arguing as follows:

> Such figures of sovereignty are far from a piece of prodigious insanity or an expression of a rupture between the impulses and interests of the body and those of the mind. Indeed, they . . . constitute the nomos of the political space in which we still live.⁹⁷

While purporting to be grounded on universal ideals of truth and reason, antiblack racist ideals are neither the products of reason, nor insanity, nor antinomies abounding between phenomena and noumena. Rather, antiblack racism, on this view, results from a fundamentally weak nihilistic desire for sovereignty.

In "On the Power of the False," Mbembe can be read as criticizing weak nihilistic responses to antiblack racism: It can be argued that the idea of good and evil on which nativism and Afro-radicalism are based so strongly resembles the "slave morality" described by Nietzsche that the two are virtually indistinguishable. . . . This was a morality produced by "weak individuals" perfectly satisfied with the limits of their own existence.⁹⁸ Here, Mbembe clearly condemned certain forms of traditionalism. I read him as arguing for strong black nihilistic approaches in response to antiblack racism. "The way out of this dead-end is not to be found in ethno-philosophy."⁹⁹ For example, consider Mbembe's critique of black Christian responses to antiblack racism:

> Right from the beginning the Christian narrative of Africa is dominated by the motif of darkness. Theologically speaking, "darkness," constitutes a primordial tragedy . . . the truth is shrouded in all kinds of superstitions. . . . Africa is seen to live at a distance from the divine. . . . The Christian project of deliverance involves throwing off the chains, that is, separating the world of appearances and falsity (sin) from the truth (redemption). . . . The proposed alternative is an initiation into the truth, a key to happiness, and a promise of a new life. In doing so, however, the world of allegory characteristic of pagan existence is not simply eradicated. Christianity establishes a new relationship between that world and the world of the event. The event is the promise of redemption. Redemption consists of a set of ideas that, because of their ability to enchant, could be defined as magico-poetic. This is true of the resurrection of the Dead.¹⁰⁰

Furthermore, Mbembe writes as follows:

> Colonization is founded on a similar universalizing project. . . . Colonial rule is supposed to operate as a regulating mechanism that ultimately leads to the

triumph of 'universal reason.' In this instance, 'universal reason,' presumes the existence of a subjectivity by the same name, whose universality is embodied in his or her humanity.[101]

Mbembe's implicit critique of what I call "white nihilism" can be seen in the summation "like Islam and Christianity, colonization is a universalizing project." His philosophies of black death, false knowledge, and what it would mean to nondogmatically think through the ontological question of what black people are, and the ethical-teleological question of what black people ought to be striving for, illuminates the space of black nihilism. Through his language of "necropolitics," Mbembe sheds light on the situation of strong black nihilism needing to forge meaning through black pessimism without relying on weak nihilism:

> Indeed, the fact is that the history of continental Africa does contain in its midst an element of terror, a cavity, which is not that which Hegel and the others call ontological. The cavity in question consists, over the long durée, of a collection of dead things and masks, a litany of horrors, which taken to their extreme, almost always produce half-human, half-animal figures that have the particular characteristic of devouring themselves. This auto-devouring is the absolute signifier. It is the power of the negative near which a truly radical thought must dwell. It might allow us to get to the root of things.[102]

Saidiya Hartman's work also helps illuminates the situation of black nihilism, of existing from a liminal space of life and death, and the need for thinking unlicensed thoughts in facing as yet unrealized hopes. Stephen Best and Saidiya Hartman's concept of "Fugitive Justice" describes the predicaments of black pessimism and nihilism while addressing the question of attitudes and dispositions that may be required for going forward in light of a well-documented antiblack racist American history. Indeed, as they said, "By 1787, it was already too late. It was not too late to imagine an end to slavery, but it was too late to imagine the repair of its injury."[103] Legal redresses of American slavery "would inevitably be too narrow, and as such it would prove necessarily inadequate."[104] The injuries of slavery must be endured and cannot be undone.

> The forms of legal and social compensation available are less a matter of wiping the slate clean than of embracing the limited scope of the possible in the face of the irreplaceable, and calling attention to the incommensurability between pain and compensation. How does one compensate for centuries of violence that have as their consequence the impossibility of restoring a prior existence . . . of repairing what was broken?[105]

Here, black nihilism is considered in light of a form of black pessimism offered through Ottobah Cugoana's writings on "captivity." Cugoana argued that, in such cases, one is forced to demand justice "in light of that which he cannot describe or convey, fully cognizant that what has been destroyed cannot be restored."[106] Hartman and Best mobilized pessimistic and nihilistic languages emphasizing the transformative roles of mourning, grief, lamentation, and death, as conducive to the establishing of further perspectives necessary for valuing black life in antiblack racist societies, where one can potentially live again. "A life lived in loss" was Cugoana's description of what I call black nihilism, where, as Hartman and Best put it, there is "a sophisticated understanding . . . between the necessity of logical remedy and impossibility of redress," which can be used to understand black nihilism as, a "loophole between hope and resignation."[107]

Pessimistic resignation from traditional values can lead to strong nihilistic black values. Strong black nihilism is neither a pessimistic resignation, nor an optimistic hope for redress; it is a pursuit of an elusive form of justice enabled by nihilistic circumstances. The question of why and how justice emerges as elusive, or "fugitive," for people living through the situation of black nihilism, must be taken up with specific attention paid to "the kinds of political claims that can be mobilized on behalf of the slave in the political present," with the purpose of gaining insight into our present political possibilities for dealing with a "melancholy recognition of foreseeable futures still tethered to this past."[108]

The political condition of black nihilism can be considered in terms of American legal cases involving attempts to sue the U.S. government for redresses of the injuries suffered in and as a result of antiblack slavery; all of which, to date, have been dismissed according to the "sovereign immunity" of the American government:

> Sovereign immunity protected the government from all charges of culpability as regards the institution of slavery. This seems to be the lesson by those who currently argue for reparations. Today, it is too late to invoke the crimes of the U.S. nation state. Few dare to speak of a "slaveholder's Constitution" (as abolitionists has a century and a half ago), to change the government with ultimate responsibility for slavery. The injuries suffered were not at the hands of the U.S. Government, but at the hands of . . . companies. . . . These most recent reparations cases are unable to name the state as an agent in the perpetuation of the injury; they foreclose the possibility of a discussion of the racial state, and as such they reinscribe the neutrality of the state.[109]

American political discourse has traditionally reinforced black pessimism and black nihilism by rendering invisible the subjects and terms of discussion necessary for redressing its effects. Black nihilism is exacerbated by the American government's failure to acknowledge its continued dependence upon philosophies precipitating black invisibility, that is, antiblack racism and white nihilism. For instance, the official registering of the "injuries of slavery" listed were "withholding of the slave's wages."[110] But, is monetary compensation all that was denied to, or demanded by, black people?

Black people live a "second death," wherein one is prefixed as "dead in law," then killed again in terms of the physical and psychological reduction of one's phenomenal capacities to a commodity of labor. And then, of course, there is the threat of actual physical death. "This brutal reduction of life is a condition from which there is no return, for which no redress is possible."[111] The social panorama of death the black body finds itself existing within leaves a scene to be investigated, which Hartman does in *Scenes of Subjection* (1997).[112] There, she illuminates the lived fact of black nihilism, in terms of "everyday life—specifically, tactics of resistance, modes of self-fashioning, and figurations of freedom—and to investigate the construction of the subject and social relations contained."[113] Through "black enjoyment," for example, she explains how antiblack racism requires a phenomenal reduction of black capacities to the status of pure objectivity so that black people can be "enjoyed," or, "used and abused by all whites."[114] She inherently describes black nihilism in black needs to express that which functions within antiblack racist societies as metaphysically "meaningless and incoherent." "Black noise," in other words, comprises languages, expressions, songs that represent the extreme and paradoxical contradictions of blackness that antiblack racists desire not to see. "These seemingly meaningless and incoherent songs, though difficult for those outside and within the circle of slavery to understand, revealed more about the horrors of the institution than did volumes of philosophy."[115] The entire spectacle of antiblack racism, and whiteness, can be viewed as a sublimating act of recoding the invisibility of black claims and pains into displays of white cheer. Black existential suffering is a value condition for the possibility of white enjoyment of life. Hartman highlights the nihilistic suffering of everyday black people in antiblack racist contexts. "The most invasive forms of slavery's violence lie not in these exhibitions of 'extreme' suffering or in what we see but in what we don't see. Shocking displays too easily obfuscate the more mundane and socially endurable forms of terror."[116] The misery of black nihilistically situated people is in part due to the fact of having to "dance" to the tunes of white nihilistic ideals. "Behind the facade of innocent amusements [of antiblack racism] lay the violence the master class assiduously denied."[117]

Black nihilists are ultimately aiming to "steal" political spaces where free, and responsible, thought can perhaps develop strength. Hartman points out that secret meetings among the enslaved literally meant "expropriation of the object of property" in order to make those meetings possible. Stolen, "fugitive," spaces beyond antiblack racist realities highlight both the possibility of their construction and the inherently violent and risky circumstances of their coming into being.[118] The notion of stealing away involves unlicensed movement, and in the case of taking seriously the concerns of black nihilism in political theory, it involves thinking unlicensed thoughts:

> Bound by the fetters of sentiment, held captive by the vestiges of the past, and cast into a legal condition of subjection—these features limn the circumstances of an anomalous, misbegotten, and burdened subject no longer enslaved, but not yet free.[119]

Finally, Lewis Gordon's thought on the Afropessimism debate supports my theorization that strong black nihilism is the appropriate way beyond the binary of black pessimism and optimism, provided it leads to political commitments. His support for my theorization can be summed up in the following extended quote:

> An ironic dimension of pessimism is that it is the other side of optimism. Oddly enough, both are connected to nihilism. . . . It emerges when people no longer want to be responsible for their actions. Optimists expect intervention from beyond. Pessimists declare relief is not forthcoming. Neither takes responsibility for what is valued. The *valuing*, however, is what leads to the second, epistemic point. The presumption that what is at stake is what can be *known* to determine what can be done *is* the problem. If such knowledge were possible, the debate would be about who was reading the evidence correctly. Such a judgment would be a priori—that is, prior to events actually unfolding. The future, unlike transcendental conditions such as language, signs, and reality, is, however, *ex post facto*: it is yet to come. Facing the future, the question isn't what *will be* or *how we do know what will be* but instead the realization that *whatever is done will be that on which the future will depend*. Rejecting optimism and pessimism, there is a supervening alternative: political commitment (Emphasis in original).[120]

How might political commitments to justice be conceived for those who historically exists beyond the bounds of humane considerations of the just? Artistic analogues for reflecting on this dimension of black nihilism are useful. Compare the Fugitive sense of justice sought by black people to the situation of the "fugitive" jazz musician, who has a negative relation to the law of music. Utilizing Bryan Wagner's term "black noise" reject the idea that the Fugitive must vanish from the scene of the music's origin before the music can be integrated into the timeframe of liberal nationalism, as Hartman suggests. Forget the idea that the black nihilist must die before the wisdom of our words can have a positive effect. The black nihilist's gift comes from occupying a fugitive space. As Best and Hartman worded it, "In the state of exception (the negative relation to law) that defines the slave's existence," or within what I call, spaces of black pessimism and black nihilism, strong upheavals can be borne.[121] What Hartman and Best describe as "the state of exception" is the existential space of black invisibility, which is a black nihilistic site, wherein unique contributions to reality, especially through language, art, and music, can be made.

Strong black nihilistic responses to antiblack racism reject its philosophical and existential underpinnings; they ultimately seek to move beyond the metaphysically affirmed values traditionally justifying (white) Human life. Strong black nihilism contains, therefore, a necessarily black pessimistic disposition toward white nihilistic values. Black pessimism and certain forms of weak black nihilism, *negritude* for example, can be developmental stages within a strong black nihilistic process. Ultimately, strong black nihilism desires not to rely on constructed black metaphysical affirmations in order to struggle against antiblack racism, but may do so, initially, as a reactively necessary move. Strong black nihilism insists upon devaluing white nihilism, that is, black pessimism, as a first step, while preparing to transvalue weak nihilism, that is, strong black nihilism, as a final step. Or, as Fanon put it, "Liberating the man of color," from certain restrictive understandings of the meaning of race is the ultimate goal of strong black nihilism.[122] We seek not merely reformation, but a new civilization premised upon "a new humanism."[123]

Through each of the above philosophers mentioned in my discussion of black nihilism, strength, and the Afropessimism debate, the cause of stealing away black nihilistic philosophical spaces wherein black people can develop and continue the work of building and preparing the way for newer forms of humanity beyond white nihilism and antiblack racism is, in one way or another, advanced. The importance of black nihilistic thought cannot be understated precisely for this reason: philosophies of black nihilism, including black pessimism and black optimism, construct terms of discourse useful for future generations of black people to identify, theorize, and strategize against the prevalence of evolving, yet weak nihilistically entrenched, antiblack racist value systems. To adopt languages enabling future generations of black people to find strong black nihilistic voices, to make undeniable "black noise," and not perish of the forces of antiblack racism's weak nihilistic impositions, is the goal of strong black nihilism. With this in mind, I would like to end this monograph by turning attention to the relationship between antiblack racism and the future prospects of strong black nihilistic generations, directed through a discussion of the existential category of black youth in relation to what I call black nihilistic hip-hop music.

NOTES

1. Frantz Fanon, *The Wretched of the Earth*, trans. Richard Philcox (New York: Grove Press, 2004), 210. Originally published in 1963.
2. "The very structure of modern [Western] discourse at its inception produced forms of rationality, scientificity, and objectivity as well as aesthetic and cultural ideals which require the constitution of the idea of white supremacy." Cornel West, *Prophesy Deliverance!* (Louisville: Westminster John Knox Press: 1982), 47.
3. Derrick Bell, *Faces at the Bottom of the Well: The Permanence of Racism* (New York: Basic Books, 1992).
4. Cornel West, *Race Matters* (Boston: Beacon Press, 1993), 17–31. See, also, Cornel West, *Prophesy Deliverance!*
5. Lewis Gordon, "The Unacknowledged Fourth Tradition: An Essay on Nihilism, Decadence, and the Black Intellectual Tradition in the Existential Pragmatic Thought of Cornel West," in *Cornel West: A Critical Reader*, ed. George Yancy (United Kingdom: Wiley Press, 1999), 53.
6. Frantz Fanon, *Black Skin; White Masks*, trans. Charles Lam Markmann (New York: Grove Press, 1967), 139.
7. Friedrich Nietzsche, *The Will to Power*, trans. Walter Kaufman (New York: Vintage Books, 1967), 12:12. Originally published (posthumously) in 1901.
8. Fanon, *Black Skin; White Masks*, 7.
9. Ibid. 8.
10. If man, as the existentialist conceives him, is indefinable, it is because at first he is nothing. Only afterward will he be something, and he himself will have made what he will be. . . . Not only is man what he conceives himself to be, but he is also only what he wills himself to be after this thrust toward existence.

Jean-Paul Sartre, *Existentialism and Human Emotions* (New York: Philosophical Library, 1957), 15.

11. Lewis Gordon, *Bad Faith and Antiblack Racism* (New York: Humanity Books), 140–159.
12. W. E. B. Du Bois, *The Souls of Black Folk* (England: Penguin, 1996).
13. Ibid. 7.
14. Frantz Fanon, *The Wretched of the Earth*, 182.
15. Fanon, *Black Skin; White Masks*, 8.
16. Ibid.
17. Ibid. 216–222.
18. Valentine Moulard-Leonard, "Revolutionary Becomings: Negritude's Anti-Humanist Humanism," *Human Studies* 28 (2005): 234.
19. Georg Wilhelm Friedrich Hegel, "A Geographical Basis for a World History," Appendix A, in *Lectures on the Philosophy of History* (Cambridge: Cambridge University Press, 1980), 176–177.
20. Moulard-Leonard, "Revolutionary Becomings," 235.
21. Georg Wilhelm Friedrich Hegel, *The Phenomenology of Mind*, trans. J.B. Baillie (New York: Dover Publications, 2012), 108–111. Originally published in 1807.

22. Hegel, *The Phenomenology of Mind*, 110.
23. Moulard-Leonard, "Revolutionary Becomings," 235.
24. Ibid.
25. Ibid.
26. Ibid.
27. Ibid. 220. See, footnote 8.
28. Oladipo Fashina, "Frantz Fanon and the Ethical Justification of Anti-Colonial Violence," *Social Theory and Practice* 15, no. 2, (Summer 1989): 179–213.
29. Fanon, *Black Skin; White Masks*, 216–217.
30. Fanon, *The Wretched of the Earth*, 50.
31. Black people, for instance, had been living and existing on the planet Earth for several hundred thousands of years before the first, phenotypically, "white" person evolved.
32. Fashina, "Frantz Fanon and the Ethical Justification," 187.
33. Fanon, *The Wretched of the Earth*, xiv.
34. Ibid. xivi.
35. Fashina, "Frantz Fanon and the Ethical Justification," 187.
36. Ibid. 189.
37. Ibid. 191.
38. Lewis Gordon, *Existentia Africana: Understanding Africana Existential Thought* (New York: Routledge, 2000), 48.
39. Frantz Fanon, *Toward the African Revolution* (New York: Grove Press, 1964), 44.
40. Fanon, *Black Skin; White Masks*, 218.
41. Ibid. 8.
42. Ibid. 114.
43. Ibid. 109.
44. Ibid.
45. Ibid. 121.
46. Fanon, *Toward the African Revolution*, 43.
47. Ibid. 34.
48. Ibid. 33–34.
49. Ibid. 40.
50. Fanon, *Black Skin; White Masks*, 120.
51. Fanon, *Toward the African Revolution*, 41.
52. Ibid. 33.
53. Ibid.
54. Ibid. 41.
55. Ibid. 42.
56. Ibid. 41.
57. Ibid. 41–42.
58. Ibid. 42.
59. Ibid.
60. Ibid.
61. Ibid.

62. Fanon, *Black Skin; White Masks*, 7.
63. Fanon, *Toward the African Revolution*, 42.
64. Fanon, *Black Skin; White Masks*, 222.
65. Frank Wilderson, III, "Biko and the Problematic of Presence," in *Biko Lives*, eds. Andile Mngxitama, Amanda Alexander, and Nigel C. Gibson (New York: Palgrave Macmillan, 2008), 95–114.
66. Wilderson, "Biko and the Problematic of Presence," 104–105.
67. Ibid.
68. Frank Wilderson, III, *Red, White &Black: Cinema and the Structure of United States of America Antagonisms* (Durham: Duke University Press, 2010).
69. Wilderson, *Red, White &Black*, 23.
70. Ibid. 55.
71. Ibid. 50.
72. Ibid. 215
73. Wilderson, "Biko and the Problematic of Presence," 105.
74. Ibid. 111.
75. Ibid.
76. Ibid.
77. Lewis Gordon, "Afro pessimism," *Contemp Polit Theory* 17 (2018), 106.
78. Marshall H. Stephen, "Political Life of Fungibility" *Theory & Event* 15, no. 3 (2013).
79. Fred Moten, The Case of Blackness, *Criticism* 50, no. 2 (Spring 2008): 177–218.
80. Moten, "The Case of Blackness," 185.
81. Jared Sexton, "The Social Life of Black Death," *InTensions* 5 (Fall/Winter 2011): 28–29.
82. Sexton, "The Social Life of Black Death," 28.
83. Ibid. 37.
84. Ibid. 34.
85. Ibid.
86. Ibid. 33–34.
87. Jared Sexton, "People-of-Color-Blindness: Notes on the Afterlife of Slavery," *Social Text* 28, no. 2/103 (2010): 31–56.
88. Sexton, "People-of-Color-Blindness," 47–48.
89. Ibid. 42.
90. Jared Sexton and Steve Martinot, "The Avant-Garde of White Supremacy," *Social Identities* 9, no. 2 (2003): 169–181.
91. Sexton and Steve Martinot, "The Avant-Garde of White Supremacy," 178.
92. Ibid. 172.
93. Achille Mbembe, "Necropolitics," *Public* Culture 15, no. 1 (Winter 2003): 11–40.
94. Here, he is drawing on Hannah Arendt's theorizing of presumed spaces within Nazi concentration camps. "[There] are no parallels . . . it stands outside of life and death." Mbembe, "Necropolitics," 12.
95. Ibid. 13.

96. Ibid. 14.
97. Ibid.
98. Mbembe, "On the Power of the False," 14, no. 3: 630.
99. Ibid. 630.
100. Ibid. 633–634.
101. Ibid. 634.
102. Ibid. 636.
103. Stephen Best and Saidiya Hartman, "Fugitive Justice," *Representations* 92, no. 1 (Fall 2005).
104. Best and Saidiya Hartman, "Fugitive Justice," 1.
105. Ibid.
106. Ibid. 2
107. Ibid. 3
108. Ibid. 5
109. Ibid. 7.
110. Ibid.
111. Ibid. 10.
112. Saidiya Hartman, *Scenes of Subjection: Terror, Slavery, and Self-Making in Nineteenth Century America* (New York: Oxford University Press, 1997).
113. Hartman, *Scenes of Subjection*, 11.
114. Ibid. 24.
115. Ibid. 35.
116. Ibid. 42.
117. Ibid. 43.
118. Ibid. 65.
119. Ibid. 206.
120. Gordon, "Afro pessimism."
121. Best and Saidiya Hartman, "Fugitive Justice," 9.
122. Fanon, *Black Skin; White Masks*, 3.
123. Ibid. 7.

Chapter 6

The Future
Black Nihilism, Hip-Hop, and Maturity

> Then came another generation, which shifted the question. Its writers and poets took enormous pains to explain to us that our values poorly matched the reality of their lives and that they could neither quite reject them nor integrate them. Roughly, this meant: You are making monsters out of us; your humanism wants us to be universal and your racist practices are differentiating us.[1]

They made a monster out of me
The monstrosity of locking me
Inside a mental box
without a lock or key
That's got to be
the cruelest, or the most absurd hypocrisy
Prophesy fulfilled;
The wills of the rotten seeds
Ill begotten, still
We rockin' these philosophies.[2]

In chapter 2, I demonstrated that the strong nihilist, or the "higher man," is also a pessimist.

> He rejects the optimism of the last man's metaphysically affirmed valuations of human meaning. The higher man goes through two stages: Initially, he is a pessimist who negates and destroys traditional values, then he becomes a strong nihilist, struggling to affirm and build newer values.

In chapter 4, I suggested that "having gone through the traditional stages of black optimism and black pessimism in weak black nihilism, strong black nihilism can emerge as an appropriate response to the white nihilism of antiblack racism, or at least one worth considering carefully." In the previous chapter, I suggested black pessimism and certain forms of weak black nihilism, *negritude* for example, can serve as developmental stages within strong black nihilistic processes. Here, I will consider black nihilism and antiblack racism in terms of its effects on black youth through a discussion of hip-hop music and culture, which, I argue, can be reflective of stages of maturity within a black nihilistic process. I will end by considering *Section 80* and *Damn* by the artist, Kendrick Lamar, as an "existentially dope" example of what I call, black nihilistic hip-hop music.[3]

Observing what can be called black nihilistic youth, and their chosen vehicles of symbolic expression, black nihilistic hip-hop music illuminates existential attitudes of large swathes of young black people growing, maturing, and attempting to produce values for blackness today. Black nihilistic youth, and black nihilistic hip-hop music, can be considered in terms of potential philosophical and political import for producing modes of valuing blackness in the twenty-first century. The seeds that would eventually germinate into hip-hop culture were planted during and after the Black American Civil Rights movements of the late 1960s. Ever since, hip-hop music and culture have dominated black youth aesthetic modes of expression in the United States. Throughout America, and the world, hip-hop culture has grown to be a massively popular lens of expression through which one can view the internal desires, ambitions, angsts, and frustrations, of many black youth. I am concerned with the struggles of black youth, today, against black invisibility and white nihilism, and these struggles can be apprehended through their artistic, especially musical and visual, productions. Antiblack racism presents a threat of existential annihilation to the category of black youth and their potential for a strong, healthy, maturation process. In particular, white nihilistic values promoting antiblack racism, as well as traditional black optimistic values renouncing it, provide distressing axiological contexts for strong black nihilistic youth maturation projects.

Like blues, swing, jazz, R&B, and funk music before it, hip-hop music emerged from cultural spaces of blackness. From early twentieth-century Folk, to Tin Pan Alley jazz, Southern, West coast, and Midwest blues, Rock and Roll, Race records, and R&B music of the 1950s and 1960s, to the Funk and Disco music of the late 1970s, popular black American music always emerged in relation to established axiological traditions wherein the philosophical import of these productions were routinely policed and/or denied. Originating as "underground" forms of expression, hip-hop produced radically subversive innovations within traditional techniques of music production. For example, by sampling, rearranging, and extending certain parts of previously recorded songs, it created new forms of musicality using elements whose meanings were already taken to be complete. Hip-hop music introduced radically new sounds and methods for creating innovative "beats," which were complemented by equally radical innovations in lyricism often evoking allegorical, dreamlike, imagery reflecting lived black realities in antiblack racist societies. Hip-hop culture, in other words, birthed the expression of a tragedy, the tragedies of black nihilistic youth at the dawn of the twenty-first century, which can be observed in the spirit of black nihilistic hip-hop music.

Hip-hop music is nihilistic in light of what it does to traditional musical forms; it selects, scratches, mixes, and remixes. It constructs new forms of musicality by transvaluing ideals in music production. Art reflects existential experiences shared by the occupants of its realities. Music, and poetry in particular, tend to be reflective of cultural ways of being that often indicate the social and political conditions inhabited or envisioned by the occupants of those realities. In thinking and writing about black nihilistic youth in the twenty-first century, it is an undeniable fact that much of the musical and poetic expressions there are reflective of struggles within voids of meaninglessness and nothingness precipitated by weak nihilism and antiblack racism, and, if we listen carefully, we can discern black pessimistic and potentially strong black nihilistic attempts at producing newer values for the meaning of black life.

Black nihilistic hip-hop music is reflective of the entire range of black nihilism, including black pessimism and weak nihilism. It is an aesthetic mode of production centered within experiences of black nihilism, which is, at first, a negative, pessimistic moment. The production of new kinds of values from the space of black pessimism, as shown in the previous chapter, is not an automatic result. In phenomenological terms, there is a concept of "apperception" that refers to something implied by a direct perception. So, if I'm looking at a house, I perceive the exterior of the house, but I apperceive the other side of the wall. I am suggesting that the negative perceptive moment of black pessimism *can* provide the "upheaval" necessary to apperceive positive formations of values. In this way, black nihilistic hip-hop music may directly reflect strong attempts at constructing new values, or it may directly reflect destruction of traditional values; often, there are elements of each displayed on a single song.

The term "hip-hop" historically references value productions of black American people born in and after the post–civil rights eras of the twentieth and twenty-first centuries.[4] In the 1970s, there was a major influx of dope, heroin, into black communities, and the seeds of hip-hop music began to form, in large part, reflecting the lived anguish and despair of black and brown youth enduring dilapidating social and economic conditions alongside massive amounts of underground pockets of accumulated, subversive, black wealth. There were young, black, rich, "hustlers," who were seriously "getting money" from illicit markets, while living, nonetheless, in and among the black and invisible. By the early 1980s, with the backing of funds from the "underground" economy, hip-hop emerged on the national stage, as a strong, youthful, black voice expressing black desires to reject black invisibility. "God is smilin' on you, but he's frownin' too / Because only God knows, what you'll go through."[5] These are lyrics from the biggest hip-hop song of 1982, "The Message," by Grandmaster Flash and the Furious Five. "So, don't push me / 'Cause I'm close to the edge / I'm trying not to lose my head."[6] The "message," was broadcast across America. It reflected an attempt to make undeniable, if not recognizable, the perspectives of a generation of youths navigating the pitfalls of antiblack racist institutions and white nihilistic values. It produced a sound that was musical, lyrical, poetic, and rooted in young, black, philosophical ruminations on life in America's post–Civil Rights era.

More than forty years have passed since "The Message" was broadcast. The seeds planted have long since germinated into the "hip-hop generation," and these generations of black people are now facing the question of what an adult version of hip-hop culture looks like. People born into this culture, or the "hip hop generationers," as Bakari Kitwana calls us, face the project of maturing within antiblack racist frameworks where possibilities for maturity become uniquely underdeveloped.[7] The question of growing up, or having grown up, in the hip-hop era begs another. What does it mean to "grow up"? What does it mean to become an adult? What is the role and meaning of the category of youth in relation to the existential spaces in which they grow? In this case, we must consider the maturation processes of black youth growing through spaces of black nihilism and antiblack racism.

As an original expression of dissatisfaction with the failures of American social and political institutions to address the existential needs of black life, hip-hop music, in part, displays pessimistic and nihilistic struggles of black youth facing white nihilistic ideals of antiblack racism. However, being situated in a pessimistic relationship with the weaknesses of traditional ideals does not necessarily lead to producing transvaluative modes of valuing. As we have seen, it is possible to oppose antiblack racism while promoting other weak nihilistic ideals in its place. We may be in the midst of a cultural shift where the limits of traditional white nihilistic and black optimistic ideals are being exhausted; perhaps this is the "message" of black nihilistic hip-hop music. Black nihilistic hip-hop music necessarily involves a form of black pessimism, which tends to bring an increase in exposure to weak nihilistic value structures. There is no shortage of appeals to black pessimistic and weak black nihilistic value structures in black nihilistic hip-hop music, which can include expressions of hedonistic desires for materialism and accumulation, alongside, perhaps, weak rejections of antiblack racism, which themselves more often belie attempts to evade black existential invisibility through appeals to economic success. Such forms of black pessimism are nonetheless driven by desires to value beyond the confines of white nihilism and antiblack racism; however, they fail. White nihilistic value structures and antiblack racist institutions have condemned the wills of countless numbers of black people, many of whom have been imprisoned, or killed by law enforcement agencies, for attempting such black pessimistic forms of resistance. Furthermore, the idea that adopting capitalistic values can save black people, or a black person, from an absurdly oppressive proximity to death and imprisonment is an increasingly untenable prospect. I will not lament certain forms of pessimism and weak black nihilism in black nihilistic youth, there is already enough of that. Instead, I want to consider their struggles for development in terms of existential maturity, or what amounts to resisting the values governing traditional ideals. I suggest considering ways in which weak nihilistic optimism contributes to the prevalence of weak nihilistic pessimism.

Traditionally black optimistic modes of valuing do not sufficiently address the lived realities of hip-hop generationers attempting to mature and produce values beyond weak nihilistic traditions. Hip-hop culture faces a problematic relationship with nihilism and maturity, perhaps, but the problem is often misstated in terms of them simply lacking the wisdom of traditional values, or put simply, a problem of being *immature* and failing to *grow up*. A discussion of the traditional notion of maturity sheds light on the subject. The term "mature" comes from the Latin term *maturus*, meaning "ripe," or having reached the most advanced stage in a process. Tom Meagher illustrates as follows:

> One imagines a banana sitting on a counter, "just ripening" as if maturation were something that "just happens." But the banana only matures through a relation with its environment: warmth and sunlight ripen it, whereas cold and darkness stifle it, leaving it green and starchy. Europe imagines itself as having ripened non-relationally, a mythic banana.[8]

Meagher's depiction of what I call (European) "Man's" imagining of himself can be read in terms of white nihilistic value processes, or the production of a "mythic banana." This myth functions as a Platonic Lie that black nihilistic youth reject. Nevertheless, the languages, symbols, and tools for philosophical and aesthetic expressions of Europe are finessed, ripped, stolen, reworked, and given new forms of meaning; some languages and symbols were scratched and effaced, some were discarded, others were repurposed and remixed, all were potentially considered in hopes of creating something that might yield fruit, life, despite originating in cold and darkness.

Imagine coming home and finding your child using your record player to spin records backwardly, intentionally scratching the records back and forth. Hearing the needle emit high-pitched frequencies as it scuffs against the vinyl, your first reaction might be that the child is ruining, or simply not valuing, musical tradition. It may be difficult, at first, for some to view the phenomenon as reflective of transcendence, and maturity, or to use the language of Jane Anna Gordon, to view the phenomenon as a form of *creolization*, where one undertakes a creative, and in this case, potentially aesthetically beautiful, eclecticism of parts, mechanisms, sources, and values, in this case, driving the birth of newer musical forms. The term *creolization* is developed in Jane Anna Gordon's work as a framework for understanding the fluid and shifting geographies of human thought and development in constructing "truth" and producing "value." Her work is fundamental for understanding ways in which Africana thought, for example, develops out of perspectives from the global south, east, west and north, in producing constantly evolving Human realities.[9] Existential maturity, on my view, is not a "final stage in a process," but rather a realization and embracement of the fluidity and constantly evolving nature of human reality, alongside desires to take one's place within the flow of Human values and ideals, which inherently involves notions of values as resultant from *creolization* processes, in Jane Anna Gordon's sense of the term. Hip-hop culture and music, from this perspective, are forms of *creolization* of traditional Western philosophical and aesthetic ideals. *Creolization* transvalues dominant languages and symbols into useful tools for black people fighting against the meaning of (white) Humanity in the antiblack racist world.

Black nihilistic maturity involves battling against black invisibility through attempts at creolizing the dominant tropes of antiblack racist societies. Here, black nihilistic maturity can be connected with the *creolizing* capacities of "subalterns" not supposed to have the "capacity for symbolic production" to perform such tasks, but nevertheless, they have "blended things supposed to be opposed (e.g., 'high' and 'low' culture, 'black' and 'white' folks) together."[10] Furthermore, according to Fred Lee, the process of *creolization* transforms "dominants and subordinates down to the very grammar and syntax of their social interactions. Creole societies forged symbolic frameworks out of fragments of shattered traditions, frameworks that transformed fragments (but not beyond recognition) into parts of new wholes."[11] Black nihilistic hip-hop music is a prime example of *creolization*, which can be heard as expressions of struggles and desires of black nihilistic youth for maturity. Black nihilistic hip-hop music offers a soundtrack for multiple generations of black youth, born after the modern American Civil Rights era, who are attempting to grow and mature, and perhaps, remix and revalue the meaning of blackness.

The problem of maturity in hip-hop is further exacerbated by its being, up to this point, primarily a youth-oriented mode of expression. However, there are now large demographics of adults around the world who have "grown up," in the nearly half a century since hip-hop first burst upon the scene as a distinct genre of music becoming a staple of everyday cultural life. Today, there are "hip-hop adults," and yet, being a movement originally rooted in the experiences of black youth, there persist problems with conflating what began as a black adolescent cultural form of expression with "black culture" itself. The phenomenon of fixing one dimension of cultural life, youth culture in particular, as a stand-in for the complexity and dynamism of black people, is a form of antiblack racism. Lewis Gordon's essay, "The Problem of Maturity in Hip Hop," for instance, demonstrates ways in which hip-hop productions are situated within larger contexts of antiblack racist denials of black humanity and adulthood.[12]

While there are undeniable exceptions, there is a fundamental problem concerning maturity in hip-hop music and culture, especially as it is portrayed within larger media contexts of antiblack racist societies; however, since antiblack racism fundamentally entails weak nihilistic systems of value attempting to delimit axiological parameters of humanity according to metaphysically affirmed idealizations of whiteness, that is, white nihilistic values, which regard themselves as synonymous with the activities of human phenomenal life, antiblack racists have constructed a (white) Human world in which only they are seen as existing as human, which also means that only they are capable of maturing. As Meagher put it as follows:

> Europe is viewed not as a relation to the world, a loose and evolving cultural formation emerging out of a peculiar and profoundly troubling history; it is, rather, imagined as a trans-historical substance, a thing that contains within itself those characteristics that make it a priori valuable, desirable, beneficent. Europe asserted itself as substance in denial of the relations that constituted it. It imagined its maturation as the entelechy of an imminent essence.[13]

The resulting imposition of black invisibility constitutes a situation of black nihilism that not only makes black life nearly impossible in many cases, but also completely eviscerates the existential category of black youth, and profoundly affects its maturation processes.

Black youth in an antiblack racist world are made to face problems of black invisibility and nihilism as children who are not yet fully developed. They are set to wrestle with some of the most despairing absurdities of human life, as children, within frameworks discursively and non-discursively opposed to the possibility of their strongly maturing through it. They are set to undergo the horrifying journeys of trying to find meaning through implosion and fragmentation from a young age. They are cast to deal with problems of black optimism, pessimism, weakness, and, if they can endure and strive, potentially, strong black nihilism.

If the meaning of black life finds itself resisting weak nihilistically fixed determinations of whiteness, then the space of black invisibility must be viewed as an assault not only on black capacities to produce meaning, but also on black capacities to transcend the value of given meanings and produce newer ones. If one cannot transcend meaning and produce newer values, one cannot grow. If one cannot grow, one cannot mature, and if one cannot grow and mature, one cannot become an adult. Paradoxically, if one cannot become an adult, then, tragically, one can never truly exist as a child. In other words, if one's humanity is demanded to exist as a nonexistence, then one's being a transcendent, fluid, for-itself, with the capacities of pre-reflection, reflection, self-determination, evaluation, judgment, that is, value production, growth, and maturity, become theoretically precluded. If one's humanity is theoretically precluded from these dimensions of growth and maturity, one can never become an adult, which, again, entails the tragic conclusion that one can never *truly* exist as a child.

Black children are not allowed to be children. Meagher's "banana" analogy can be extended to capture this point. "What makes bananas viable as a global export commodity is that they may be harvested in the tropics and then refrigerated to prevent their maturation prior to reaching market destinations. There is a commercial interest in delaying their maturity."[14] The analogy, applied to black youth, means they are "refrigerated," or frozen, while they are still young and developing, in order to prevent their "maturation prior to reaching market destinations." Alternatively, one could say, in the case of black youth, they are "forced ripe," and set to "spoil," or decay quickly. Here, black maturity functions paradoxically, it demands physical growth of the black body without accompanying developments of the mind, especially in terms of offering critiques of the (white) Human world and its underlying philosophies. Ask yourself, if you were a black youth of strong nihilistic will, beginning to pessimistically doubt the objective "goodness" of the values of your social world, which means, in part, recognizing its desire to reduce your mind to your body, that is, make you a commodity of sex, entertainment, and labor, and/or provide the statistical expectation that you will be destitute, dead, or in prison by the age of nineteen, what activities might you be engaged in as soon as adolescence permits? What philosophies might you produce? Might not you find yourself seeking to transcend all traditional boundaries in hopes of maximizing the potential of your expectantly limited life? What kinds of values might you value? Might you not have a couple of kids of your own already? Might you not also try and make as much money as possible, by any means possible? "Fuck minimum wage; I feel like I got minimum days."[15]

Antiblack racist societies depend upon white nihilistic values, which themselves depend upon an obliterating of the existential category of black adulthood, and by extension, black youth and maturity. It eradicates, eviscerates, and otherwise perverts the whole affair of human development existing within a single black body. It forces black youth, in particular, to wrestle with the very adult task of nihilistically dealing with erasure in a (white) Human world. Black children don't get to be children in antiblack racist worlds because this world seeks to deny black phenomenal existence entirely and utterly, big and small, young and old.

Running up against these sorts of existential limitations, "breaking down," and then attempting to live and value in spite of them, that is, nihilism, is the domain of adult "responsibility." Under the rubric of white nihilistic values, (European) "Man" sets himself up to be a universal "adult," lording over the lives of perpetually infantilized black people as "children." Hence, the project of maturity faced by black youth, in particular, in antiblack racist societies involves facing "adults" who desire the preclusion of their maturity. Adults are the gatekeepers of values in the world; they provide the boundaries and contexts of meaning within which it makes sense to be a child, wherein children are enabled to understand themselves as valuable or not, "good" or "bad." Adults are responsible for establishing the boundaries of goodness and badness in ways that children are not. They are responsible for setting the poles governing these categories, which means they are responsible for determining, shifting, augmenting, eradicating, sustaining, and so on the valuative frameworks within which the meaning of values operate. Children who are set to mature into strong adults are enabled to eventually assume adult responsibility over the poles of valuing, for determining the worth and the meaning of their values. That is, children who grow into adults, on my view, are enabled to raise and answer for themselves questions concerning the value of traditional values. They become "adults," by virtue of becoming determiners of values and boundaries for subsequent generations of people to find themselves within. However, white nihilistic conceptions of (European) "Man" attempt to preclude such notions of black maturity by enforcing institutions that rely on values desiring black invisibility. It is in this sense that black "grown-ups" never get to truly function as adults in an antiblack racist world because their perspectives are treated as "childlike," or nonexistent, *and* black children never get to truly function as children because they are made to prematurely wrestle with adult existential affairs of black invisibility and nihilism. In the processes of developing from childhood to adulthood, black people face continual reinforcing of the antiblack racist trope that black people have nothing meaningful to contribute to Humanity, especially at the level of theoretical critique.

As Meagher points out in his analysis of maturity, "The child faces an imperative to develop as a moral agent, but a general relief from the anguish of adult responsibilities facilitates this."[16] Thus, children encounter worlds in which "the domains of its responsibility are clearly demarcated. An adult, by contrast, is responsible for responsibilities: adults engage in projects through which burdens and duties accrue and intensify."[17] Maturity, on this view, requires attempting to assume "responsibility" for a world of values already produced, populated, and filled by others. "Immaturity," here, is an uncritical acquiescence or rejection of traditional ideals, such as, for example, the moral poles of "goodness" or "badness," ordering the value structures of one's society. It is not that one cannot maintain traditions, certain ideals have emerged and persisted for good reasons. Rather, the point is that to uncritically maintain traditions without raising the question of the relevance of certain ideals for meeting contemporary needs, on my view, is a failure to existentially "grow up." In other words, one may conclude that traditions and ideals rooted in weak nihilism, and white nihilism, are forms of existential immaturity, reflecting what Simone De Beauvoir called the "spirit of seriousness." "This means that the world in which he lives is a serious world, since the characteristic of the spirit of seriousness is to consider values as ready-made things."[18] Or, to use Meagher's words, antiblack racism and white nihilism exhibit a form of the spirit of seriousness, which is "a way of regarding values as ready-made such that one is, ultimately, not responsible for what one values. One becomes responsible for following rules, but not for proposing, debating, or refashioning them."[19]

Black nihilistic youth of the hip-hop generation face struggles through maturity in a white nihilistic, antiblack racist context. Here, the traditions of their oppressors *and* their forbearers, all the grown-ups involved, appear exhausted. We are left facing traditional whiteness and traditional blackness as forms of weak nihilism, as a form of immaturity. Black nihilistic youth, who were to be "seen, and not heard," are attempting to be both "seen" and "heard." Black nihilism, as reflected through hip-hop music, can be seen, and heard, as dealing with problems of maturity that have the potential to create open-ended, *creolized*, projects of value construction, attempts to move forward, toward "ever-greater responsibilities, toward an intensification of the anguish and shame that accompany adult accountability." I see and hear black nihilistic hip-hop music as a thrilling, anguished filled, reflection of multiple dimensions of the black nihilistic situation encountered by black youth in their struggles with maturity:

> This anguish is also an exhilaration, for where immaturity seeks to quarantine my freedom from the possibility of contamination by the projects of others,

it retards and diminishes it in so doing; maturity intensifies the anguish of responsibility precisely because it liberates me to be touched by others, to be responsible for how I respond to a world that is not under my control but that will bear my influence.[20]

Strong black nihilism entails a desire to become existentially mature, which in this context, requires fighting to be seen and heard as a black perspective who is contributing to the development of the values of Humanity. Black youth attempting to mature and become adults in this way, who attempt to value freely and strongly, *creolize* the traditions of white nihilism and black optimism. They often face massive opposition and are tragically set to fail in light of their most gallant efforts.

The project of black existential freedom in an antiblack racist society is an inherently dangerous political undertaking requiring adult levels of maturity and resilience to sustain itself, given that it challenges core values on which Western political life is built. For this reason, black political struggles against antiblack racism tend to almost always get met, on various levels, with white dismissal, resistance, hostility, or dangerous intensifications of desires for black invisibility, death, all of which is too much to allow young, maturing, black consciousnesses to face alone:

> The vulnerability of political life can be crushing. Adults are responsible for overcoming its slings and arrows, but such outrageous fortune can overwhelm a child and retard maturation. Children may need to be protected from the shame that political activity necessitates: to be political is to "see" oneself being "seen," to face the insecurity of accountability to others. Adult life demands such shame.[21]

Challenging limitations, dreaming of fantastic futures and worlds in anticipation of assuming ownership over this one, is the domain of youth. Wading and navigating through the murky, shitty, waters of our society's politics is the shameful task of us adults. Children, it is said, are not demanded to suffer such shame; but black children in antiblack racist worlds don't get to be children. As it goes, neither will they get to be *seen* as "adults." Whose world is this? If I am black, and if I am young and black in particular, not mine, not ours, unless I make it so. It is a world that belongs to grown-ups who appeared to have no questions in the face of traditions, and so many who challenged nothing when it came to presumptions of white superiority; antiblack racist societies are maintained by generations of white acquiescence, by generations of "good (white) boys" and "good (white) girls."

Black children don't get to exist as children in antiblack racist societies because the notion of black youth could only be such in relation to discursive frameworks where there are healthy understandings of what it means to be a black adult. However, discursive frameworks for self-determined, existentially free, and mature conceptions of blackness are precisely what white nihilism and antiblack racism seek to eviscerate. Kill the seed before it grows.

Antiblack racism infects the developmental processes inherent in the maturation of black youth by distorting fundamental relationships with freedom, possibilities of choice, and eventual self-determinations of value, which are otherwise germane to the category of youth. Black youth are demanded to "grow up," in a sense that precludes them from ever becoming "adults." They face a host of objectifying and dehumanizing realities implicit to the lived experiences of blackness, while too often being instructed to remain existentially immature in acquiescing to a world of imposed traditions. It is according to these realities that many black youths have grown in a hip-hop era where they continue to witness the knee of (European) "Man" being pressed against the necks of their fathers and mothers, their black "grownups." Black nihilistic hip-hop youth have taken a defiant, vulgar, oppositional stance in response to this reality. They thus reject all traditional offers of black optimism in response to antiblack racism, especially those that would kneel in prayer, submission, or fellowship, alongside people with white nihilistic desires.

Black children ought to be positioned to eventually assume the role of critical engagement, devaluing and transvaluing, and developing newer values, beyond white nihilistic values of antiblack racism. They ought to be encouraged to strongly grow and mature through black nihilism, not condemned for working their way through it; they are already facing a society that is theoretically and politically opposed to their healthy mature development. They ought to be protected from premature exposure to implosive dimensions of "adult" political struggles. However, if protecting children from certain forms of political responsibility is the goal, then "a danger lurks: the polis that excludes children in order not to hear them is thereby pursuing its decreolization."[22] Here *decreolization* is being used to describe mechanisms seeking to reduce the dynamism of Human meaning by denying its interrelational and intersubjective dimensions, or what I call, weak nihilism. Antiblack racist(s), today, advocate for an ironic form of *decreolization*, which seeks to deny *creolized* perspectives on Human life emergent from cultural blends occurring, at least, since modern European colonial conquest of the "New World."

European colonial conquest imposed white nihilistic philosophies and erected antiblack racist institutions imposing vicious "savagery" on black and brown civilizations, which presupposed the idea that Human perspectives were introduced into the "New Worlds" each time Europeans landed on its shores. However, unless one plans on remaining forever subject to the existential desires and political whims of weak nihilism, then one must recognize that "political life demands of adults that they be shaped by the demands of generations to come; the needs of the future must creolize the plans of the present."²³ In other words, black nihilistic youth expressions, and the sometimes vulgar and blunt nature through which they tend to articulate themselves, should not be summarily dismissed:

> [Maturity cannot] reasonably be taken as a prerequisite for political participation, for such is a recipe for elders to sit shamelessly while they mortgage children's future. Rather, that adults face political responsibility demands maturity of them; that children must prepare for adulthood means they may be protected from being political but must be given means to become political. Both the adult's project of meeting this demand and the child's project of preparing for it require, in turn, openness to anguished and exhilarating processes.²⁴

This quote can be extended, through my analysis, to include a call for strong black nihilistic maturity, understood as a black nihilistic form of *creolization* is necessary for the project of black existential freedom.

On God: Black Nihilism and Traditional Black Christianity

Perhaps the most insidious element of antiblack racism and white nihilism is the burden it places on the project of black maturity through black invisibility, which amounts to perverse desires to suck black children into the adult worlds of pessimism and nihilism, for the purpose of making them fodder for the enjoyment and pleasure of the (white) Human world. Taking this point seriously while seeking to understand the travails involved in attempting to value beyond weak nihilistic traditions may explain, for instance, the rejection of black traditionalism and Christianity that Cornel West identified in his analysis of black nihilistic youth in America. As I demonstrated in chapter 4, one traditional response to antiblack racism in America has been a black optimistic Christian "leap of faith in God or its description of what it is to be a person, what one should hope for and how one ought to act." However, West admits, "all these descriptions bear the stamp of interpreters, the social and personal problems they faced, and the particular . . . solutions they offered."²⁵ He concedes that the black American Christian view reflects "personal" interpretations of black existence and what it means to struggle against antiblack racism alongside implicit commitments to a metaphysically affirmed basis for valuing humanity. He also conceded, however, that he did not fully understand why this program was, today, rejected by black nihilistic youth in America, or as he put it, "why the cultural structures that once sustained black life in America are no longer able to fend off the nihilistic threat."[26] Perhaps the reason is that, as a traditional black optimist, he sought to discourage nihilism in black youth by describing its possibilities solely in terms of moral debauchery and destructiveness, or an unrestricting of human will that ends in radical annihilation of self and others. Perhaps it is because this view does not see or hear the vulgarity, defiance, and processes of devaluation, what may properly be called, black pessimism, there, as reflective of developments of maturity aspiring to value beyond traditional black optimistic ideals. Traditional black optimists tend to treat black nihilistic youth as if they are valueless peoples whose valuelessness is a function of their rejection of ultimate sources of value. They tend to describe black nihilistic youth as criminally minded individuals without moral qualms, driven by capitalistic values toward a will for destruction.[27] Capitalistic market-moralities, antiblack racism, existential invisibility, and not being grounded in traditional values, according to them, creates nihilistic black youth, or a condition that requires reflection on the meaning of a "possible triumph of the nihilistic threat in black America," according to Cornel West.[28]

I read what it means for the nihilistic threat in black America to "triumph," differently. From my perspective, going through stages of black pessimism and nihilism may potentially lead to strong black nihilism; we ought to encourage black pessimistic and weak nihilistic youth to complete the strong black nihilistic journey. Strong black nihilism is the ability to insist upon oneself as a source of values in ways that reflect understandings of existential freedom and responsibility for oneself and others in constructing Human reality. On my view, black existential freedom, responsibility, and maturity, that is, strong black nihilism, is the recipe for "triumph" over white nihilism and antiblack racism, and not, as some traditionalist's might think, a recipe for the triumph of antiblack racism. The processes of black nihilism can be developed into an honest and open confrontation with inherent contradictions and interdependencies of human nature, which in this case are blackness and whiteness, that may encourage recognition of the mutual freedom and incompleteness that each of us have in constructing our world. All of this, however, requires existential maturity.

What is also required is a recognition that our shared responsibilities for constructing values in the Human world involves processes by which some of us must work our way through struggles of black nihilism. Yet, this should be allowed because of black nihilism's potential to produce healthy and mature responses to antiblack racism. Black nihilism involves insisting on the values of freedom and responsibility in the face of its denials, but it may require going through stages of black pessimistic nihilism and/or weak black nihilism. Simple obsessions with pleasure, and capitalistic materialism, for example, are not directly reflective of strong black nihilism, or maturity, but neither are they exhaustive of the potentials of pessimism and weak forms of black nihilism. On my view, simple desires for hedonistic pleasures are destined for exhaustion and boredom, which are tropes of pessimism, as Schopenhauer wrote extensively on regarding the futility of human desire, especially in the form of pleasure. However, this stage of pessimism is not all there is to the potentialities of black nihilism. Collapsing black nihilism into hedonism, valuelessness, or as suffering from something "like alcohol and drug addiction . . . a disease of the soul" must be rejected. All forms of nihilism are not like "addictions" that must be overcome, although some are.

My position on black nihilism and antiblack racism is that traditional values undergirding antiblack racism, as well as black optimistic traditions of response, ought to be ultimately rejected by black nihilistic youth as weak. Traditional black Christianity, for example, does not transvalue the weak nihilistic modes of valuing constituting the modern category of the (white) Human being informing antiblack racism, it only rejects its antiblack racist moral and political conclusions. I have tried to show that valuing weak nihilistic ideals distorts the inherent strength of freedom in human phenomenal capacities to creatively construct strong values into forms of weakness that ultimately bear the "stamp of interpreters" who appear to harbor moral resentment against the human existential condition. Trying to grow, mature, and redetermine the meaning of their black existence, but finding it absurd to rely on white nihilistic, antiblack racist, and black optimistic traditions, is the nihilistic situation faced by many black youth in the twenty-first century.

Black youth in antiblack racist societies are encouraged to be weak from multiple directions. Black nihilistic youth attempting to value against antiblack racism are left to struggle within a world that denies them on two fronts. They wrestle with impediments from white nihilistic value structures, as well as admonishments from black optimistic traditions. Traditional black optimists, on my view, respond to the absurdities of black life by trying to deny them. They proceed to wrongly treat black nihilistic youth *as* an absurdity of black life. That is, antiblack racist's respond to black nihilistic youth by attempting to deny, arrest, eradicate, or erase them, and traditional black optimists respond by attempting to shame, guilt, slander, or undermine them. Nothing is left for black nihilistic youth attempting to insist upon the value of themselves outside of a defiant rejection of both. Strong nihilists, on my view, seek a criterion for healthily embracing and persevering through the absurdities of the human existential condition. In other words, if antiblack racism presents an absurd, inherently weak, white nihilistic, world of pre-given values that black life must struggle to make itself meaningful in spite of, then strong black nihilism, and not weak black nihilism, may be a better disposition from which to respond.

Strong black nihilism and existential maturity involve a commitment to valuing humanity in terms of renouncing metaphysically affirmed ideals as bases where public and political affairs are concerned. It also involves attempting to construct strong nihilistic conceptions of humanity wherein the value of each human consciousness is understood in fundamentally, mutually, and reciprocally, acknowledged terms as respected bearers (or future bearer) of "responsibility" for the world: a determiner in the process of constructing Human realities. However, this means augmenting the final lines of West's chapter on black nihilism where he beckoned for black leadership to have "the audacity to take the nihilistic threat by its neck and turn back its deadly assaults."[29] Perhaps we should replace "turn back" with "transcend" and "deadly" with "weak." Black leadership must have the audacity to take the nihilistic threat and *transcend* its *weak* assaults. Black leadership must have the audacity to become strong black nihilists. Strong black nihilism attempts to transcend white nihilism and antiblack racism. Strong black nihilism is not something to be turned back or rejected; it is something to be developed and fostered in the face of white nihilism. It is something worth encouraging black youth to embrace, however, this point can be missed if one conflates black nihilism with black pessimism. Pessimism involves realizing the fall of decadent traditions of values; nihilism involves attempting to value in light of pessimism. It is a mistake to conflate nihilism with pessimism. Such a mistake can lead to misreading signs of potentially developing strong black nihilistic responses to antiblack racism. Misreading the signs may also lead to not recognizing strong black nihilism as a philosophical disposition against decadent traditional values, which can be a productive outcome of pessimistic and nihilistic processes. Instead, consider black pessimism in terms of its potential to lead to strong black nihilism. Perhaps black pessimistic and nihilistic youth have not lost the armor of their traditional values and are now working through the processes of forging new weapons. Cornel West said, "The genius of our black foremothers and forefathers was to create powerful buffers to ward off the nihilistic threat, to equip black people with cultural armor to beat back the demons of hopelessness."[30] Perhaps, black nihilistic youth are making radical use of their traditional "armor." The strength and vitality of youth lies in its capacity to value beyond tradition.

In other places, I have advocated for serious consideration of analyses of blackness seeking to produce values beyond traditions of black optimism and pessimism. In an essay entitled, "Beyond Tradition," I argue for the need to consider the role of nihilism in reflecting on what it means to value blackness anew in the twenty-first century.[31] In another essay entitled, "The New Wave: Hip Hop Adults," I argue for the need to create spaces for nurturing and facilitating the development of strong nihilistic black youth through engagements with their musical and artistic productions.[32] Traditions help to protect children within the space of youth, but if youth are to mature into adults, they must be taught to assume "responsibility" as evaluators of traditions and determiners of the values. In this sense, black nihilistic youth should not be viewed as having lost traditional values; they should be viewed as youths maturing in ways that have potentially devalued traditional values. West's traditional black Christian optimism, for example, cannot accommodate such a distinction because of its Kierkegaardian commitments; there, any devaluation of Christ as a source of values is dreadful. However, on my view, traditional black optimistic Christian ideals and values are themselves, often dreadful, and indicative of existential immaturity. Furthermore, black devaluation of values is, strictly speaking, pessimism. As a black pessimist, one can be weak nihilistic, in terms of valuing not valuing; but one cannot, as traditional black optimist purports, be nihilistic in terms of not having values; that is impossible. Black pessimistic and nihilistic youth ought to be read as struggling to mature, that is, produce values outside of weak nihilism, in the face of antiblack racist and black optimistic traditions of resistance. The point is not to question the loss or retention of traditional values in black nihilistic youth, but to understand the processes of devaluation and transvaluation being displayed.

I do not take the position that nihilism in black youth is a problem of a lack of values. Rather, I believe nihilistic youth are engaged in processes of devaluation and inversion of traditional values. The preponderance of Christian symbology, crucifixes, praying hands, and so on, highly visible in the form of creatively augmented neck, face, arm, and torso tattoos, jewelry, clothing, and so on depicting a suffering Christ, for instance, are commonplace; they are semiotic embodiments and testaments to black nihilistic inversions of traditional Christian ideals. The phrase "on God . . ." has literally become a commonly used colloquial expression of black nihilistic hip-hop youth for affirming even the most mundane and trivial elements of their individual will.

Hip-hop adults, today, many of whom are rearing children and young adults of their own, are poised to defiantly, and vulgarly, challenge and assume responsibility over societies traditionally premised upon them being erased or relegated to the role of perpetual children. What may have behooved previous generations of black people to maintain a variety of traditionally optimistic beliefs as to why black liberation from antiblack racist oppression may be ordained, today, is viewed from black pessimistic and nihilistic perspectives to have become exhausted; they have run their course. Those ideals are now being devalued and inverted by black nihilistic youth, and nowhere is this more evident than in black nihilistic hip-hop music, where considerations of the meaning of blackness are prevalent.

Black Nihilistic Hip-Hop Music

Similar to Lucius Outlaw's arguments in "Against the Grain of Modernity: The Politics of Difference and the Conservation of Race," which addressed the need to retain race languages and certain discursive frameworks for blackness in spite of the universalistic languages of modern Enlightenment thought, hip-hop music and culture can be seen as a vehicle for "going against the grain," of traditional Enlightenment forms of value and thought originating in black youth experiences, which seek to make use of traditional Western ideals for the purposes of constructing radically newer forms of reality. Outlaw argued that one must be careful not to throw the proverbial "baby out with the bath water," when it comes to considering Western discursive tools for thinking against the grain of modernity in producing Human understandings.[33] In the same vein of going against the grain, hip-hop music and culture originated as an attempt to devalue and produce countervalues for traditional meanings of blackness, youth, and maturity. Black nihilistic youth live traditional facts of blackness in ways that remain in need of further articulation; but what is clear, at least to me, is that whatever else might be said of black American life more than half a century after the signing of modern American Civil Rights Bills, this era has been demarcated by the birth and growth of the hip-hop generation, and it has been a period of marked black nihilism.

What signs might indicate struggles of maturity in a direction toward black pessimistic understandings of traditional modes of American orderings of reality, which may lead to potential strong nihilistic responses to antiblack racism? What would those horns, strings, and drums sound like? What is the musical key of strong black nihilism? What is its tone? What kinds of melodies might announce the ominous coming of newer ways of black being, violently scratching against the weaknesses of whiteness and antiblack racism? What kind of lyrics might announce a coming of newer values for blackness? Hip-hop music; it has announced itself as a loudly persistent, base-filled, thumping genre that both symbolizes the decadence of modern Western ideals alongside hope-filled aspirations of transvaluation and new possibilities for worlds to come.

The music of Kendrick Lamar captures many of the dimensions of black nihilism that I am describing. His albums, *Damn* and *Section 80*, display travails of black youth facing horrors of black invisibility while attempting to mature and grow. He depicts intoxicating ascents, and sobering crashes, as he reports tales of trying to value from the zone of nonbeing, as a youth, facing opposition from traditional white nihilists and traditional black optimists. Frantz Fanon's depictions of such travails are captured by his chapter on the "lived experiences of blackness," in *Black Skin; White Masks* (1952). Fanon suggested that through battles of resistance there comes to be a movement of consciousness, which brings both the black and the white back in touch with their humanity. Fanon referred to the violence, and vulgarity, inherently involved in rejecting antiblack racism and white nihilistic values. He acknowledged the necessarily disruptive element black humanity carries along with it in antiblack racist environments. Mature black humanity is theoretically outlawed by the Western world. Raising critical inquiries concerning the weak nihilistic status of (white) Humanist discourses implies a violent offense. It is an alleged attacking of the innocence and purity of whiteness, a condemning of the objectively "good." In a society that stands to, quite literally, "lose the world," if such condemnation is permitted, any, and all, attempts to criticize the philosophies of (European) "Man" are deemed necessarily vulgar and violent.[34]

Kendrick's *Section 80* begins with an explicitly vulgar and violent rejection of traditional conceptions of race and ethnicity. The first scene in the album announces, "I recognize all of you, every creed and color. With that being said: Fuck your ethnicity!"[35] Kendrick elaborates, "Now, I don't give a fuck if you're black, white, Asian, Hispanic, god damn it! It don't mean shit to me, fuck your ethnicity."[36] He sends out a call to black pessimistic and nihilistic youth, and anyone listening is given sound advice: "Everybody throw your hands up high; if you don't give a fuck, throw your hands up high." One is being called to anticipate an exhilarating, anguished, angst filled journey for which strength and maturity demand "letting go" of the security of traditional ideals. I imagine the angst of being on a roller coaster that has just begun moving and knowing that subduing the anguish of my fears involves me being willing to not "give a fuck," to "throw my hands up high," during the scariest ascents and descents. What follows is a harmonious, melody-filled, tragic, scary, but beautiful, musical and lyrical journey through the mind and thoughts of one of America's most gifted black nihilistic hip-hop artists. *Section 80* symphonically offers lyrical testaments to the travails and struggles of black nihilistic youth attempting to grow and mature. Kendrick honors these experiences, and hip-hop music in general, as a vehicle for transformation, for going against the grain of whiteness and antiblack racism, which, according to him, "saved my life."[37]

As an artistic project, the varied themes of *Section 80* go beyond exclusive commentary on race. However, the project's countless allusions to problems of black nihilism and maturity is undeniable. For example, when Kendrick says, "I'm easily pedaling / with the speed of a lightning bolt / as a kid I killed two adults / I'm too advanced / I lived my twenties at two years old / The wiser man / Truth be told, I'm like 87," he offers lyrical support for my theorization that nihilistic black youth are producing values in ways that devalue traditional conceptions of black "adulthood."[38] He clearly performs a devaluation of traditional black optimistic ideals, which in this case is represented through a blurring of the lines of distinction within black Christian moral and ethical thought, when he says, "Wicked as eighty reverends / in a pool of fire with devils holding hands / From a distance don't know which one is the Christian / Damn."[39] He informs the listener that, from his perspective, the ideals of black Christianity, as they relate to traditional conceptions of black maturity, are, at least, questionable. He grips the listener and drags them downward, through rings of black pessimism, where devaluation of traditional black and white values is the order of the day. This is a path black nihilists take in route to facing "adult" problems of producing newer meanings for one's life. Kendrick laments the situation of black nihilistic youth having to raise themselves. "Who can I trust in 2012 / nobody, not even 'myself.'"

The black nihilistic undertones of *Section 80* are, perhaps, best displayed on the song, "A.D.H.D." There, it sounds as if Kendrick is directly responding to traditional admonishments of black Christianity. "Uh, uh . . . fuck that / Eight doobies to the face."[40] Here, Kendrick provides lyrical support for my theorization that the predicament of black nihilistic youth is one in which their "age don't exist," because they are situated as neither children nor adults. "Got a high tolerance when your age don't exist."[41] He elucidates this predicament and its seductive calls for "not giving a fuck," or "throwing your hands up high," and for displaying a high tolerance, or strength, necessary for dealing with that which is intoxicatingly absurd. Kendrick drops us right in the middle of this dizzying spell. "Man, I swear my nigga trippin' off that shit again."[42] He describes youth struggling with nihilistic tolerance. He paints a picture describing him picking his friend up and sitting him in cold water while ordering someone to bring Vicodin to counter nausea. He explains that this is brought on by a feeling that one feels every day, including today, that no one relates to the struggles of black youth and, outside of this demographic, they are all alone. "Cause you are . . . you are / A loner . . . loner."[43] Seeking strength from alternative sources, including potions and herbs, alongside adamant, defiant attitudes of "not giving a fuck," mixing to create a dangerously combustible recipe of attitudinal response to their situation, Kendrick simply states, "Marijuana endorphins make you stronger / Stronger."[44] There is an ominous sense of the (white) Human world's meaninglessness, a sensing of the decadence of decayed ideals that is displayed in Kendrick's philosophical poetry, which is swiftly followed by a resolute determination: "Our lives is caught up in the daily superstition / The world is 'bout to end / Who gives a fuck? We never do listen."[45]

Black nihilistic youth desires to be "stronger" while undergoing pessimistic descent is captured in Kendrick's depiction. The essence of black nihilistic youth struggles through vulgar processes of devaluation are brought to life through his poeticism. The song, "Chapter Six," is a slow burning repetition of a black pessimistic chant. "Riding with the boys and girls and we're high /

All we want to do is have a good time / Young, wild, and reckless is how we live life / Pray that we make it to twenty-one."[46] "Chapter Six" sets up a blunter depiction of black nihilistic youth singing out their pessimistic frustrations. In the song entitled "Ronald Reagan Era," Kendrick makes it clear: black youth are "far from good / Not good from far."[47] That illusory, fugitive, experience of freedom, sometimes, rests in fleeting moments of contentment, compliments of a cold beer and big spliff. "We don't give a fuck! / Drink my 40 oz. of 'freedom' while I roll my blunt / Cause the kids just ain't alright."[48] Kendrick continues, "Just ride with me, just die with me. . . . When you fight, don't fight fair / 'Cause you'll never win."[49] "The Reagan Era" displays pessimistic determinations of black nihilistic youth to "not fight fair," in proximities to death and erasure. Black nihilistic youth understand the need to fight in response to an unfair war, which they know they may "never win."

In "Poe Man's Dream" Kendrick, again, depicts frustrations of black nihilistic youth with traditional black optimistic value structures. He further conjures melodious waves of pessimistic reprieve for living and smoking "good." He invokes a conception of "goodness" radically altered from traditional understandings. Smoking "good" means smoking good weed. He reflects black nihilistic youth's pessimistic struggles to make "good" out of absurd circumstances when he says, "I used to want to see the penitentiary, way after Elementary / thought it was cool to look the judge in his face when he sentenced me."[50] He offered an encompassing, vividly detailed, depiction of the slippery terrain of black nihilistic youth struggles. Kendrick displays angst and vulnerability in existing as a black youth growing in a world of erased black adults. "My Mama is stressing, my daddy tired / I need me a weapon." The weapons sought, he realizes, he must forge for himself. The development of black nihilistic weapons requires moving through pessimistic attitudes toward traditional black optimism. This is reflected when Kendrick says, "Every minute, hour, and second / ministers try / to save me; how am I going to listen / when I can't even hear God?" This line is a direct rejection of traditional Christian metaphysical ideals. The inability to "hear" God from the existential zone of nonbeing, wherein black consciousness is disconnected from knowledge and wisdom of the source of universal value, that is, God, means black youth reject the value of optimistic traditions of black Christianity. This rejection is based on a recognition of those traditions' failures to adequately devalue or transvalue weak nihilistic structures situating their reality. On this view, the traditionally optimistic nature of black Christianity is rejected and replaced by black pessimism and nihilism. Or in Kendrick's words, "Heaven or Hell / Base it all on my instincts / My hands dirty / You're worried 'bout mud in your sink." This line, in particular, reflects pessimistic attitudes of black nihilistic youth against traditional ideals of black Christianity.

Announcing that the axiological poles of "heaven and hell" are things that he must now determine the value for, Kendrick offers lyrical support for my theorization that black youth are prematurely set to assume the adult task of defining/defending the meaning of black existence without the aid of fallen traditions. He is forced, initially, to "base it all on my instincts." In the midst of this, black nihilistic youth face allegations of "sin" from traditional black Christians. However, in light of the previous discussion of *creolization*, traditional moral values of "sin" can be seen to depend upon ideals of purity that produce politically naive conceptions of maturity, freedom, and justice. The ideal of purity, which here includes piety and innocence, is, perhaps, a framework only befitting of children, those who are not yet "guilty" of having produced, evaluated, maintained, rejected, or otherwise assumed responsibility for the values governing their reality. The levels of maturity and responsibility being sought through Kendrick's confessional admission of "dirt on my hands" transcends the limits of traditional black Christian ideals, which results in a potential misreading of the processes of transformation undertaken. Kendrick reflects this when stating that they are worried about mud in their presumably white porcelain "sink."

Kendrick completes the imagery inverting traditional optimistic ideals of black adulthood by depicting defiant, vulgar, desires to transvalue traditional conceptions of blackness and maturity. This is a tragic sojourn where black youth seek to mature in a world of others, as a mutual source of value production, seeing endlessly into the universe of values, gazing, as a star does, through the cosmos. "I deal with you like my son / Stare at the Sun / And you'll be looking in my eyes, homie." He flat out says that he is going to deal with the traditional black optimistic perspective as immature, as his "son." How defiant! His critique of traditional black optimism gets summed up with "Stand for something or fall or for anything / And you're working with two left feet at the skating rink." Standing for something references a need to produce newer, and/or critically engage and radically alter certain traditions of meaning. Working with two left feet at the skating rink is a reference to the set up for blackness to "fall," or fail, in terms of freedom, maturity, and adulthood.

After being initially burst apart, the black nihilist proceeds to exhaust the limits of the antiblack racist society's traditions, at first, by attempting to live its credos of moralism and rationalism in good faith. Then, after being rejected on that front, the black nihilist is forced to attempt alternative conceptualizations of "value." A black pessimistic disposition against white nihilistic ideals, at this stage, is necessary, however, it is a disposition that is subject to the pitfalls of weak nihilism. Black pessimism and nihilism set the stage on which blacks are designed to fall, or collapse, into weak nihilism. *Section 80* can be read as a pessimistic attempt to devalue and invert the value of traditional white nihilistic ideals.

Frantz Fanon undergoes a similar black pessimistic descent in the first half of chapter five of *Black Skin; White Mask* entitled "The Lived Experiences of Blackness." There are important elements of Fanon's analysis there that offer insights into Kendrick's depictions of pessimism and black nihilistic youth. *Section 80* can be interpreted, from this perspective, as a testament to black pessimism that tests the limits of white nihilistic ideals. Fanon also demonstrated the theoretical limits of traditional black optimistic responses to antiblack racism.

Fanon addressed themes fundamental to the struggles for adulthood and maturity faced by black people in an antiblack society. He wrote as follows:

> I came into the world imbued with the world to find a meaning in things, my spirit filled with the desire to attain to the source of the world, and then I found that I was an object in the midst of other objects.[51]

> Sealed into that crushing objecthood, I turned beseechingly to others. Their attention was a liberation, running over my body suddenly abraded into nonbeing, endowing me once more with an agility that I had thought lost, and by taking me out of the world, restoring me to it. But just as I reached the other side, I stumbled, and the movements, the attitudes, the glances of the other fixed me there, in the sense in which a chemical solution is fixed by a dye. I was indignant; I demanded an explanation. Nothing happened. I burst apart. Now the fragments have been put together again by another self.[52]

Fanon described being sealed in a world of antiblackness ordered by weak nihilistic valuations of (white) Humanity, from which he must extricate himself, but through which he must confront his blackness as a shattered being, as a "thing" to be known, but never a perspective that produces knowledge. Living through this paradoxical predicament and attempting to strongly produce values for blackness in spite of existential invisibility is black nihilism. As Lewis Gordon, points out in *What Fanon Said* (2015), in the chapter entitled, "Living Experience, Embodying Possibility":

> Fanon announces the experience of a world that denies his inner life; he examines this supposed absence *from the point of view of his inner life*. The paradox of the black experience is thus raised: Black experience should not exist since Blacks should not have a point of view. Nonetheless, black experience is all that should exist since a Black's subjective life should not be able to transcend itself to the level of the intersubjective or the social. The prejudice is familiar: Black's live, at best, on the level of the particular, not the universal. Thus, black experience suffers from a failure to bridge the gap between subjective life and the world. It is an experience that is, according to racist logic, not experience.[53]

In other words, black youths are set to grow within antiblack racist frameworks that demand they interpret their life experiences in ways that theoretically preclude existential maturity. They are set to grow within a world that demands denying that black phenomenal life is partially constitutive of the intersubjective dimensions of Human value construction. This preclusion from black adulthood is described, through Fanon, by Gordon. In Gordon's words:

> Reaching to the social world, [Fanon] finds himself sealed in a world without reciprocity. He finds himself in his situation of epistemic closure. Epistemic closure is a moment of presumably complete knowledge of a phenomenon. Such presumed knowledge closes off efforts at further inquiry. The result is what we shall call *perverse anonymity* (Emphasis in original). Anonymity literally means to be nameless. Namelessness characterizes most generalizable features of the social world. It is usually characterized by the indefinite article, "a." One sees "a student" or "a passerby" or "a police officer" or a "man" or a "woman." In ordinary encounters, we admit limited knowledge of individuals who may occupy these roles or social identities. The encounters become skewed, however, when we presume complete knowledge by virtue of individuals who exemplify an identity. The schism between identity and being is destroyed, and the result is a necessary being, an over determined, "ontological" reality. To see someone this way is to close off possibilities. It takes the form of the command and the declaration instead of the interrogative; one does not, in other words, ask questions because one presumes that one already knows all there is that needs to be known. The person seen in this way is never spoken to, never queried, but simply spoken of, about and, at best, ordered with special words.[54]

Gordon's and Fanon's works support my theorization that the lived experiences of black youth generally entail a black nihilistic affair. Black phenomenal perspectives are demanded to function through a perverse form of anonymity, black invisibility, as "*a* black," or "*a* black youth," which becomes overdetermined at the level of possibilities for producing alternative meanings. The black pessimistic and nihilistic predicament, which Gordon describes as a "realization of a situation that stimulates an existential struggle against sedimented, dehumanized constructions," was described by Fanon when he wrote as follows:

> I was responsible at the same time for my body, for my race, for my ancestors. I subjected myself to an objective examination, I discovered my blackness, my ethnic characteristics; and I was battered down by Tom Toms, cannibalism, intellectual deficiency, fetishism, racial defects, slave ships. . . . On that day, completely dislocated, unable to be abroad with the other, the white man, who

unmercifully imprisoned me, I took myself far off from my own presence, far indeed, and made myself an object. What else could it be for me but in amputation, an excision, a hemorrhage that spattered my whole body with black blood? But I did not want this revision, this thematization. All I wanted was to be a man among other men. I wanted to come lithe and *young* into a world that was ours and to help build it together (Emphasis mine).[55]

Section 80 can be viewed as reflecting the same situation described here by Fanon. One becomes disillusioned by the white nihilism of antiblack racist values. One begins to reject the histories and traditions of societies dependent upon such ideals. As Gordon explains, "Although black's live in history, it seemed as though Blacks were invisible to it; Blacks seemed to be, as Hegel claimed in the introduction to his philosophy of history, patently not historical."[56] In light of these tragic realities, black nihilistic music attempt to make their voices "historical."

Another album by Kendrick Lamar, *Damn*, continues his black nihilistic trajectory, and finds parallel in the second half of chapter five, in Fanon's *Black Skin; White Masks*, as well as *The Wretched of the Earth* (1961). In *Black Skin; White Masks*, as Gordon describes, "Against reason and history," Fanon "attempted *poetic* (Emphasis in original) resistance, resistance on the level of affect." This was, perhaps, a reactively necessary move. Having found reason and morality in (European) "Man" limited, Fanon resorted to a form of mysticism, a traditionalism that predates European colonial encounters, which was a move against white nihilistic values, but nevertheless, entangled in weak nihilistic desires. Traditional black Christianity demonstrates a similar succumbing through its production of anti-racist forms of weak nihilistic blackness. Kendrick's broad and sweeping appeals to Afro-Judaism, in *Damn*, too, are ultimately, anti-racist appeals to weak nihilistic ideals. With that in mind, we should remember that Fanon's demonstrative reports of the limitations of weak black nihilistic responses to antiblack racism were the products of an extraordinarily mature, and philosophically gifted, black adult. He had the strength not only to undergo, but to analyze and report back the lived experiences of black nihilism. Kendrick's maturation process is still in development and being played out, publicly, on the global stage of hip-hop. I do not cite Kendrick's work, here, because he is necessarily a strong black nihilist who remains to be seen; I cite him because, in my opinion, he vividly and beautifully captures predicaments of black nihilistic struggles. Black nihilistic hip-hop music involves attempts at valuing through black pessimism that, often, requires weak nihilism as a stage to be worked through. The question of whether Kendrick Lamar, as a black nihilistic hip-hop artist, is a strong black nihilist or not is not important for this analysis. What is of primary importance, here, are the descriptions of black nihilism found in *Section 80* and *Damn*.

The existential problems that *Damn* reflects are struggles of maturing black subjectivities facing weak nihilistic pitfalls of tradition. *Damn* portends a black nihilistic youth response to antiblack racism, white nihilism, and traditional black optimism. It is a prime example of black nihilistic hip-hop music whose themes capture black invisibility and creative responses. Black nihilistic hip-hop music addresses deeply held concerns of black nihilistic youth seeking to make their struggles visible, and audible, if not aesthetically beautiful. In this way black nihilistic music, and *Damn*, are what I call "existentially dope."[57] In general, the term "dope" should be read as an adjective describing something as interesting or intriguing. More precisely, the term is applicable to phenomena that are interesting in unexpected and/or transgressive ways, demonstrative of new thoughts and expressions. In other words, something that reflects creativity and ingenuity is "dope." Since, existentialism explores various ways human consciousness experiences and orders the meanings of its realities, black nihilistic music is "existentially dope" because it excites creative sensibilities concerning possibilities for alternative understandings and ordering of black existence.

In *Damn*, Kendrick's deployment of Afro-Jewish religious themes marks a significant shift from the reactive forms of black pessimism displayed in *Section 80*. After demonstrating the limits, and failures, of traditional black optimistic responses through radical inversion and devaluation, he attempts to construct alternative value structures. He does so by invoking religious and metaphysical narratives of traditional (African) Hebrew philosophies. He seeks to respond to the contemporary situation of black invisibility by endowing blackness with meaning from a source of value that historically predates the philosophies of (European) "Man." Here, Fanon's words should be borne in mind:

> This passionate quest for a national culture prior to the colonial era can be justified by the colonized intellectuals shared interest in stepping back and taking a hard look at the western culture in which they risk becoming ensnared. Fully aware they are in the process of losing themselves, and consequently of being lost to their people, these men work away with raging hearts and furious mind to renew contact with their people's oldest, inner essence, the farthest removed from colonial times.[58]

"I got so many theories and suspicions / I'm diagnosed with real nigga conditions / Today is the day I follow my intuition."[59] Kendrick specifically references "Yah," an ode to "Yahweh," the Hebrew God, in the song "Yah." His appeals not only explicitly renounce the modern racial label "black" but also appear to avoid serious critiques of histories of racial formation, and *creolization*, at least, since the modern Enlightenment period. "I'm an Israelite /

don't call me black no more / That word is only a color / it ain't facts no more."⁶⁰ His claim that he will no longer accept being called "black," as "that's just a color," is an inversion of the rigidity of the meaning of blackness in white nihilistic terms. Announcing it as "just a color" attempts to strip it of its traditional meaning. This, however, is rooted in a narrative that identifies the meaning of antiblack racist domination, and black suffering, as fated realities resulting from historical impieties of ancestors. The rejection of "black" as a self-descriptor in an antiblack racist world is, thus, a reactive move that is profoundly different from the active sense in which precolonial African populations didn't have a need, or a context, within which to refer to themselves as "black." At any rate, *Damn* delves into a region of black life where defiance, bravery, and strength are required to move through darkness. There are no guarantees of light, or impending day, but there remains something to make walking through the darkness worthwhile: nihilism; valuing in spite of darkness.

Sometimes, especially for black people in an antiblack racist society, things can suddenly become dark. This is captured in the opening sequence of *Damn*. Ominous music plays while Kendrick attempts to assist a blind lady in finding her lost items. Bang! She shoots him and smoothly explains that *he* has *lost* something, his innocence, his childhood, his life. What starts out as a good faith moralistic gesture quickly erupts into a tailspin of rejection, resentment, pessimism, and nihilism—a response to being rejected while having good faith. Kendrick attempted to help a blind American Lady Justice trying to find what she seems to have lost. But, when the seeming disability of antiblack racists to recognize black humanity is unveiled as a willed denial, in that moment, innocence and optimism dies. The pessimistic "fall" of black youth in antiblack racist societies begins with appeals to morality that get revealed as dangerously naive. The American Lady Justice beguiles black youth, teaching them from an early age that the blindness from which their invisibility proceeds is not the result of some bureaucratic oversight, but a function of white nihilistic desires.

Damn offers a plethora of subtle and not so subtle appeals to Afro-Judaic existential motifs alluding to precolonial understandings of metaphysical reality in hopes of providing a basis for responding to black invisibility, white nihilism, and antiblack racism. Perhaps the best example, however, is the song "Fear." There, Kendrick paints a picture chronicling three decades of black struggles with maturity within nihilistic circumstances. He tragically and vividly portrays this picture through hermeneutics displaying angsts and the inner turmoil of black nihilistic youth. He asks, "Why God? Why, God, do I gotta suffer?"⁶¹ His black pessimism is clearly heard: "Earth is no more, why don't you burn this motherfucker?"⁶² In another song, when he says, "I'm high now . . . I'm high now . . . / Life's a bitch, pull them panties to the side, now," his descriptive metaphors for antiblack racist reality suggests a vulgar response, literally, "fuck it."[63] Antiblack racism constructs a universe of white nihilistic meaning out of which we are meant to experience the desires of white people as universal and implacable, but which betrays weakness and finitude, ironically, by constantly demonstrating its need to deny black humanity in order for the sham to work. The project of maturing through these conditions demands insisting upon original relationships to humanity, that is, attempting to nihilistically value blackness in spite of constant threats of erasure and/or physical murder. One has to have an appropriate amount of nihilistic strength, defiance, to insist upon valuing blackness within such a reality. To nihilistically insist upon the values of blackness, here, requires doing so from an attitude of "whatever happens, happens." There must be an appropriate amount of "fuck it" involved in black nihilistic attempts at self-determination in an antiblack racist society. Kendrick teeters between the pessimism of impending death and the nihilistic strength to say "fuck it" while moving forward.

What a dangerous attitude that must constantly be on guard against weak nihilistic forms of irresponsibility. Fanon pointed out as follows:

> Generally speaking the bards of negritude would contrast old Europe versus young Africa, dull reason versus poetry, and stifling logic versus exuberant Nature; on the one side there stood rigidity, ceremony, protocol, and skepticism, and on the other, naïveté, pestilence, freedom, and, indeed, luxuriance. But also irresponsibility.[64]

Consider the depths of Kendrick's representation of black pessimism when he says, "I don't think I can find a way to make it on this earth / I'll probably die anonymous / I'll probably die with promises."[65] In this verse, Kendrick laments the possibility of being killed by Police: "I'll probably die from one of these bats and blue badges / Body slammed on black and white paint / my bones snappin."[66] As if that isn't bad enough, he also laments the alternative, dying from the stress and anxiety of worrying about being killed. "Or maybe die from panic, or die from being too lax / Or die from waiting on it, die 'cause I'm moving too fast."[67] In the end, the tragic, obvious, conclusion is unavoidable. "I'll probably die 'cause that's what you do when you're Seventeen / All worries in a hurry / I wish I controlled things."[68] Some of life's deepest worries are faced by black nihilistic youth in a ludicrously short span of time. "All worries in a hurry." Black youth don't get to be children. "I wish I controlled things." Black youth don't get to be adults. Death results from "panic." Death results from "being too lax." Death results from angst, anguish, and worrying about worrying too much. Death abounds on all sides; everywhere we turn, there it is. "I'll probably die 'cause that's what you do when you're Seventeen."[69] Antiblack racist worlds destroy black childhood.

The angst of nonexistence, long before having one's body "slammed on black and white paint," presents a form of existential violence against black people, and black youth, that is faced as a constituent element of black nihilistic maturity. In "Fear," Kendrick admits that by the age of twenty-seven, he had grown accustomed to fear, which was accumulated ten times over throughout the years. His biggest fear, at that point, was losing all that he had managed to gain. His newfound life made all of him magnified, but he displayed concern over "losing it all."

He practiced running from fear. He openly engaged intersubjective dimensions of identity formation between blacks and whites by considering the roles of "how they look at me," and admitting that he is, perhaps out of immaturity, in fear of "being judged." His distrust of any success or economic gain was an obvious indication of pessimism; however, this sense of impending loss also occasions further attempts at valuing in response to failure. The next move may be to construct a teleological meaning for black failure, which is exactly what one finds in Kendrick's concluding verse. He suggests, pessimistically, that black suffering is inevitable, which is foreshadowed by the song's prelude, a voice message of Kendrick's cousin, Carl, who is also heard after the song:

> I know you feel like, you know, people ain't been praying for you. But you have to understand this, man. We are a cursed people. Deuteronomy 28:28 says, "the Lord shall smite thee with madness, and blindness, and astonishment of the heart." See, family, that's why you feel like you feel, like you got a chip on your shoulder. Until you get the memo, you will always feel that way.[70]

At the end of the song, Carl continues as follows:

> Verse two says, "you only have I known of all the families of the earth; therefore, I will punish you for all your iniquities." So, until you come back to these commandments . . . We're gonna be in this place; we're going to be under this curse because [God] said He's going to punish us, the so-called Blacks.[71]

Kendrick's final verse ends with a capitulation: "God damn you; God damn me / God damn us; God damn we / God damn us all."[72]

I understand Kendrick's capitulation to an ultimately weak black nihilistic paradigm; it is a stage in the process of black nihilism, one that is borne of a black pessimism that may, nevertheless, lead to a strong black nihilism. Black nihilistic hip-hop music is an existentially dope vehicle for facilitating this process; it attempts to value blackness while adopting pessimistic attitudes against both white nihilistic and black optimistic ideals. As a result, black nihilistic hip-hop tends to promote values viewed as deviant from both traditions. Kendrick's depiction of black youth's loss of innocence in his opening scene reflected the damning circumstance of having to exist as a black moral subjectivity in an antiblack racist context. Facing rejection, he demonstrates the black nihilistic project of maturity involving tasks of constructing alternative forms for valuing blackness, which *Damn* attempts by resurrecting certain Afro-Judaic ideals to replace the narratives for blackness found in traditional black Christianity. Antiblack racism induces weak nihilistic responses. Kendrick sank into the temptations of weak nihilistic responses to antiblack racism. This is evidenced by his ultimate collapse into his interpretation of certain metaphysically affirmed narratives of Afro-Judaism as a means for providing a justificatory potential for black suffering. He sought to alter the meaning of blackness within this world via narratives of black religious piety from a world that predates this one. Or, as he put it, he responded out of "fear," of not being able to "evolve in the light of God."

While it is true that the majority of mass media–produced images of black nihilistic youths often promote hedonism, materialism, and capitalism, alongside weak rejections of antiblack racism that evade questions of maturity and responsibility, we can consider *Damn* as symbolic of a demographic of black nihilistic youth attempting to reflect maturely on its philosophical meaning in relation to black suffering and invisibility within antiblack racist contexts, for which Kendrick offered an Afro-Judaic inspired critique. *Damn*, and the song "Fear," in particular, can be read as arguing for a metaphysical teleology of blackness that assigns a transcendent value to black suffering different from the one proffered by white nihilistic ideals. It inverts the white nihilistic quality of antiblack racist values by displacing the historical achievements of colonialism, locating them as a derivative, a consequence, of black spiritual failures on the part of ancient ancestors. The cause and effect of black suffering, on this view, is the result of black failures and not white successes. However, this move serves to delimit the potentiality of future human valuing according to a predetermined framework of meaning. The values of (European) "man," here, are cast aside, reduced to being a side effect of black spiritual failures, a black self-induced fall from original situatedness, but this approach, like traditional black Christianity, is ultimately weak, because it advocates for a moving forward that simultaneously calls for an arresting of the potential of future value production. It defines the future exclusively in terms of the past. In other words, the future, on that picture, effectively depends upon black metaphysical ideals combating and replacing white metaphysical ideals.

We should consider the weak black nihilism expressed in *Damn* through the lens of Fanon's thought, where he describes the poetry of the "colonized creator" as a "poetry of revolt; but which is also analytic and descriptive."[73] For example, in Fanon's critique of Sartre's *Black Orpheus*, Fanon described what I consider to be the weak dimensions of black nihilism, as a stage in a process for which one needs to be "lost in the night." Having found reason and rationality in antiblack racist societies infected with white nihilistic desires for black invisibility, where it plays a cat and mouse game with black consciousness, disappearing and making a fool out of black moralistic and rationalistic appeals whenever they appear, then reappearing insisting on civility and decorum when black people get violent or vulgar, Fanon, too, resorted to unreason in the face of antiblack racism through a "nostalgia for the past."[74] Fanon warned that although the job of the poet, here, is "to clearly define the people, the subject of his creation," he must also recognize that "it is not enough to try and disengage ourselves by accumulating proclamations and denials. It is no longer enough to reunite with the people in a past where they no longer exist."[75] In *Black Skin; White Masks*, Fanon hermeneutically described black optimistic and pessimistic processes that can appear through black nihilism:

> It was hate; I was hated, despised, detested, not by the neighbor across the street or my cousin on my mother's side, but by an entire race. I was up against something unreasoned. The psychoanalysts say that nothing is more traumatizing for the young child than his encounters with what is rational. I would personally say that for a man whose only weapon is reason there is nothing more neurotic than contact with unreason.
>
> I felt knife blades open within me. I resolved to defend myself. As a good tactician, I intended to rationalize the world and to show the white man that he was mistaken.[76]

He continued as follows:

> With enthusiasm I set to cataloging and probing my surroundings. As times changed, one had seen the Catholic religion at first justify and then condemned slavery and prejudices. But by referring everything to the idea of the dignity of man, one had ripped prejudice to shreds. After much reluctance, the scientists had conceded that the Negro was a human being; in *vivo* and in *vitro* the Negro had been proved analogous to the white man: the same morphology, the same histology. Reason was confident of victory on every level. I put all the parts back together. But I had to change my tune.
>
> That victory played cat and mouse; It made a fool of me. As the other put it, when I was present, it was not; when it was there, I was no longer. In the abstract there was agreement: The Negro is a human being. That is to say, amended the less firmly convinced, that like us he has his heart on the left side. But on certain points the white man remained intractable.[77]

In response to the white nihilistic values of (European) "man," or what Fanon described as the "affective ankylosis of the white man," who is firmly convinced that black humanity has "come too late, much too late. There will always be a world—a white world—between you and us," indeed, it is understandable that black nihilistic youth may need to get lost in the night. As Fanon remarked, "It is understandable that I could have made up my mind to utter my Negro cry."[78] Gordon described the appeal of what I call weak black nihilism to so many black people in antiblack racist worlds:

> Yet one could easily see its immediate attraction to many alienated Blacks who want a metaphysical as well as a physical difference from those who persecute them. Fanon's "place" was, in a word, announced. He was in a cat and mouse game with reason because he was reaching for something supposedly allergic to his "nature." His place was in the world of "emotion," a world of "affect," of rhythm, song, and dance. . . . If whiteness represented the outer, the objective, the realm of reason, the Black's realm will be radically inner and subjective and at home in the realm of unreason.[79]

Damn should be understood as Kendrick's aesthetic representation of the pessimistic and nihilistic "negro cry" of black youth, where, as Gordon says of Fanon's *negritude*, "he had found a terrain on which whites will lose: the terrain of the irrational."[80] The vulgarity of the black nihilistic negro cry shares affinity with the adoption of the term *nègre*, in *negritude*, by the founder of the literary and poetic movement, Aimé Césaire. The term was intended to be a strongly defiant, and vulgar, affirmation of the pejorative use of the French term.[81] In Fanon's words, "From the opposite end of the world a magical negro culture was hailing me. Negro Sculpture! I began to flush with pride. Was this our Salvation?":[82]

> I had rationalized the world and the world had rejected me on the basis of color prejudice. Since no agreement was possible on the level of reason, I threw myself back toward unreason. It was up to the white man to be more irrational than I. Out of the necessities of my struggle I had chosen the method of regression, but the fact remained that it was an unfamiliar weapon; here I am at home; I am made of the irrational; I weighed in the irrational. Up to the neck in the irrational. And now how my voice vibrates![83]

Gordon explains, however, "as in any analysis of failure, [Fanon's] search for *nègre* greatness encounters its impasse."[84] Fanon's critique of Sartre's *Black Orpheus*, as expressed in *Black Skin; White Masks*, cited the preface to Sartre's essay:

In fact, *negritude* appears as the minor term of a dialectical progression: the theoretical and practical assertion of the supremacy of the white man is its thesis; the position of *negritude* as an antithetical value, is the moment of negativity. But this negative moment is insufficient by itself, and the Negroes who employ it know this very well; they know that it is intended to prepare the synthesis or realization of the human in a society without races. Thus negativity is the root of its own destruction, it is a transition and not a conclusion, a means and not an ultimate end.[85]

Fanon responded as follows:

When I read that page, I felt I had been robbed of my last chance. I said to my friends, "The generation of younger black poets has just suffered a blow that can never be forgiven." Help had been sought from a friend of the colored peoples, and that friend had found no better response than to point out the relativity of what they were doing. For once, [Sartre] had forgotten that consciousness has to lose itself in the night of the absolute, the only condition to attain to consciousness of self. In opposition to rationalism, he summoned up the negative side, but he forgot that this negativity draws its worth [produces values] from an almost substantive absoluteness. A consciousness committed to experience is ignorant, has to be ignorant, of the essences of the determinations of its being. . . . Sartre's mistake was not only to seek the source of the source [of values] but in a certain sense to block that source.[86]

Seventy years have passed since Fanon's sage advice that black nihilistic "generations of younger poets" must be given time to develop. We can see Fanon's depiction of the analogy I began with, of something, or someone, attempting to block the "source" of human valuing. (European) "Man," even in Sartre's radical manifestation, commits the "mistake," of not only seeking "the source of the source [of values] but in a certain sense to block that source." Perhaps Sartre's mistake, here, was inadvertent. Nevertheless, according to Fanon, the damage of pointing out the "reason" motivating the "unreason" of weak black nihilistic opposition to antiblack racism was done. Or, as Fanon wrote the following:

In opposition to historical becoming, there had always been the unforeseeable. I needed to lose myself completely. . . . One day, perhaps in the depths of that unhappy romanticism. . . . In any case I needed not to know. This struggle, this new decline had to take on an aspect of completeness. Nothing is more unwelcome than the commonplace: "You'll change, my boy; I was like that too when I was young . . . you'll see, it will all pass."

> The dialectic that brings necessity into the foundation of my freedom drives me out of myself. It shatters my unreflected position. Still in terms of consciousness, black consciousness is immanent in its own eyes. I am not a potentiality of something, I am wholly what I am. I do not have to look for the universal. No probability has any place inside of me. My negro consciousness does not hold itself out as a lack. It is. It is its own follower.[87]

Sartre spoke of "black souls," while suggesting *negritude* was a form of antiracist racism, or as I consider it, weak black nihilism, that was ultimately meant to defeat itself. Fanon's point in response was that "being lost" in the black nihilistic night requires *that* truth to be a self-realization; it wasn't Sartre's "place" to point out the dialectical relativity of black nihilistic struggles. Fanon, in other words, needed to "not know," for the black nihilistic moment of *negritude* to do its antithetical work. Gordon worded it as follows:

> [Fanon] rebuked Sartre for a rationalist impulse that violated a needed, ironically Platonic Lie. Reflection was the death knell of the black; It was that from which he was attempting to escape. Sartre, he suggests, should have encouraged his self-delusion, his narcissistic search for his desired mirror image, if but for the sake of instantiating Sartre's argument of maximizing the negative moment of the antiracist, anticolonial struggle for the spirited chest of the *nègre*. It needed to be the *nègre's* moment, his resistance, his upsurge.[88]

According to Gordon, "What Sartre didn't understand was that he was in effect counseling the death of blackness through eventual absorption into the light of whiteness. This expectation of a racist society is a phenomenon of which Fanon was aware throughout his life." This expectation is also one of which black nihilists are made aware from a young age. As Gordon points out, in the final lines of Fanon's unfinished play, "*Les mains parallèles*," *Parallel Hands*, Fanon inscribes a summation of the rejection of what I call white nihilistic values and black invisibility, "To no longer see mute whiteness / To no longer see death."[89]

Fanon ended his chapter on the lived experiences of blackness by weeping. He wept because, despite extraordinary efforts, he was left "without responsibility, straddling Nothingness and Infinity." He was left without avenues supporting the "responsibility" required for maturity and black adulthood. What else can one do at this point? Fanon admits, he cried. Gordon points out that the functions of laughter, defiance, and crying, are psychoanalytic languages reflective of the cathartic processes of psychological "breakthroughs."[90] Fanon performatively demonstrated this fact by having a "breakdown" at the end of the chapter on "the lived experiences of blackness," which situated his "breakthrough" in the subsequent chapter on "the

Negro and Psychopathology." As Gordon put it, he was "now able to face the psychopathological implications of his situation."[91] What is of particular import for my analysis is the ways in which Fanon's and Gordon's work can be used to support my theorization that black pessimism as a form of black nihilism can be indicative of developments in which black youth are attempting to maturely face their world.

If creativity and possibility are the domain of youth, then antiblack racism seeks to effectively eviscerate the fundamentally creative features, if not the entire category of, black youth. As Kendrick put it, "I'm talking Fear / Fear of losing creativity." The obligation of black adulthood, then, is to provide the necessary structures wherein possibilities for black youth are not collapsed into what Lewis Gordon calls a "Peter Pan-ism."[92] In other words, we must take seriously the concerns and expressions of the hip-hop generation, which is now inquiring about what it means to be an adult within a society that disavows black existential maturity.[93] Perhaps the hip-hop generation is disposed against taking for granted the weak nihilistic values of antiblack racism and black optimism. Or as Kendrick put it, "I'm talking Fear / Fear that it's wickedness or weakness / I'm talking Fear / Whatever it is; both is distinctive."[94] *Damn*, from this perspective, appears precocious and indicative of an elevated sense of maturity, not one without limitations or contradictions, but one, as compared to many of his artistic contemporaries, that seeks to engage levels of maturity that most "grown-ups" find horrifying.

What kinds of lyric poets call for reordering traditional black and antiblack realities? What kind of music might announce the coming of newer forms of blackness being cast into the world? Perhaps the answers to these questions cannot be fully known ahead of time, but we should be on the lookout for signs of their potential unfolding.

Damn is an aesthetic critique of white nihilism, antiblack racism, and traditional black optimism, offered through the lens of black nihilism. It uses the pessimistic languages of death and desire in order to capture all that is decried by traditionalism as "sin," before ultimately becoming exhausted and seeking newer standards for valuing. It exemplifies a youthful expression of blackness desiring transcendence through affirmations of black nihilistic will, set against antiblack racist and black traditionalist challenges to maturation. *Damn* reflects tensions and contradictions germane to the existential life of black youth in antiblack racist societies articulated through the lens of a maturing, black nihilistic, American consciousness. While the Afro-Judaic response to black nihilism in *Damn* resembles Cornel West's Black American Christian response in the sense that both appeal to metaphysically affirmed ideals, it should be kept in mind that existential contradictions between being and nothingness are anguished and despair-filled encounters from which many adults have fled, but which Kendrick faces and wrestled with, openly, as a youth on a public stage.

> I can't take these feelings with me / So, hopefully they disperse within fourteen tracks / carried out over wax / searching for resolution until somebody get back / Fear / Wondering if I'm living through fear or living through rap.

We must bear in mind Fanon's words that such creators might press on in their black nihilistic attempts toward further forms of knowledge. In Fanon's words:

> This creator, who decides to portray natural truth, turns, paradoxically enough, to the past, and so looks at what is irrelevant to the present. What he aims for in his inner intentionality is the detritus of social thought, external appearances, relics, and knowledge frozen in time. The colonized intellectual, however, who strives for cultural authenticity, must recognize that national truth is first and foremost the national reality. He must press on until he reaches that place of bubbling trepidation from which knowledge will emerge.[95]

One must attempt to be strong in living through the damning contradictions inherent to the predicaments of black youth maturing within antiblack racist worlds. At this point, has Kendrick succeeded in becoming a strong black nihilist? No; I don't think so. "God damn you. God damn me. God damn us. God damn we. God damn us all." Black nihilistic music reflects desires to *become* strong; it reflects abilities to confront and deflate false hopes in decadent ideals; it challenges one to have the courage to do so; to reevaluate the entire affair of human valuing under oppressive circumstances; to walk, wander, into the possibilities that lay beyond the values of this world; this is the task of black nihilism. For black nihilists such as myself, Kendrick's searing pessimism and passionate nihilism, reflected by uncanny lyricism, is existentially dope, for all the reasons mentioned, while nevertheless raising the question of stronger forms of black nihilistic developments.

Finally, the existential themes I have been raising through my discussion of "black nihilistic hip-hop" can be connected with Nietzsche's explicit thought on nihilism, poetry, and music. In *The Birth of Tragedy from the Spirit of Music* (1872), Nietzsche depicted what could potentially be understood as, nihilistic hip-hop lyricists, when he described the lyric poet's potential to become a *philosopher-artist*. Nietzsche's description of lyric poet's creative processes mirrors the processes of black nihilistic hip-hop lyricist. Nietzsche wrote as follows:

> In the state prior to the act of writing, he does not claim to have had before or within him an ordered causality of ideas, but rather a musical mood. . . .

A certain musical atmosphere of moods precedes it, and the poetic idea only comes afterwards.

Whether freestyling, making up lyrics spontaneously, or delicately crafting written rhymes and verses, the hip-hop lyricist begins by perceiving a musical mood, an internalized atmosphere provided by the melodies and rhythms of musical sounds, or beats. Nietzsche's description of the Apolline lyric poet combining with the Dionysiac music maker captures the existential dopeness of hip-hop music reflected through its DJ/Producer and MC relationship:

> If we add to [the Dionysiac spirit of music] the most important phenomenon . . . the unification, or indeed the identity of the lyric poet with the musician. . . . First of all, as a Dionysiac artist, he has been thoroughly united with the primal Oneness, its pain and contradiction, and produces the copy of that primal oneness as music, if we can rightly call music a repetition and recast of the world; but now, under Apolline dream influence, this music is revealed to him as an allegorical dream-image. That reflection of primal pain in music, free of images and concepts, redeemed by illusion, now creates a second mirror image as a single allegory or example. The artist has already abandoned his subjectivity in the Dionysiac process, the image that now reveals to him his unity with the heart of the world is a dream scene symbolizing the primal contradiction and primal suffering, as well as the primal delight in illusion. The "I" of the lyric poet therefore sounds from the very depths of being: his "subjectivity" in the sense used by modern aestheticians is a falsehood. . . . The Dionysiac musical enchantment of the sleeping man now sends out sparks of images, lyric poems which, at the peak of their evolution, will bear the name of tragedies.[96]

Black nihilistic hip-hop music, I have been arguing, is a musical form birthed by the spirit of tragedy. The perspectives of black nihilistic artists, and lyricists in particular, produce "sounds from the very depths of being." Their "subjectivity," in the sense of modern ideals, is a "falsehood," which sends out "sparks of images, lyric poems, which at the peak of their evolution, will bear the name of tragedies."

Hip-hop music has grown in fortune and global fame, and due to corporate institutional factors in media and entertainment playing co-opting roles militating against strong constructions and developments of black youth culture, it has tended to struggle with maturity in a black nihilistic sense. Simultaneously, it has become a major conduit for the global "visibility" of large swathes of generations of black people and youth. The hip-hop era marked the first generation of black people seeking to come into visibility in the post–Civil Rights era in America. We continue to face realities of anti-black racism and black invisibility experienced as particularly nihilistic for our generations. Black nihilism is one lens through which one can understand our struggles. The "hip-hop generation" is grappling against both antiblack racism and black traditionalism. If we read their expressions as projections of values that simultaneously criticize the givenness of antiblack racist values while also trying to conceive of alternative bases for inverting those values, then, for example, we can acknowledge black nihilistic hip-hop music, at least, as being existentially dope in its often dark and despairing demands that something exists in the place of fallen ideals.

As Fanon reminded us, "Every generation must discover its mission, fulfill it or betray it, in relative opacity."[97] Since black nihilism involves forging new values in the face of dead or dying ones, then it must be realized that the determination of each generation's mission is also begat by the fluidity of transmissions, achievements, shortcomings, and struggles of previous generations. In this spirit, younger and older generations of contemporary black people must embrace the project of working together to create newer values in anticipation of future peoples, worlds, and needs, which we can only hope to anticipate and supply in the most liberatory forms. Unfortunately, black nihilism is often decried as a lack of values that has nothing to offer the project of black freedom and maturity. Black nihilism, however, is not a disease that afflicts the black soul in the sense of needing to be avoided or cured, or something that can be countered by reinvigorating traditional values. Black nihilism is a descriptive term designating processes of maturity struggling to develop through the decadence of oppressive and weak value systems, which get confronted in anguish while projects of producing value continue.

The response to antiblack racism and white nihilism expressed by young black nihilists ought to be judged from the consideration that these are youth attempting to value through an "adult" terrain. The weak, young, and immature, tend to perish of the lived experiences of blackness and nihilism. They tend to crash and burn before maturely facing the question of how to put oneself back together; before facing the question of how to value anew. Fanon described the harrowing journey of black life undergoing these processes, attempting to announce itself in good faith as a member of the human world, being shattered, rejected, and struggling to find a way forward. The process described is one of black nihilistic maturation in a world that demands black people to exist as children, where strength and existential freedom emanating from a black body is questioned, challenged, denied, and presumed to entail an abomination of objective "goodness."

Not only are Fanon's analyses relevant for understanding processes of becoming existentially mature and black nihilistically strong within antiblack racist societies in the twenty-first century, but public demonstrations of white nihilism and antiblack racism continue to demonstrate the validity of Nietzsche's critique of modern (European) "Man," which, today, may be extended and applied to his children. America is a traditionally white nihilistic and antiblack racist society. Its philosophical forbearers identified racial whiteness as relevant for producing human phenomenological perspectives. A cultural life world built on such weak nihilistic situating of Humanity fundamentally dismisses the historical and contemporary perspectives of the majority of the world's human beings. It is a solipsistic point of view from which to consider human valuations. White nihilism, thus, fixes the meaning of human reality solely according to its own limited viewpoint. The remaining human denizens of the world are rendered, or seriously militated against, from experiencing the values undergirding the social and political structures of the world as germinating from and being reflective of a contingent sociogenic process; they are viewed and enforced as natural and inevitable. Black people are made to pray over white people's decisions.

The necessity and inevitability that the (white) Human world regards itself with "stinks" of weakness. In order to transcend the historical contingency of antiblack racism, to become a secondary citizen within the (white) Human world, one is demanded to acquiesce to white nihilistic ideals or assert their a priori value; this is a proposition that is absurd and should be met with a strong, if not vulgar, oppositional stance. To point out the contingency of the self-appointed necessity of whiteness is to remind a fragile, weak nihilistically situated people of that which they need to deny in order to continue valuing life. The existence of black perspectives, let alone ones that insist on original abilities to produce values, is apperceptively recognized by antiblack racists as challenging denials upon which the force of their value systems depend. Thus, there is a fear of strong black life on the part of antiblack racists that signals the fragility and weakness of whiteness. It is not that simply valuing anti-whiteness is threatening to the antiblack racist, but that black phenomenological existence itself is seen as a threat to white existence. Thus, black strength from youth, in particular, is met with a call for erasure, denial, and/or murder. It is by virtue of willing value structures that require killing black phenomenal existence that whiteness draws its sustenance. This means whiteness needs blackness to exist, but not as a form of life; rather, whiteness needs blackness to exist as a form of death.[98]

The strong black nihilist, in response to fear and death, does not need to depend on universalistic narratives. The strong black nihilist rejects weak nihilism; in particular, he rejects all forms of valuing that demand black people value in ways that have been, in the words of Nelson Maldonado Torres, "epistemically colonized."[99] The strong black nihilist, in other words, fights against epistemic colonization of the terms for which the meanings of Humanity and blackness are produced. The strong black nihilist insists upon being able to produce values and images for blackness for themselves, beyond epistemic colonization; he fights against those who would arrest, imprison, and kill his strength of phenomenal willing, which is the source of *all* human values.

What a strong black nihilistic adult future will look like cannot, and should not, be known ahead of time. Black nihilistic culture, like all cultures, comes into being and undergoes processes of development. What is needed, at this time, I'm suggesting, is a facing of the problems of black maturity where individuals are encouraged to embrace projects of creating possibilities while within existentially free, strong nihilistic, value paradigms. This means encouraging black nihilistic youth toward strong black nihilistic adulthood, which further requires engaging their perspectives, and this can be facilitated by looking through the lenses of their musical expressions, which I call black nihilistic hip-hop music.

Black nihilistic hip-hop music is an existentially rich form of aesthetic expression, and an informative lens through which to hear what so many black youths, today, are saying. This also means, finally, giving up on the idea that one can become "too old" for hip-hop. Rather, we must accept the challenges that each generation faces, which necessarily includes facing what it means to "grow up." This generation, my generation, faces the question of maturity in terms of what it means to grow up as a black nihilistic adult. There is a positive humanism that antiblack racism threatens, which often demands mastering the task of walking through darkness without the need for light, without the need for weak nihilistic guarantees; this is strong black nihilism. Where might we look for signs pointing toward strong black nihilistic futures? Follow the sounds of black nihilism and hip-hop.

Frantz Fanon ended *Black Skin; White Masks* with a prayer; not to God, but to himself. Before doing so, he offered a rhetorical question inviting all of Humanity to participate in strong nihilistic constructions of reality:

> Was my freedom not given to me then in order to build the world of the *You*? (Emphasis in original) At the conclusion of this study, I want the world to recognize, with me, the open door of every consciousness.
> My final prayer:
> O' my body, make me always a man who questions!

Here, "You" refers to the unmediated world of strong, existentially free, and mature Humanity "devoid of overdetermined presumptions."[100] This book is my prayer that I offer for black nihilistic youth; and it is a prayer I offer for us all. This public prayer is not directed toward God. My values concerning God are my own, personal, business. Rather, my prayer is directed at each of our own consciousnesses, our senses of strength, life, vitality, freedom, youth, and maturity. I call upon our black bodies and minds to release themselves from the "enmeshed web of social pathologies," governing these foul systems that hate us, toward an expression that better suits a "mature, free consciousness—the embodiment of questioning," or that which I call strong black nihilism.[101] May we always have the strength to insist upon the value of ourselves.

As for tradition, may we always remember that each tradition must justify itself before those currently facing existence. We, those who are alive and conscious, are an original source of value production. May we always remain strong in our valuative dispositions. May we continue to mature, to loudly, undeniably, and through our existentially dope brand of cultural expressions, dream, fight for, and forever seek newer possibilities, newer values, newer ways of being, for blackness, for Humanity; may we always reject the denigration of "Man"; and, in the face of antiblack racism and white nihilism, may we always, from the very depths of our black souls and chests, in the most defiant, vulgar, strong, and hopeful sense of the term, forever, proclaim, "Fuck that!"

Amen.

NOTES

1. This is from Jean-Paul Sartre's famous "Preface" to Fanon's last book. Frantz Fanon, *The Wretched of the Earth*, trans. Richard Philcox (New York: Grove Press, 2004), xliv. Originally published in 1963.

2. Carter Woodz (2019). "The Truth." https://www.amazon.com/Love-Lost-Explicit-Carter-Woodz/dp/B07T3F5J82.

3. See, Kendrick Lamar, *Section 80*, Top Dawg Records, 2011. See, also, Kendrick Lamar, *Damn*, Top Dawg Records, 2017.

4. Clearly, I am an existentialist; so, I don't believe there are any essential values necessarily produced by any particular group of people. However, as an existentialist, it makes sense to talk about conditions under which certain dominant modes of valuing are formed, produced, and transmitted across generational lines. I do not suggest that every black person, or otherwise, born after 1969 is a member of the hip-hop community, or that every member of the hip-hop community struggles through pessimism and nihilism, or that every person will find themselves in the following analysis.

5. Chase, C., Robinson, S., Fletcher, Glover, M. (1982). "The Message." Genius. Accessed May 26, 2021. https://genius.com/Grandmaster-flash-and-the-furious-five-the-message-lyrics#song-info.

6. Ibid.

7. Bakari Kitwana, *The Hip Hop Generation* (New York: Basic *Civitas* Books, 2003).

8. Tom Meagher, "Creolization and Maturity: A Philosophical Sketch," *Contemporary Political Theory* 17 (2018): 383.

9. See, Jane Gordon, *Creolizing Political Theory: Reading Rousseau Through Fanon* (United States: Fordham University Press, 2014).

10. Fred Lee, "Creolizing Political Theory with Extraordinary Racial Politics," *Contemporary Political Theory* 17 (2018): 377.

11. Ibid.

12. Lewis Gordon, "The Problem of Maturity in Hip Hop," in *Hip Hop & Philosophy: Rhyme 2 Reason*, eds. Derrick Darby and Tommie Shelby (Chicago: Open Court Books, 2005), 105–116.

13. Meagher, "Creolization and Maturity," 383.

14. Ibid.

15. Lil' Snupe. (2014). "No Games." Genius. Accessed May 26, 2021. https://genius.com/Lil-snupe-no-games-lyrics#song-info. Lil' Snupe was murdered on June 20, 2013.

16. Meagher, "Creolization and Maturity," 384.

17. Ibid.

18. De Beauvoir, *The Ethics of Ambiguity*, 35.

19. Meagher, "Creolization and Maturity," 384.

20. Ibid. 385.

21. Ibid.

22. Ibid.

23. Ibid.

24. Ibid.

25. Cornel West, *Prophesy Deliverance!* (Louisville: Westminster John Knox Press: 1982), 96–97.

26. Cornel West, *Race Matters* (Boston: Beacon Press, 1993), 24.

27. "It must be recognized that the nihilistic threat contributes to criminal behavior." West, *Race Matters*, 25.

28. Ibid.

29. Ibid. 31.

30. Ibid. 23.

31. Devon Johnson, "Beyond Tradition: A Short Philosophical Rumination on Africana Philosophy and Nihilism in the 21st Century," *American Philosophical Association: Newsletter on Philosophy and the Black Experience* 16, no. 2 (Spring 2017): 22–23.

32. Devon Johnson, "Hip Hop Adulthood: Nihilism, Hip Hop, and Black American Youth in the 21st Century," *Social Alternatives: The Critical Philosophy of Race and Decoloniality* 38, no. 4 (2019): 42–47.

33. See, Lucius Outlaw, *On Race and Philosophy* (New York: Routledge, 1996). See, also, "Against the Grain of Modernity: The Politics of Difference and the Conservation of Race," *Man and World* 25 (1992): 443–468.

34. This is why white violence, vulgarity, and hate get cast toward peaceful black protests.

35. Kendrick Lamar. (2011). "Fuck Your Ethnicity." Genius. Accessed May 26, 2021. https://genius.com/Kendrick-lamar-fuck-your-ethnicity-lyrics#song-info.

36. Ibid.

37. Ibid.

38. Kendrick Lamar. (2011). "Hol' Up." Genius. Accessed May 26, 2021. https://genius.com/Kendrick-lamar-hol-up-lyrics.

39. Ibid.

40. Ibid.
41. Ibid.
42. Ibid.
43. Ibid.
44. Ibid.
45. Ibid.
46. Kendrick Lamar. (2011). "Chapter Six." Genius. Accessed May 26, 2021. https://genius.com/Kendrick-lamar-chapter-six-lyrics.
47. Ibid.
48. Kendrick Lamar. (2011). "Ronald Reagan Era." Genius. Accessed May 26, 2021. https://genius.com/Kendrick-lamar-ronald-reagan-era-his-evils-lyrics.
49. Ibid.
50. Ibid.
51. Frantz Fanon, *Black Skin; White Masks*, trans. Charles Lam Markmann (New York: Grove Press, 1967), 109.
52. Ibid.
53. Lewis Gordon, *What Fanon Said* (New York: Fordham University Press, 2015), 48.
54. Gordon, *What Fanon Said*, 49.
55. Fanon, *Black Skin; White Masks*, 112–113.
56. Gordon, *What Fanon Said*, 52.
57. Devon Johnson, "Existentially Dope," *The Philosophers' Magazine* 86 (2019): 36–43.
58. Fanon, *The Wretched of the Earth*, 148.
59. Kendrick Lamar. (2017). "Yah." Genius. Accessed May 26, 2021. https://genius.com/Kendrick-lamar-yah-lyrics.
60. Ibid.
61. Ibid.
62. Ibid.
63. Kendrick Lamar. (2017). "Fear." Genius. Accessed May 26, 2021. https://genius.com/Kendrick-lamar-fear-lyrics.
64. Fanon, *The Wretched of the Earth*, 151.
65. Lamar, "Fear."
66. Ibid.
67. Ibid.
68. Ibid.
69. Ibid.
70. Ibid.
71. Ibid.
72. Ibid.
73. Fanon, *The Wretched of the Earth*, 162.
74. Fanon, *Black Skin; White Masks*, 121.
75. Fanon, *The Wretched of the Earth*, 163.
76. Fanon, *Black Skin; White Masks*, 118.
77. Ibid. 119–120.

78. Ibid. 122.
79. Gordon, *What Fanon Said*, 55.
80. Ibid.
81. Ibid. 54.
82. Fanon, *Black Skin; White Masks*, 123.
83. Ibid.
84. Gordon, *What Fanon Said*, 55.
85. Jean-Paul Sartre, *Black Orpheus* (United States: Présence africaine, 1948), xl ff.
86. Fanon, *Black Skin; White Masks*, 134.
87. Ibid. 135.
88. Gordon, *What Fanon Said*, 56.
89. Ibid. 57. See, also, Frantz Fanon, *Alienation and Freedom* (India: Bloomsbury Publishing, 2018).
90. Gordon, *What Fanon Said*, 59.
91. Ibid.
92. Gordon, "The Problem of Maturity in Hip Hop," 106.
93. There are large subcultures of "hip-hop adults" engaging questions of maturity. For example, Juan Vidal addresses these concerns through themes of parenthood, and the influence hip-hop music has had in shaping our generation's conceptions of adulthood, freedom, and child rearing. See, Juan Vidal, *Rap Dad: A Story of Family and the Subculture That Shaped a Generation* (India: Atria Books, 2020).
94. Lamar, "Fear."
95. Fanon, *The Wretched of the Earth*, 161.
96. Friedrich Nietzsche, *The Birth of Tragedy* (London: Penguin Books, 1993), 5: 29.
97. Fanon, *The Wretched of the Earth*, 145.
98. For further elucidation on the situation of blackness and lived-death, see, Abdul Jon Mohamadd, *The Death-Bound-Subject: Richard Wright's Archaeology of Death* (Ukraine: Duke University Press, 2005).
99. "Decolonization is waiting to occur not only in regard to material and cultural levels but also vis-à-vis epistemic levels." Nelson Maldonado-Torres, *Against War: Views from the Underside of Modernity* (United Kingdom: Duke University Press, 2008), 246.
100. Gordon, *What Fanon Said*, 70.
101. Ibid.

Bibliography

Allison, David B., ed. *The New Nietzsche: Contemporary Styles of Interpretation.* Cambridge: MIT Press, 1985.
Appiah, Anthony, and Amy Gutmann. *Color Conscious: The Political Morality of Race.* Princeton, NJ: Princeton University Press, 1996.
Aristotle. "Metaphysics." In *The Basic Works of Aristotle*, edited by Richard McKeon, translated by W.D. Ross. New York: Random House, 1941.
———. *Nicomachean Ethics.* Cambridge: Hackett Publishing, 2019.
———. *The Basic Works of Aristotle.* Edited by Richard McKeon. New York: Random House, 1941.
Beauvoir, Simone de. *The Ethics of Ambiguity, Tr.* Translated by Bernard Frechtman. New York: Citadel Press, 1962.
Bell, Derrick. *Faces At The Bottom Of The Well: The Permanence Of Racism.* New York: Basic Books, 1993.
Benston, Kimberly. "Black Dada Nihilismus: Phillis Wheatley, Malcolm X, and the Traumatic Politics of Conversion." *Journal of Power and Ethics* 2, no. 3 (January 1, 2001): 149–85.
Bernasconi, Robert, and Tommy Lee Lott, eds. *The Idea of Race.* Indiana: Hackett Publishing, 2000.
Bernier, Francois. "A New Division of the Earth According to the Different Species or Races of Men Who Inhabit It." In *The Idea of Race*, edited by Robert Bernasconi and Tommy Lee Lott, 1–4. Indiana: Hackett Publishing, 2000.
———. *Bernier's Travels in the Mogul Empire.* New Jersey: Ross & Perry, 2001.
Best, Stephen, and Saidiya V. Hartman. "Fugitive Justice." *Representations* 92, no. 1 (2005): 1–15.
Blaustein, Albert P., and Robert L. Zangrando, eds. *Civil Rights and African Americans: A Documentary History.* Evanston: Northwestern University Press, 1991.
Bois, William Edward Burghardt Du. *The Autobiography of W. E. B. DuBois: A Soliloquy on Viewing My Life from the Last Decade of Its First Century.* New York: International Publishers, 1968.

Buffon, Georges-Louis Leclerc. *Buffon's Natural History of Man, the Globe, and of Quadrupeds, Vol. 1.* Cambridge: Fb&c Limited, 2018.

Camus, Albert. *The Rebel: An Essay on Man in Revolt.* Translated by Anthony Bower. New York: Vintage Books, 1991.

Cotkin, George. *Existential America.* Maryland: John Hopkins University Press, 2003.

Curry, Tommy J. *The Man-Not: Race, Class, Genre, and the Dilemmas of Black Manhood.* Philadelphia: Temple University Press, 2017.

Darby, Derrick, Tommie Shelby, and William Irwin, eds. *Hip Hop and Philosophy: Rhyme 2 Reason.* Chicago: Open Court Publishing, 2005.

De Genova, Nick. "Gangster Rap and Nihilism in Black America: Some Questions of Life and Death." *Social Text*, 43 (1995): 89–132.

Deleuze, Giles. "Active and Reactive." In *The New Nietzsche: Contemporary Styles of Interpretation*, edited by David B. Allison, 80–106. Cambridge: MIT Press, 1985.

Descartes, René. *Meditations on First Philosophy: With Selections from the Objections and Replies.* Translated by Michael Moriarty. Oxford: Oxford University Press, 2008.

———. *Philosophical Essays and Correspondence.* Edited by Roger Ariew. Indianapolis: Hackett Pub, 2000.

———. *Oeuvres de Descartes: Vie & Oeuvres de Descartes; Étude Historique, Par Charles Adam. 1957.* Edited by Charles Adam and Paul Tannery. Paris: J. Vrin, 1957.

Dictionary. "'Nihilism' - Definition." In *Merriam-Webster.Com*, May 24, 2021. https://www.merriam-webster.com/dictionary/nihilism.

Dienstag, Joshua Foa. *Pessimism: Philosophy, Ethic, Spirit.* Princeton: Princeton University Press, 2006.

Du Bois, William E. B. *The Souls of Black Folk.* New York: New American Library, 1969.

Ephraim, Charles Wm. *The Pathology of Eurocentrism: The Burden and Responsibilities of Being Black.* New Jersey: Africa World Press, 2003.

Eze, Emmanuel., ed. *Postcolonial African Philosophy: A Critical Reader.* Oxford: Blackwell Press, 1997.

———. "The Color of Reason: The Idea of Race in Kant's Anthropology." In *Postcolonial African Philosophy: A Critical Reader.* Oxford: Blackwell Press, 1997.

Fanon, Frantz. *Alienation and Freedom.* Translated by Steven Corcoran. New York: Bloomsbury Publishing, 2018.

———. *Black Skin, White Masks.* New York: Grove Press, 1968.

———. *The Wretched of the Earth.* Translated by Philcox Richard. New York: Grove Press, 2004.

———. *Towards the African Revolution: Political Essays.* Translated by Haakon Chevalier. New York: Grove Press, 1988.

Fashina, Oladipo. "Frantz Fanon and the Ethical Justification of Anti–Colonial Violence." *Social Theory and Practice* 15, no. 2 (Summer 1989): 179–212.

Fichte, J. G. *The Science of Knowledge: With the First and Second Introductions.* Translated by Peter Heath and John Lachs. Cambridge: Cambridge University Press, 1982.

Gabbard, David. "Meaning Matters: Education and the Nihilism of the Neocons." *Journal of Thought* 41, no. 3 (2006): 39–44.

Galton, Francis. "Eugenics: Its Definition, Scope and Aims." In *The Idea of Race*, edited by Robert Bernasconi and Tommy Lee Lott, 79–83. Indiana: Hackett Publishing, 2000.

Gillespie, Michael Allen. *Nihilism before Nietzsche*. Chicago: University of Chicago Press, 1996.

Gordon, Jane Anna. *Creolizing Political Theory: Reading Rousseau through Fanon*. New York: Fordham Univ Press, 2014.

Gordon, Lewis R. *An Introduction to Africana Philosophy*. Cambridge: Cambridge University Press, 2008.

———. *Bad Faith and Antiblack Racism*. New Jersey: Humanity Books, 1999.

———, ed. *Existence in Black an Anthology of Black Existential Philosophy*. New York: Routledge, 1997.

———. *Existentia Africana: Understanding Africana Existential Thought*. New York: Routledge, 2000.

———. *Fanon and the Crisis of European Man: An Essay on Philosophy and the Human Sciences*. New York: Routledge, 1995.

———. *Her Majesty's Other Children: Sketches of Racism from a Neocolonial Age*. Maryland: Rowman & Littlefield, 1997.

———. "The Problem of Maturity in Hip Hop." In *Hip Hop and Philosophy: Rhyme 2 Reason*, edited by Derrick Darby, Tommie Shelby, and William Irwin, 105–16. Chicago: Open Court Publishing, 2005.

———. "The Unacknowledged Fourth Tradition: An Essay on Nihilism, Decadence, and the Black Intellectual Tradition in the Existential Pragmatic Thought of Cornel West." In *Cornel West: A Critical Reader*, edited by George Yancy. 38–58. Massachusetts: Blackwell Publishing, 2001.

———. *What Fanon Said: A Philosophical Introduction to His Life and Thought*. New York: Fordham Univ Press, 2015.

Gordon, Lewis R., Annie Menzel, George Shulman, and Jasmine Syedullah. "Afro Pessimism." *Contemporary Political Theory* 17, no. 1 (February 2018): 105–37.

Gordon, Lewis R., Anne Norton, Sharon Stanley, Fred Lee, and Thomas Meagher. Review of *Creolizing political theory in conversation: Creolizing political theory: Reading Rousseau Through Fanon*, by Jane Anna Gordon. *Contemporary Political Theory* 17, no. 3 (August 2018): 363–92.

Hartman, Saidiya V. *Scenes of Subjection: Terror, Slavery, and Self-Making in Nineteenth-Century America*. Oxford: Oxford University Press, 1997.

Hayes, III, Floyd. "Cornel West and Afro-Nihilism: A Reconsideration." In *Cornel West: A Critical Reader*, edited by George Yancy, 245–60. United Kingdom: Wiley, 2001.

———. "The Concept of Double Vision in Richard Wright's The Outsider." In *Existence in Black an Anthology of Black Existential Philosophy*, 173–84. New York: Routledge, 1997.

Hegel, Friedrich. *The Philosophy of History*. Translated by J. Sibree. New York: Dover Publications, 1956.

Hegel, G. W. F. *The Phenomenology of Mind*. Translated by J. B. Baillie. Massachusetts: Courier Corporation, 2012.

Hegel, Georg Wilhelm Friedrich. *Lectures on the Philosophy of World History*. Translated by H. B Nisbet. Cambridge: Cambridge University Press, 1980.
Howells, Christina M. "Sartre and the Language of Literature." *The Modern Language Review* 74, no. 3 (1979): 572–79.
JanMohamed, Abdul R. *The Death-Bound-Subject: Richard Wright's Archaeology of Death*. North Carolina: Duke University Press, 2005.
Jefferson, Thomas. *Notes on the State of Virginia*. London: Burlington House, 2002.
Johnson, Devon. "Beyond Tradition: A Short Philosophical Rumination on Africana Philosophy and Nihilism in the 21st Century." *American Philosophical Association Newsletter*, Philosophy and the Black Experience, 16, no. 2 (Spring 2017): 22–23.
———. "Existentially Dope." *The Philosophers' Magazine*, 2019.
———. "Hip Hop Adulthood: Nihilism, Hip Hop, and Black American Youth in the 21st Century." *Social Alternatives*, The Critical Philosophy of Race and Decoloniality, 28, no. 4 (2019): 42–47.
Kant, Immanuel. *Anthropology from a Pragmatic Point of View*. Translated by Robert Louden. Cambridge: Cambridge University Press, 2006.
———. *Critique of Pure Reason*. Translated by Allen Wood and Paul Guyer. Cambridge: Cambridge University Press, 1998.
———. *Groundwork for the Metaphysics of Morals*. Edited and translated by Allen Wood. New Haven: Yale University Press, 2002.
———. *Perpetual Peace: A Philosophical Essay*. Translated by M. Campbell Smith. New York: Garland Pub., 1972.
Kaufmann, Walter, ed. *Philosophic Classics: Bacon to Kant*. New Jersey: Prentice Hall, Inc., 1961.
Kierkegaard, Sören. *Fear and Trembling*. Translated by Sylvia Walsh. Cambridge: Cambridge University Press, 2006.
———. *The Sickness Unto Death: A Christian Psychological Exposition of Edification and Awakening by Anti-Climacus*. Translated by Alastair Hannay. England: Penguin UK, 2004.
Kitwana, Bakari. *The Hip-Hop Generation: Young Blacks and the Crisis in African-American Culture*. New York: Basic Books, 2003.
Lamar, Kendrick. *Damn*. Top Dawg Records, 2017.
———. *Section 80*. Top Dawg Records, 2011.
Liptack, Christopher. "Justices Void Oversight of States, Issue at Heart of Voting Rights Act." *The New York Times*, June 26, 2013, sec. A1.
Locke, John. *An Essay Concerning Human Understanding*. Cambridge: Hackett Publishing Company, 1996.
Maldonado-Torres, Nelson. *Against War: Views from the Underside of Modernity*. North Carolina: Duke University Press, 2008.
Marshall, Stephen H. "The Political Life of Fungibility." *Theory & Event* 15, no. 3 (2012). muse.jhu.edu/article/484457.
Martinot, Steve, and Jared Sexton. "The Avant-Garde of White Supremacy." *Social Identities* 9, no. 2 (June 1, 2003): 169–81.
Mathew R. Hachee. "Kant, Race, and Reason." Michigan State University, May 24, 2014. https://www.msu.edu/~hacheema/kant2.htm.

Mbembé, Achille. "Necropolitics." Translated by Libby Meintjes. *Public Culture* 15, no. 1 (2003): 11–40.

———. "On the Power of the False." *Public Culture* 14, no. 3 (September 1, 2002): 629–41.

Mills, Charles W. *The Racial Contract*. New York: Cornell University Press, 1997.

Mngxitama, A., A. Alexander, and N. Gibson, eds. *Biko Lives!: Contesting the Legacies of Steve Biko*. New York: Springer, 2008.

Moten, Fred. "The Case of Blackness." *Criticism* 50, no. 2 (2008): 177–218.

Moulard-Leonard, Valentine. "Revolutionary Becomings: Negritude's Anti-Humanist Humanism." *Human Studies* 28, no. 3 (November 2005): 231–49.

Nietzsche, Friedrich Wilhelm. *Beyond Good and Evil*. Translated by R.J. Hollingdale. England: Penguin, 2003.

———. *On the Genealogy of Morals*. Translated by Walter Arnold Kaufmann and R. J Hollingdale. New York: Vintage Books, 1989.

———. *The Anti-Christ, Ecce Homo, Twilight of the Idols: And Other Writings*. Edited by Aaron Ridley. Translated by Judith Norman. Cambridge: Cambridge University Press, 2005.

———. *The Birth of Tragedy and The Genealogy of Morals*. Translated by Francis Golffing. New York: Anchor Books, 1990.

———. *The Will To Power*. Translated by Walter Kaufmann. United Kingdom: Vintage Books, 1968.

———. *Thus Spoke Zarathustra*. Translated by Thomas Common and Davey Nicholas. Hertfordshire: Wordsworth Editions, 1997.

———. *Twilight of the Idols and The Anti-Christ*. Translated by R.J. Hollingdale. England: Penguin, 1968.

Outlaw, Lucius. "Against the Grain of Modernity: The Politics of Difference and the Conservation of 'Race.'" *Man and World* 25 (January 1, 1992): 443–68.

———. *On Race and Philosophy*. New York: Routledge, 2016.

Rugaber, Christopher. "Healthy US Economy Failed to Narrow Racial Gap." *AP News*. September 28, 2020. //apnews.com/article/virus-outbreak-race-and-ethnicity-health-united-states-hispanics-d575192ae495ac0415f587f02b79bae0.

Russell, Bertrand. *A History of Western Philosophy*. New York: Simon and Schuster, 1972.

Sartre, Jean-Paul. *Being and Nothingness: An Essay in Phenomenological Ontology*. Translated by Hazel Barnes. New York: Washington Square Press, 1992.

———. *Black Orpheus*. Translated by S. W. Allen. United States: Présence africaine, 1976.

———. *Existentialism and Human Emotions*. Translated by Bernard Frechtman. New York: Philosophical Library, 1957.

Schopenhauer, Arthur. *Essays and Aphorisms*. Translated by R. J. Hollingdale. England: Penguin, 1970.

———. *Parerga and Paralipomena: Short Philosophical Essays*. Translated by E. F. J. Payne. Oxford: Clarendon Press, 2000.

———. *Studies in Pessimism*. Translated by T. Bailey Saunders. New York: Cosimo, Inc., 2007.

———. *The World as Will and Representation, Vol I*. Translated by E. F. J. Payne. New York: Dover Publications, 2012.

———. *The World as Will and Representation, Vol. II*. Translated by E. F. J. Payne. Massachusetts: Courier Corporation, 1966.

Sexton, Jared. "People-of-Color-Blindness: Notes on the Afterlife of Slavery." *Social Text* 28, no. 2 (103) (June 1 2010): 31–56.

———. "The Social Life of Social Death: On Afro-Pessimism and Black Optimism." *InTensions* 5 (Fall/Winter 2011): 1–47.

Snupe, Lil'. *R.N.I.C.* Millenium Era, 2014.

Taney, Roger B. "Dred Scott v. Sandford: Court Opinion." In *Civil Rights and African Americans: A Documentary History*, edited by Albert P. Blaustein and Robert L. Zangrando. Evanston: Northwestern University Press, 1991.

The Furious Five, Grandmaster Flash &. *The Message*. Sugar Hill, 1982.

Vidal, Juan. *Rap Dad: A Story of Family and the Subculture That Shaped a Generation*. India: Atria Books, 2018.

West, Cornel. "Black Strivings in a Twilight Civilization." In *The Cornel West Reader*, edited by Cornel West. 87–118. New York: Basic Books, 1999.

———. *Democracy Matters: Winning the Fight Against Imperialism*. England: Penguin Books, 2004.

———. "Nietzsche's Pre-Figuration of Postmodern American Philosophy." In *The Cornel West Reader*, 188–210. New York: Basic Books, 2001.

———. *Prophesy Deliverance!: An Afro-American Revolutionary Christianity*. Westminster: John Knox Press, 2002.

———. "Prophetic Christian as Organic Intellectual: Martin Luther King, Jr." In *The Cornel West Reader*, 425–34. New York: Basic Books, 2001.

———. *Race Matters*. 2nd ed. Massachusetts: Beacon Press, 2001.

———. "Subversive Joy and Revolutionary Patience in Black Christianity." In *The Cornel West Reader*, 435–39. New York: Basic Books, 1999.

———. *The Cornel West Reader*. New York: Basic Books, 2000.

Wilderson, Frank B. "Biko and the Problematic of Presence." In *Biko Lives!: Contesting the Legacies of Steve Biko*, edited by Andile Mngxitama, Amanda Alexander, and Nigel C. Gibson, 95–114. Contemporary Black History. New York: Palgrave Macmillan US, 2008.

Wilderson III, Frank B. *Red, White & Black: Cinema and the Structure of U.S. Antagonisms*. North Carolina: Duke University Press, 2010.

Williston, Byron. "'Complete Nihilism' in Nietzsche." *Philosophy Today* 45, no. 4 (August 1, 2001): 357–69.

Woodz, Carter. *Love Lost*. 2019.

Wright, Richard. *The Outsider*. New York: Random House, 2021.

Yancy, George, ed. *Cornel West: A Critical Reader*. United Kingdom: Wiley, 2001.

Index

absolute-I, 28, 30, 60
actional, 90, 97, 130, 132
adult(s)/adulthood, 18, 152, 158–63, 167–75, 185
aesthetics and aesthetic production, 18–19, 27–29, 32, 44–46, 53, 61, 64, 72, 83, 86, 146, 152–53, 155–56, 176, 182, 185, 187, 190; absorption, 37–38, 46; representations of tragedy, 44; moral interpretations of, 45
Africa, 3, 72–73, 140–41
African Americans, 86–87, 111, 112n25
Africana philosophy, 2, 57n7
Africana thought/thinkers, 83, 156
African people/Africans, 5–6, 13, 71, 73, 80n14
Afro-Judaism, 175, 180
Afropessimism, 18, 132–35, 137, 144–45
"All Lives Matter," 80
amor fati, 33, 55
anguish, 4, 17, 98–99, 103, 160–61, 163, 169, 178, 185, 188
anonymity, 174
antiblack racism, 1–5, 8, 10–11, 14–19, 23–24, 29, 32, 34, 53, 56, 67–71, 73, 75–79, 83–92, 106–10, 119–21, 125–26, 128–33, 135–40, 143, 145, 152, 154–57, 160–66, 168–69, 175–81, 183, 188, 190–91, 197, *passim*; against maturity, 152, 154–55, 157, 160–61, 163, 185; historical contingency of, 189; nostalgia for the past, 181; threat to positive humanism, 145, 190; values, 2, 4–5, 10–11, 14–19, 23–24, 29, 32, 43, 56, 68–70, 79, 83–84, 86–88, 91–92, 104, 107–10, 119, 126, 135–38, 145, 152–55, 157, 161–62, 164–69, 175, 180, 185; vulgar response to, 1–2, 4–5, 18, 162–64, 178
antiblack world, 13–15, 28, 76–79, 84, 104, 108–10, 120–22, 124–25, 127–35, 137, 156–57, 159, 161, 177, 179–80, 186
anxiety, 63, 75, 102, 178
apollonian, 34, 44
Aristotle, 2, 20n4, 109, 117n147
art, 18, 32, 35, 38, 45, 53, 61n43, 62n44, 100; Apollinian, 44; of living, 37, nihilistic art, 19; ritual, 97; strong art, 53. *See also* aesthetics
artist(s), 19, 38, 53, 61n43, 169, 175, 186–87
attic tragedy(ies), 44–45
Augustine of Hippo, Saint, 26, 31, 49
authenticity, 186
authority, 89

201

axiological, 15–16, 35, 83, 91, 120, 152, 157, 172

bad conscience, 88, 111n115
bad faith, 17, 100–103, 121
Baptist Christianity, 90–91
Beauvoir, Simone de, 48, 65n98, 98–99, 114n91, 160, 192n18
Bell, Derrick, 22, 84, 86, 111n3, 119, 132, 146n3; on pessimism, 16–17, 84–88, 110, 121
Bernier, François, 72, 80nn15–18
Best, Stephen, 18, 139, 141, 145, 149nn103, 104
black (color), 6, 20–21, 23, 72, 85, 121, 138, 145, 169, 177, 182, 183, *passim*
black adult(s), 2, 4, 6–9, 13, 18, 21, 24–25, 72, 75, 86, 90, 92, 99–100, 108, 119, 122, 124, 129, 139–41, 143, 158–59, 162, 167, 190
black bodies, 13, 25, 90, 108, 124, 190
black christianity, 16, 18, 90–97, 99, 105, 113n44, 130, 140, 163, 170–71, 175, 180, *passim*
black consciousness, 25, 90, 108, 124–25, 137, 161, 171, 184, *passim*
black existentialism, 104
black existentialist, 3–5
black invisibility, 3–4, 90–91, 94–97, 104, 107, 119–21, 122, 124–25, 127, 129, 133–35, 137–38, 143, 145, 152, 154–59, 161, 168, 173–74, 176–77, 180–81, 184, 187, *passim*
Black lives matter, 78
black nationalism, 95–96
black nihilistic hip hop music, 145, 152–56, 160, 167, 168, 176, 179, 187–88, 190
black noise, 138, 143–45
black optimism, 16–18, 84, 87–88, 91–92, 104–5, 119–20, 132, 135–38, 144–45, 152, 161–62, 166–67, 171–72, 176, 185, *passim*
black pessimism, 16, 17–19, 83–89, 99, 100, 110, 119, 131, 134–35, 138, 152–55, 158, 164, 166, 170–72, 175–79, 185–86, *passim*
black strivings, 96–97
black youth, 18–19, 152–74, 176, 180, 182, 185–90, *passim*
Buffon, George LeClerc, 80

Camus, Albert, 107, 116n134
capitalism, 5, 104, 133, 155, 164, 180
Cartesian Circle, 10
Cartesian dualism, 11
Cartesian rationalism, 7
Christian god, 11, 21; theodicy, 90; theologies, 26, *passim*
class, 46, 139
cogito, 7
colonialism, 13, 68, 116, 122, 180
colonization, 3, 24, 138, 140–41; epistemic, 189
colorblind racism, 85
commitment: actional, 97; to God's will, 99; to valuing hummanity, 166
consciousness, 4, 6–16, 20–21, 25, 30, 36–39, 41–42, 51, 53–54, 58, 60, 62, 64, 73–74, 80, 90, 92–93, 100–103, 108, 121–25, 128, 131–32, 134, 137, 161, 166, 169, 171, 176, 183–85, 190–91; delimiting, 16; experiences of, 10, 14; ironic, 92; limits of, 12; original, 2; phenomenal, 25, 36, 128; self-, 36, 58n15, 60n28; servile, 124, *passim*
creolize, 161, 163
critique, 2, 18, 84, 97, 160; and Afro-Judaism, 180; Fanon's of "Black Orpheus," 17, 181; Fichte's of rationality, 39; Gordon's of West's nihilism, 109; Jacobi's of Idealism, 31; Kant's of pure reason, 57, 59; Kendrick's of black optimism, 175; of the master-slave dialectic, 123; Mbembe's of black Christianity, 140–41; Nietzsche's of modern European philosophy, 12–13, 45, 70, 95; radical, 91; self, 24; of "the

talented tenth," 94; West's of black Christianity, 16, 90, *passim*
Cugoano, Quobna Ottobah, 142
Curry, Tommy, 21n12

death, 7, 39, 64n63, 105, 137, 139–40, *passim*
dehumanization, 5, 83, 85, 152, 174, *passim. See also* oppression
Deleuze, Giles, 51, 66
Descartes, René, 7, 9–11, 20n10, 21nn20–22, 26–28, 31–32, 42–43, 49, 56–58nn14, 15, 61, 57nn9–11, 59n22, 61n38, 68, 70, 73
despair, 29, 89, 92–99, 105, 109, 113–15, 113n45, 114n95, 153, 157, 185, 188
dialectic(s), 12, 45, 123–25, 127–28, 131, 184
dignity, 101, 104, 125–26, 130, 181
dionysian/dionysian man, 44, 50–52, 55
Dostoevsky, Fyodor, 106
Du Bois, W.E.B., 84, 94–97, 114, 122, 146

economic(s), 89, 111n6, 143, 154, *passim*
ego, 26, 68, 74
empiricism, 7, 20, 21
Ephraim, Charles, 108, 116
epistemic certainty, 26
epistemic closure, 174
epistemology, 13, 26, 32, 61
essence, 2, 9, 20, 31, 45, 58, 60, 67, 103, 115n107, 121, 123, 157, 176, 183
essentialism, 2–3, *passim*
eternal recurrence, 32, 53–55, 86, 123
ethics, 25, 139; of ambiguity, 98; of resignation, 53; stoic, 64n62
Europe, spirit of, 10–12, *passim*
Europeans, 45, 71, 162
European man, 3, 6–7, 10–11, 14–17, 20, 23–43, 45–46, 49–51, 53–56, 66n116, 67–79, 83, 85, 93, 110, 120, 124, 127, 155, 159, 162, 169, 175–76, 180, 182–83, 188
evil, 12, 37, 47, 61n38, 72, 75, 77, 79, 90, 92, 94, 126, 140, *passim*
exhaustion, 28–31, 75, 165
existential dope, 176
existential invisibility, 3, 69, 119, 129, 133, 155, 164, 173
existentialism, 100, 104, 110n2, 114n95

facticity, 100, 101
failure, 4, 84, 87, 135; to relate to God, 93, *passim*
Fanon, Frantz, 3, 5, 6, 9, 14, 17–22, 56, 110, 116, 119–37, 145–49, 168–69, 173–78, 180–88, 190, 191, 193, 194; on black nihilism, 121–25; on "Black Orpheus," 17, 181; of the master-slave dialectic, 127; on negritude, 173–75; on violence, 126–32, *passim*
Fashina, Oladipo, 125–27, 147
Fichte, Johann, 27–32, 35–39, 43, 53, 56, 59–61, 121
Foucault, Michel, 139
freedom, black, 94; as consciousness, 8; from exhaustion, 31; in imagination, 28; intelligible, 65; in valuing, 34, *passim*

genocide, 68, 134
Gillespie, Michael, 52, 57–61, 64–65
God, 11, 21nn21–22, *passim*
Gordon, Jane Anna, 156, 191n9
Gordon, Lewis R., 8–9, 20, 22n29, 56n3, 57n7, 102, 105, 108, 127, 144, 157, 173, 185; on anonymity, 174; on anxiety, 102–3; on negritude, 182–85; on nihilism, 105–10; on self consciousness, 8, *passim*
government, 142–43
Greek (ancient), 44–45, 68, 73
guilt, 165

Index

Hartman, Saadiya, 18, 121, 139, 149nn103–19; on fugitive justice, 141–45
Hegel, G.W.F., 13, 21, 73–74, 79–80, 141, 175; on black humanity, 73–74, 79, 80n12; on dialiectical consciousness, 123–25, 127
Heidegger, Martin, 106
higher man, 50–52, 151
hip hop Adults, 157, 166–67, 194n93
hip hop culture, 152–57, 176
hip hop music, 19, 44, 145, 152–57, 160, 166–69, 175–76, 179, 185–88, 190, 194n93
history, 55, 62n44, 75, 85–86, 91, 110n2, 141, 157, 175
home, 59n21, 156, 182
hope, 18, 63n53, 66n116, 142, 163; loss of, 89, 106
humanism, 125, 128, 131–33, 151, 190; new, 145; weak nihilistic, 78; Western, 2, 13, 72, 78, *passim*

identity, 21n20, 92, 100, 174, 187; formation, 3, 179; in patterns, 10, relation, 20n4, 36, 93; self-, 60
imagination, 28–31, 39, 53, 60, 61, 74, 87
individualism, 19
innocence, 109, 169, 172, 177, 180; of becoming, 47; is the child, 52
intersubjective(ity), 101, 103, 128, 136, 162, 173–74, 179

Jacobi, 19, 31, 32, 49, 55, 61, 79, 121
jazz, 144, 152
Jefferson, Thomas, 75, 81, 89
justice, 4, 15, 51, 73, 86, 109, 139, 142, 144, 172
justice, 109, *passim*
justification, 13, 30, 125

Kant, Immanuel, 13, 27–28, *passim*
Kierkegaard, Søren, 16, 92, 93, 97, 105, 106

Lamar, Kendrick, 19, 152, 168–73, 175–80, 182, 185, 186, 191–93
last man, 50–53, 151
laws, 58n, 59n20, 107, 116n141; logical, 68; moral, 83; of nature, 57n14
legitimacy, 2, 23, 29, 78, 85, 108
liberal nationalism, 144
Lincoln, Abraham, 56, 74
Locke, Alaine, 83
Locke, John, 13, 21, 70, 83
logic, 10, 26, 65n103, 71, 129–30, 178; of antiblack racism, 77; of improvisational immanence, 137; of Manicheism, 127; of pessimism, 41; racist, 173; time-ordered, 37
love, 8, 42, 55, 104, 123, 129, 132; of fate, 33, 55

Martinot, Steve, 18, 139, 148
Marxism, 139
master-slave dialectic, 123, 127
maturity, 18, 152, 154–61, 163–66, 168–70, 172–74, 177, 179, 180, 184, 185, 187, 188, 190
Mbembe, 18, 139–41, 148, 149; on black death, 139–41
Meagher, 155, 157, 158, 160, 191, 192
memory, 63n49
metaphysical affirmations, 36, 38–40, 45, 48, 50, 52–54, 67–68, 74, 97, 145; ideals, 68, 88, 94, 97, 104, 120, 185; values, 68
metaphysics, 11; of recognition, 123; theological, 41
methodology, 17, 84, 94, 104
Mills, Charles, 20, 24, 56, 84
modernity (European), 11, 25, 94, 107
monsters, 151
moralism, 12, 46, 172
morality, 5, 13, 15; of African chattel clavery, 78; pessimistic, 39, 41, 45, 47, 61
Moten, Fred, 18, 136–37, 148nn79–90
myth, 116n141, 155

negation, 5, 7, 14, 55, 58, 61, 75, 91, 96, 100, 123–24, 136
negritude, 17, 137, 145, 152, 178, 182–84
negro, 72–73, 75, 122, 129, 181–82, 184–85
Nietzsche, Friedrich, 9, 32–36; on *amor fati*, 33; antiblack racism, 71, 75–78; on European nihilism, 94; on (ancient) Greeks, 44–45; on nihilism, 40–48; on pessimism, 43; on strength, 50, 53–56; on thought, 68; on weakness, 42, *passim*
nihilism, 1–20, 23–56; Afro-, 18, 107–8, 132–37, 144–45, 175–77, 180, 185; black, 7, 9, 16–18, 36, 78, 83–84, 86–89, 97, 99–100, 103–8, 110, 119–21, 125, 128–29, 131–33, 135–39, 142–45, 152–59, 162–91; complete, 40; European nihilism, 40, 56, 69, 73, 94; incomplete nihilism, 40; stages of, 41, 49; strong, 44, 49–52, 54–55, 78, 98, 121; strong black, 18, 104, 110, 120–23, 131–32, 135–36, 141–42, 144, 145, 152, 158, 161, 164–66, 168, 179; strong pessimistic, 49, 51, 54; weak, 40; weak black, 16, 103–4, 110, 133–35, 145, 164–65; weak pessimistic, 49–51; white, 25, 56, 70, 74–75
not-I, 28, 29, 59, 60
noumena, 27, 28, 30, 31, 36, 37, 58, 59, 140

ontology, 137; Christian metaphysical, 32, 105; political, 133; settler, 134
opinion, 75, 137, 175
oppression, 2, 72, 84, 89–90, 106, 108, 131, 133, 138, 167
optimism, 16–20, 45, 50–51; black, 84, 88, 91, 104–5, 110, 132, 136–38, 144, 152, 161–62, 166–67, 171–72, 176, 185; idealism of, 41; Kantian, 42; Socratic, 44; veils of, 30, *passim*

options, 74, 95, 104, 120, 129
overman, 54

Patterson, Orlando, 133
Paul, Jean, 21–22
pessimism, 15–20, 24–29, 32–32–55, 71, 79–100; black, 110–21, 132–38, 141–42, 144–45, 152–53, 155–58, 164, 166–67, 172–76, 178, 185, *passim*. *See also* Afropessimism
pessimistic hammer, 50, 55, 135
phenomenal affirmations, 53
phenomenal resignation, 38, 39, 41, 46, 47, 134, 135
phenomenology, 131
philosopher-artist, 186
philosophical anthropology, 9, 11
Platonic lie, 155, 184
police, 14, 174, 178
polis, the, 109, 162
political, the, 142, *passim*
politics, 161; of conversion, 105–6, 115; of difference, 168; necro-, 139, 141
poverty, 105, 111n5
power, 36, 48, 54, 58, 85; God's, 11, *passim*
pride, 182
property, 89, 100, 144
Protestant Christianity, 90–91
psychopathological, 185
purity, 130, 169, 172

race, 24, 85, 104, 121, 128, 135, 139, 145, 181, 189; white, 75, *passim*
racial contract, 24
racial essentialism, 2
racism, 3, *passim*
rape, 120
rationalism, 7, 10, 12, 13, 20n11, 21n22, 41, 43, 45, 56, 94, 96–97, 172, 183
reasonability, 4, 14, 92
religion, 73; Catholic, 112n25, 181, 191
resentment, 34, 46, 50, 77, 107–8, 116n141, 132, 165, 177; man of, 122

responsibility, 8, 65n103, 85, 97–99, 101–3, 105, 120, 142; adult, 159–64, 166, 167, 180, 184
ressentiment, 46, 53, 88, 107, 108

Sartre, Jean-Paul, 9, 126–27; on bad faith, 101; on consciousness, 12; on dishonesty, 98–99; on language, 97; on negritude, 17, 184; on nihilism, 103; on transcendence/facticity, 100–101, *passim*
Scheler, Max, 107, 116n137
Schopenhauer, Arthur, 14, 25, 32; on art, 38; on morality, 39; on pessimism, 33–36; on resentment, 34; on resignation, 38; on time, 37, *passim*
science, 10, 45, 57n8, 58n16
second death, 143
Sexton, Jared, 18, 132, 136–39
social death, 133, 136, 137
social world, 158, 174
Socrates, 45–46, 49
solidarity, 5
solipsism, 70
sovereign, 142
sovereignty, 139–40
Spinoza, Baruch de, 31
spirit of modern Europe, 10, 11
spirit of seriousness, 48, 102, 160
state of exception, 139, 145
suffering, 37, *passim*
symbolic, 2–6, 11, 28, 44, 79, 91, 152, 156, 180
synthetic a priori judgments, 27

theodicy, 90

transcendence, 44, 100–101, 103–4, 122–23, 156, 185
transvaluation, 35, 54–55, 105, 121, 167–68; of all values, 54; transvalue, 40, 50, 99, 120, 165, 171–72

universal reality, 32, 34, 42, 45, 53, 69, 102, 123
universal truth, 27, 31, 40, 41, 50, 91
universal will, 13, 14, 33–35, 37, 39, 44, 47, 48, 53

values(ing), 7, 15; project of human, 6; value projections, 14, *passim*
violence, 4, 17, 22n29, 104, 106, 126–27, 134, 141, 143, 169; existential, 179
vitality, 166, 190; of black life, 110; of Greek life, 45; of life, 41
vulgar, 1–5, 162, 163, 169–70, 172, 178, 181–82, 189, 191

weak nihilistic values, 42
West, Cornel, 16, 84, 88; on optimism, 16–17, 84, 87–88, 97, 105, 110, *passim*
white bodies, 24
whiteness, 15, 17, 24–25, *passim*
white nihilistic values, 87, 120–21, 129, 145, 152, 162
Wilderson, III, Frank, 18, 132–35, 137–38
Williston, Byron, 52
will to power, 32, 107, *passim*

zone of non-being, 85, 129, 168

About the Author

Devon R. Johnson is a professor of Philosophy, a poet, and a hip-hop artist, who has released several works under the moniker Carter "Doctor" Woodz. He was born in 1981, in Carol City, Florida, and was raised by his Jamaican family, in Miramar, Florida. He studies, teaches, writes, and performs, on the subjects of Africana philosophy, nihilism, maturity, and hip-hop. He is a "first-generation" college student whose work focuses on existential struggles faced in association with youth, maturity, and race, within oppressive realities. In particular, his work highlights philosophical connections between certain forms of hip-hop music and the existential category of nihilism through questionings of traditional conceptions of human strength, maturity, and freedom.

Dr. Johnson/Dr. Woodz has performed, written, and/or recorded over 100 songs, becoming an honorary member of "Philly's" historically vibrant, independent artist music scene, while completing his doctoral degree at Temple University, in Philadelphia, Pennsylvania. As an artist, Dr. Woodz continues to produce works influenced by and reflective of his black existentialist philosophical positions. He truly lives, inhabits, and produces lyrics and philosophy, from the space of a *philosopher-poet*. As an academic, Dr. Johnson is currently a professor in the philosophy department at the University of Tampa, in Florida, and is a member of the Caribbean Philosophical Association, as well as the American Philosophical Association.

www.ingramcontent.com/pod-product-compliance
Lightning Source LLC
Chambersburg PA
CBHW020118010526
44115CB00008B/885